G000155172

THE FUTURE OF
LABOUR MOVEMENTS

SAGE STUDIES IN
INTERNATIONAL SOCIOLOGY
Editorial Board

Editor

Robert J. Brym, *University of Toronto, Canada*

Associate Editors

Paul Bernard, *University of Montreal, Canada*

Y.B. Damle, *Pune, India*

Elizabeth Jelin, *CEDES (Centro de Estudios de Estado y Sociedad), Buenos Aires, Argentina*

Endre Sik, *Institute for Social Sciences, Budapest, Hungary*

THE FUTURE OF LABOUR MOVEMENTS

edited by
Marino Regini

SAGE Studies in International Sociology 43
Sponsored by the International Sociological Association/ISA

© International Sociological Association/ISA 1992

First published 1992
Reprinted 1994
First paperback edition 1994
Reprinted 2007
All rights reserved. No part of this publication may be reproduced, stored in a retrieval system, transmitted or utilized in any form or by any means, electronic, mechanical, photocopying, recording or otherwise, without permission in writing from the Publishers.

 SAGE Publications Ltd
1 Oliver's Yard, 55 City Road
London EC1Y 1SP

SAGE Publications Inc
2455 Teller Road
Thousand Oaks, California 91320

SAGE Publications India Pvt Ltd
B-42 Panchsheel Enclave
PO Box 4109
New Dehli 110 017

British Library Cataloguing in Publication Data

Future of Labour Movements. – (Sage Studies in
International Sociology Series; Vol. 43)
  I. Regini, Marino   II. Series
  331.8

ISBN 978-0-8039-8761-6
ISBN 978-0-8039-7977-2 (pbk)

Library of Congress catalog card number 92–050572

Typeset by Mayhew Typesetting, Rhayader, Powys
Printed in Great Britain by Biddles Ltd, Guildford and
King's Lynn

Contents

List of Tables and Figures   vi
Notes on Contributors   vii
Preface   xi

Introduction: the Past and Future of Social Studies of
Labour Movements   1
Marino Regini

1 The Strength of Union Movements in Advanced
   Capitalist Democracies: Social and Organizational
   Variations   17
   Jelle Visser

2 Labour Movements and Political Systems: Some
   Variations   53
   J. Samuel Valenzuela

3 The Resurgence of Labour Quiescence   102
   Michael Shalev

4 The Emerging Realignment Between Labour Movements
   and Welfare States   133
   Gøsta Esping-Andersen

5 Trade Unions and the Disaggregation of the Working
   Class   150
   Richard Hyman

6 The Fate of Articulated Industrial Relations Systems: a
   Stock-taking after the 'Neo-liberal' Decade   169
   Colin Crouch

7 Europe's Internal Market, Business Associability and the
   Labour Movement   188
   Luca Lanzalaco and *Philippe C. Schmitter*

8 Trade Unions and Decentralized Production: a Sketch of
   Strategic Problems in the German Labour Movement   217
   Horst Kern and *Charles F. Sabel*

9 Training and the New Industrial Relations: a Strategic
   Role for Unions?   250
   Wolfgang Streeck

Index   270

List of Tables and Figures

Tables

1.1 Union membership and union density in eighteen
advanced capitalist democracies, 1970–89   19
1.2 Union density rates in manufacturing, financial
services, public services, and among males and females   27
1.3 The changing social composition of labour movements,
1950–89   29
1.4 The representatives of central union organizations,
1950–89   31
1.5 Number of affiliates, major unions, and membership
shares in European union confederations, 1950 and
1989   33
3.1 Industrial conflict in the OECD bloc, 1960–89   105
6.1 Working days lost per 1,000 dependent employees in
employment, 1971–80   175
6.2 Economic performance, 1970–74   176
6.3 Working days lost per 1,000 dependent employees in
employment, 1986–90   183
6.4 Economic performance, 1986–90   184
7.1 The differences between representing class interests and
producer interests to capitalists   193
7.2 Functional specialization between trade and employers'
peak associations in some countries   194

Figures

3.1 The four strike profiles of the 'golden age' (1960–67)   106
3.2 The post-1967 surge and the post-1979 slide in
participation in strikes   108
3.3 Six cases of exceptional rise or fall in relative
involvement, 1960–89   109
3.4 European strike profiles in the 1980s   114
3.5 The descending paths of strikes and unemployment   116
3.6 The impact of organization on militancy   118
3.7 Branch shares in total strike volume   120
3.8 Japan: forms of conflict   122
7.1 A diagram of the four logics of associability   195

Notes on Contributors

Colin Crouch is Fellow and Tutor in Politics at Trinity College, Oxford. He has written extensively on the politics of industrial relations in Western European countries, including *Trade Unions, the Logic of Collective Action* (1982) and *Industrial Relations and European State Traditions* (1992). He edited *The Resurgence of Class Conflict in Western Europe since 1968* (two volumes, 1978, with A. Pizzorno) and *European Industrial Relations: the Challenge of Flexibility* (1990, with G. Baglioni). He is currently working on a study of occupational training in certain European countries.

Gøsta Esping-Andersen is Professor in the Department of Political and Social Sciences at the European University Institute, Florence. He has worked extensively in the areas of comparative welfare-state research and on employment and labour markets. He is the author of *Politics against Markets* (1985) and *The Three Worlds of Welfare Capitalism* (1990). His forthcoming *Changing Classes* will be published by Sage.

Richard Hyman is Convenor of Graduate Studies in the Industrial Relations Research Unit, University of Warwick, and Secretary of the ISA Research Committee on Labour Movements. His publications include, *Strikes, Industrial Relations: a Marxist Introduction* and *The Political Economy of Industrial Relations*. He is co-editor of *Industrial Relations in the New Europe*.

Horst Kern is Professor of Sociology at the Goettingen University in Germany. His main areas of research are industrial sociology, empirical studies and international comparisons. Among his most noted publications are those written in collaboration with Michael Schumann: *Industrierarbeit und Arbeiterbewussein* (1970) and *Das Ende der Arbeitsteilung?* (first published in 1984 and translated into five languages). Some of his other publications are *Kampf um Arbeitsbedingungen* (1979), *Empirische Sozialforschung* (1982) and *Madame Doctorin Schlozer* (1989, with Baerbel Kern).

Luca Lanzalaco is a post-doctoral Fellow at the Centre for Comparative Politics at the Bocconi University in Milan. He has written several articles about business interest associations, industrial relations and political theory. His recent publications include *Dall'impresa all'associazione. Le organizzazioni degli imprenditori: la Confindustria in prospettiva comparata* (1990).

Marino Regini is Professor of Economic Sociology in the University of Trento and president of the ISA Research Committee on 'labour movements'. His publications include *State, Market and Social Regulation* (1989, with P. Lange), *I dilemmi del sindacato* (1981), *Confini mobili. La costruzione dell'economia fra politica e società* (1991) and numerous articles and essays in several languages.

Charles F. Sabel is the Ford International Professor of Social Science at MIT. His publications include *The Second Industrial Divide* (1984, with Michael Piore) and *Strategie di riaggiustamento industriale* (1989, co-edited with Marino Regini).

Philippe C. Schmitter is Professor of Political Science at Stanford University. Previously he taught at the European University Institute in Florence and at the University of Chicago. He is the co-author of *Transitions from Authoritarian Rule* (with Guillermo O'Donnell) and *The Organization of Business Interests* (with Wolfgang Streeck).

Michael Shalev teaches in the Departments of Sociology and Political Science at the Hebrew University of Jerusalem. He is the author of *Labour and the Political Economy in Israel* (1992) and has written on the comparative political economy of the OECD nations.

Wolfgang Streeck is Professor of Sociology and Industrial Relations at the University of Wisconsin-Madison. He was previously Senior Fellow at the Wissenschaftszentrum, Berlin and has held visiting appointments at the European University Institute, Florence, the University of Warwick and the Centre for Advanced Studies in the Social Sciences, Madrid. He has published on trade unions, business associations, industrial relations, economic change in advanced industrial societies and European integration. Among his most recent works are *Beyond Keynsianism: The Socio-Economics of Production and Employment* (1991, co-edited with Egon Matzner) and *Social Institutions and Economic Performance: Studies of Industrial Relations in Advanced Capitalist Economies* (1992).

J. Samuel Valenzuela is Professor of Political Sociology and Development and Senior Fellow of the Kellogg Institute for International Studies at the University of Notre Dame. His research has centred on comparative labour studies, especially labour movement formation and the relationships between labour and politics in different regimes, and on processes of political democratization. He is the author of *Democratización vía reforma: la expansión del sufragio en Chile* (1976) and his most recent publication is *Issues in Democratic Consolidation: the New South American Democracies in Comparative Perspective* (1992, co-edited with Scott Mainwaring and Guillermo O'Donnell).

Jelle Visser is Associate Professor in Sociology of Organizations at the University of Amsterdam, and has written many books and papers on the sociology of trade unions and comparative industrial relations. His latest book, *In Search of Inclusive Unionism*, was published in 1990 as a special issue of the *Bulletin of Public Relations* with Kluwer Publ.

Guido Romagnoli *in memoriam*

Preface

This volume is the first collective product of the International Sociological Association Research Committee on 'Labour Movements', which was established a few years ago with the aim of encouraging studies in this field. Labour movements as such have rarely been a unitary object of study. The social sciences have contributed major insights into specific aspects of their activity, but have been less successful in offering comprehensive understandings of their multifaceted aspects. Thus labour economists have pioneered quantitative studies of industrial conflict, unionization, and even collective bargaining, in an effort to grasp the economic significance of trade unions as collective actors. Political scientists have not only offered alternative explanations of conflict, but also, and especially, analytical frameworks with which to understand the political role of labour. Labour lawyers have considered industrial relations to be a system which is normatively structured by both collective bargaining and the law. Finally, sociologists (and to some extent social psychologists) have studied various aspects of labour movements – ranging from collective mobilization to trade unions as organizations, to their activity in the industrial and state arenas – by drawing on such different fields as the sociology of social movements, of organizations, or industrial and political sociology.

Thus labour movements have become one of the main topics addressed by an interdisciplinary approach in the social sciences. An interdisciplinary approach has many merits, for example the different angles from which a subject of study is examined, and the different analytical frameworks competing to yield more and more sophisticated explanations. There is, however, one major shortcoming, which relates to the academic division of labour. Scholars working in one discipline usually have little incentive to extend their coverage of the literature, their inside knowledge of scientific debate, and so forth, to other disciplines. On the other hand, for all their importance, subjects standing on the borders of different disciplines can hardly be central to any of them. As a result, studies on borderline subjects rarely go beyond in-depth analyses of specific aspects to provide a comprehensive overview – not to mention theoretical understanding – of what is known on the subject in general.

Social studies of labour movements share these features. In spite of an impressive amount of work on specific aspects of labour movements, especially over the last twenty years, we still lack both a comprehensive assessment of what we know about them and plausible overall scenarios concerning their future.

This volume is a first collective effort to remedy the situation. It originates from an international conference organized by the above-mentioned ISA Research Committee (at that time 'Working Group') at the University of Trento in December 1989, with the financial support of the Department of Social Policy at that University. Leading specialists on labour movements working in the fields of sociology and political science were invited to address both the more traditional concerns of scholars in this area and new aspects that appeared crucial to the future of labour movements as they entered the last decade of this century. The conference was co-organized by the editor of this volume and by Guido Romagnoli, who prematurely died before it took place and to whose memory the volume is dedicated.

The book, however, is far from being a collection of conference papers. In fact, many of the papers given at the conference have been omitted, others have been added. All of them have been carefully revised, with the general aim of filling gaps and presenting the reader with a highly consistent treatment of the subject. The outcome has been a more focused volume than was originally anticipated. For one thing, the book concentrates on Western countries, though in some cases it extends to others where labour movements have been a significant actor. Moreover, while all the authors have expert knowledge and draw extensively on different social sciences, the book is entirely the work of sociologists (except for one chapter written by political scientists).

Finally, this volume is an act of faith – or, better, it expresses a deep intellectual belief in the future of labour movements. After a decade in which different trends seemed to conspire against the continuing economic, social, and political relevance of labour movements, too many specialists and observers of the industrial relations scene have jumped to the conclusion of a 'withering away' of labour movements. This volume tries, among other things, to show how premature such a conclusion is, even though it argues that a profound rethinking is required of the past experience of labour movements and the scope of their future action.

Marino Regini
Trento (Italy)

Introduction: the Past and Future of Social Studies of Labour Movements

Marino Regini

Although generalizations on labour movements have been proposed ever since their appearence on the stage of history, except for particular periods they have followed quite different trajectories in different countries. Each national labour movement has had its character shaped by the specific features of the industrial and political systems concerned and by the constraining force of its own tradition.

Nevertheless, over the last twenty years similarities have begun to emerge, and a comparative sociology of labour movements, based on systematic studies of Western European and North American countries,[1] has achieved a considerable degree of sophistication in discerning both common trends and national or regional variations. However, there is still no generally unifying theory in the field, nor even one that is widely agreed to. In the 1970s, empirical falsification and the violent criticisms brought against various attempts in the two previous decades to uncover universal tendencies – namely, the 'withering away of the strike', the 'institutionalization of class conflict', and the 'embourgeoisement of the working class' as phenomena having to do with the 'inner logic of industrialization' (see Ross and Hartman, 1960; Dahrendorf, 1959; the critical treatment by Goldthorpe et al., 1969; and Kerr et al., 1960, respectively), or the emergence, on the other hand, of a 'new working class' giving rise to a new phase of social antagonism (Mallet, 1963) – dissuaded scholars from drawing too broad generalizations. Nevertheless, some consensus has gradually emerged, at least over the major trends and challenges that to a greater or lesser degree characterize all labour movements in the West, and also over the analytical tools to use in their comparative analysis.

In this introduction, I shall begin by briefly reviewing these trends and scholarly concerns. I shall argue that most Western labour movements have passed through three major stages of development in the last twenty-five years or so. As each stage has been dominated by one, different group of issues, the interest of social scientists in labour movements has correspondingly shifted. And this has given rise to new concepts, approaches, and areas of study which have taken the place of their predecessors. Secondly, my thesis will be that each of the groups of issues central to these three stages will again have a role to play in the 1990s. Each of them, in fact, raises still unanswered questions concerning labour movements: so much so that no balanced scenario for the year 2000 can be drawn up if only one of them is considered to the neglect of the others.

1   Trade Unions and Workers: the Phase of Collective Mobilization

In most Western European countries, the late 1960s and early 1970s were characterized by an (often sudden and unforeseen) increase in industrial conflict and rank-and-file militancy, which in some cases occurred outside the institutions of industrial relations. The most impressive cases of collective (not only worker) mobilization were probably those of France (Touraine, 1972) and Italy (Pizzorno et al., 1978; Regalia, Regini and Reyneri, 1978). However, industrial conflict reached high levels in the Anglo-Saxon world as well (Crouch and Pizzorno, 1978), and sudden outbursts of militancy erupted everywhere in the West which involved even such traditionally cooperative systems as those of Sweden (Korpi, 1970) and West Germany (Müller-Jentsch and Sperling, 1978). Although the figures on strikes show a significant upswing in this period, they are not sufficient to capture the scope of this collective mobilization. In fact, rank-and-file militancy did not always take the form of the strike; other manifestations of active dissatisfaction, sometimes of insubordination, were also frequent occurrences in the workplace; and sharp criticism or even attacks on union leadership were commonplace (Hyman, 1972).

This suggests that the central issue at this stage of labour-movement development was the relationship between trade unions and workers. At stake, in fact, was their (varying) ability to accommodate workers' demands by forcing them into the traditional channels of representation and intermediation. This strained relationship stemmed both from changes in the composition of the working class and in workers' demands, and from the problems facing trade unions as organizations.

Each labour movement responded differently to these tensions to find solutions that were satisfactory to varying degrees. In the medium term (that is, during the 1970s), however, most European trade unions benefited from this wave of militancy, as many employers and public institutions found themselves compelled to grant them recognition as their indispensable partners in the industrial order. Hence, the central preoccupation slowly became that of dealing with the consequences of greater labour strength, an issue, as we shall see, to which a clear answer was forthcoming in the second stage.

In this first stage of development, therefore, the main concerns of students of labour movements were the social and economic causes and the economic and institutional consequences of collective mobilization. The phenomenon of mobilization itself was subject to a great deal of study, whether in the form of quantitative analyses of trends in industrial conflict aimed at identifying long-run determinants, or in the form of case studies of 'cycles' of collective mobilization in which trends in industrial conflict were just one element in a more general trajectory involving social movements and labour organizations.

Both types of study became areas of intense effort to develop interdisciplinary comparative analyses of social phenomena. This search for economic, political, and socio-cultural variables in explanation of long-run trends involved economists (who already had a long and rich tradition in this field), sociologists (see, for example, Korpi and Shalev, 1980) and political scientists (see, for instance, Hibbs, 1976), not to mention the several historians who made important contributions to the subject (such as Shorter and Tilly, 1974). The same applies to the various attempts to identify and explain 'cycles of collective mobilization' or 'conflict waves' (Pizzorno, 1978; Shorter and Tilly, 1974; Tarantelli, 1978).

Some of the causes of collective mobilization in the late 1960s and early 1970s were to a large extent common to all the advanced industrial democracies. Almost everywhere, in fact, economic-industrial growth had proceeded in such a way as to provoke a strong build-up of potential protest.

At the micro-level of the firm there had been wide-ranging reorganization of production, which in the terminology of the time was called 'rationalization' and which today is usually interpreted as the expansion and consolidation of 'Fordism' (Piore and Sabel, 1984; Boyer, 1986), or, better, a Fordist-Taylorist organization of production. The effects of this rationalization, or of rampant Fordism, are well known because they were widely studied by the sociology of work – especially in France and the United States – during the 1960s and 1970s. Work rhythms were stepped up, work loads and physical toil were increased; jobs were fragmented so that workers lost their occupational identities; and opportunities for workers to pursue careers were curtailed. It was not only for cultural or ideological reasons that several Western countries saw a proliferation of analyses based on the Marxian concepts of alienation (Blauner, 1964) and exploitation (Braverman, 1974). These concepts seemed able to capture the widespread dissatisfaction of workers with their jobs which was an important basis for protest.

At the macro-national level, during the 1950s and throughout the 1960s, strong economic growth and the consequent tensions on the labour market provoked a massive migration – internal or external, depending on the country – of workers to satisfy the demand for less skilled labour; workers who were employed in the more precarious, less satisfying, and more exhausting jobs. Thus, while a situation of quasi-full employment gave workers relative job security and therefore increased their bargaining power, in all the major European countries there had formed large armies of mostly young and unskilled immigrant workers, who were socialized neither to factory discipline, nor to urban living, nor to the rules of collective action expressed through the institutional channels of interest representation. This lack of socialization, this difference with respect to native workers, was undoubtedly a factor that divided the working class and therefore weakened trade-union action. At the same time, however, it caused the build-up of an enormous potential for protest, which did or did not explode in ensuing years depending on various national factors.

Finally, a significant role was played by student movements and by political minorities, mainly consisting of middle-class intellectuals (Tarrow, 1988). In various European countries, these produced the ideology needed to unify workers' demands and to give purpose and long-term goals to confrontational behaviour, and they encouraged the social invention of new forms of conflict and of new demands.

In some countries, however, this combination of protest potential and of resources for collective action gave rise to only limited mobilization; in others (France and especially Italy) the break with the previous pattern of labour relations was radical. In these latter countries, in fact, other decisive factors came into play. First, the labour-exclusive model which had predominated since the late 1940s prevented the state from transferring distributional conflicts into the political arena (Korpi and Shalev, 1980) and produced a non-worker-orientated welfare system with severe bottlenecks in the provision of social services and limitations on workers' security. Secondly, trade union weakness in both the state and the industrial arena meant that many new grievances and demands could not be dealt with by institutional means (such as representative agents and collective bargaining) but took the form of expressive and non-negotiable, hence highly disruptive, behaviour.

Providing an explanation of collective mobilization was, as we have seen, a central concern for social studies of labour movements during this period. Equally important, however, was study of trade unions as organizations. The discovery that the degree of union weakness could to a large extent explain the forms of workers' mobilization on the one hand, and the renewed importance of trade unions resulting from that mobilization on the other, generated a series of studies on centralization–decentralization trends, on trade-union democracy, on organizational incentives to participation, and similar issues. While the sociology of social movements benefited most from the studies carried on in this period, the sociology of organizations also received new inputs and provided studies of labour movements with concepts and theories developed in analyses of different social phenomena.

2 Labour and the State: the Phase of Concertation

Although collective mobilization declined almost everywhere during the 1970s, either slowly or abruptly, labour organizations retained their strength to some degree; in some cases, they became even stronger as collective mobilization was progressively institutionalized. However, relatively strong trade unions were clearly a major constraint on the choice among different policy options facing employers and governments as they responded to the double challenge of rising inflation coupled with growing recession and unemployment. In the absence of better alternatives, in many countries these actors came to regard the participation of trade unions in the management of economic policies as a 'second-best solution', and this is why the 1970s (and early 1980s) can be considered to be the decade of neo-corporatism, or of social concertation. The literature on these trends is too large to be adequately summarized here, let alone reviewed (among the most important references, see Schmitter and Lehmbruch, 1979; Berger, 1981; Lehmbruch and Schmitter, 1982; Goldthorpe, 1984; Pizzorno, 1978).

The central issue during this phase was no longer the relationship between trade unions and workers (though questions concerning the ability of the former to represent the latters' interests in a period of strong centralization were often raised); rather, the chief concern was now the (problematic) relationship between labour and the state. One interpretation of this relationship focused on the varying ability of labour movements to transfer their newly acquired strength into the political arena, and on the consequences of this process (for example, Korpi, 1983). A different approach was to view this relationship in terms of the incorporation of trade unions into the political institutions of capitalism and of the transformation of their role as representative organizations of the working class (for example, Panitch, 1977).

These formulations have a distinctive flavour of the decade they were born in and now seem rather outdated; nevertheless, the debate produced many important findings and brought major refinements to the categories used in analysis of the political economies of Western societies. Not only did study of corporatist trends in some countries help understanding of different trends in others – for example, the pluralist pressure politics that predominated in the United States (Schmitter, 1974) or the 'labour-exclusionary' model in 1950s Italy and France (Lange, Ross and Vannicelli, 1982) – but more accurate studies of neo-corporatist experience, either long-term and stable as in Austria or the Scandinavian countries, or unstable as in Italy and the United Kingdom, also brought to light the many features of the political and institutional system that allow or constrain social concertation. The organizational and political preconditions or consequences of concertation were surveyed in some countries (Streeck, 1982; Crouch, 1977); while 'functional equivalents' of these preconditions were detected in others (Lehmbruch, 1982; Regini, 1984), where the potential 'crises of representation' brought about by trade-union participation in political bargaining could, under given conditions, be managed by various instruments of organizational and ideological control over the rank and file. From even this brief summary it should be clear that the sociology of social movements – so prominent in the early 1970s – had almost no role to play in the study of labour movements in the years that followed. Although the sociology of organizations retained some of its previous influence, the leading field was now political sociology (and political science).

What features of concertation can we now see, in hindsight, as typifying this stage of development of labour movements, and at the same time responsible for its withering away in the years that followed? As defined and practised by most labour movements, concertation was, first, a highly politicized form of negotiation: not only in the rather obvious sense that it involved governments as well as employers in the bargaining process, but also because it had the predominantly symbolic objective of 'exchanging legitimation' among the three partners. Secondly, it involved a highly centralized political exchange: again, not so much so for the obvious reason that it was conducted at the national (hence central) level, but because it was the central mechanism of the whole system of industrial relations; the pivot around which all relations among actors rotated and to which plant-level bargaining was subordinated. Thirdly, the problems addressed in this type of centralized political bargaining were identified in a comprehensive, aggregate way, and so too were the solutions: the crucial issue was how to contain aggregate labour costs in order to curb inflation, and compensations for labour were conceived in equally aggregate terms (lower levels of unemployment, some control over management decisions, and so on). It was these features that came most radically under assault in the following period – to which we now turn.

3 Labour and Management: the Phase of Flexibility

By the mid-1980s, in virtually all the advanced industrial democracies it was evident that concertation was no longer the major focus of labour-movement activity. This was so not only in those countries where political conditions were unfavourable (such as the United Kingdom), but even in those (France, Spain) whose governments actively promoted the political involvement of labour. As I have already argued, the very features that made concertation appealing in the 1970s were responsible for its crisis, now that it appeared so clearly inadequate to the challenges of a new decade dominated by the issues of intensified industrial competition and restructuring, management initiative, and forms of micro-adjustment at the plant level.

Changes toward a 'post-Fordist' organization of production, variously described as 'flexible specialization' (Piore and Sabel, 1984), 'flexible mass production' (Boyer, 1986), 'new concepts of production' (Kern and Schumann, 1984), or 'diversified quality production' (Streeck, 1989), led to a growing diversification of the labour force; that is, in workers' interests, demands, and importance for production (Regini, 1987). Employers became less interested in patterns of industrial relations designed to deal with aggregate problems and solutions. And the discovery of the centrality of firm and labour flexibility in determining economic performance in international markets (Dore, 1986) had largely the same effect: managers were now convinced that they had to search for differentiated, rather than uniform, responses to the variability of conditions in different workplaces. As a consequence of these and other factors, there was a general shift in the 'centre of gravity' of economic and industrial-relations systems from the level of macro-economic management to the micro-level of the firm; and management, rather than the state, became the central actor in the process of economic adjustment as it regained the initiative and the authority that it had lost in the previous decade and brought radical changes to firms as productive and social systems.

There is a further aspect, however, one that was not easily detectable in the early years of this phase. In some industries and countries, the very shift in initiative at the firm level helped forms of micro-concertation of industrial adjustment to emerge (Streeck, 1984; Regini and Sabel, 1989) which were based on the pragmatic recognition by labour that firms had to adjust to the growing instability of markets, and the realization by management that they could take advantage of industrial relations institutions rather than fight them.

The central issue at this stage was, therefore, the building of new relationships between labour and management. However, in marked contrast with the two preceding stages of development, the literature is largely uncertain as to which factor should be singled out as the driving force behind the trends I have just described. Is it the weakening of trade unions due to market and political factors; the fight for de-regulation waged by management; the objective constraints and imperatives of flexibility which firms have to cope with in a situation of increased competition and market volatility; or is it a physiological (possibly cyclical) shift from the dominance of a macro-political level to that of a micro-industrial one?

This uncertainty, which sometimes resists translation into scientific debate, has made for a plurality of approaches to the analysis of this stage of development which coexist without fully interacting. One major focus for social scientists has been the description of change in labour markets, technology, and the organization of production, and of its consequences on the ability of labour movements to represent workers' interests. Another approach has been to analyse management's changing objectives and strategies (under the broad headings of flexibility, de-regulation, and the like) and of their implications for personnel management and industrial-relations policies. The different features of the institutional arrangements or the industrial-relations systems that account for the various solutions advanced for the common problem of adjustment have also been researched (see, for example, Soskice, 1988). At this stage of the development of labour movements, industrial sociology and industrial relations are clearly the fields of social sciences most frequently called upon to provide concepts and analytical tools.

4 Open Questions and Scenarios for the 1990s

After a look at the recent past, I shall now address a number of still unanswered questions concerning the development of labour movements. The starting point for my discussion is the fact that certain features characterizing the 1980s now seem to be changing almost everywhere. For instance, the industrial restructuring required to adjust to the changed economic situation that virtually dominated the previous decade has by now been largely accomplished, though with varying degrees of success. Also, the crisis of large corporations, which in many countries was paralleled by an impressive growth of small firms and of an informal economy, has been attenuated and in many cases overcome. Most importantly, labour weakness, as an effect of unemployment and recession combined with a variety of other factors, in most countries has either been remedied or at least no longer paralyses efforts at mobilization and negotiation. Other features, however, can be expected to persist in the new decade. The need for the continuous reorganization of production and the importance of product quality and flexibility for international competition will still produce their effects on labour movements, acting as both constraints and opportunities. The same can be said for the expansion of the tertiary sector, of non-manual workers, and of non-standard types of employment.

Proceeding in reverse order with respect to the discussion above, let us now examine the changing relationships between labour and management. What patterns will prevail in the new decade? Are the different responses currently given to the common imperative of flexibility to be seen as conjunctural – that is, typical of a phase of intense capitalistic restructuring and likely soon to be redefined – or as structural and permanent alternatives?

Certain indicators would seem to suggest that the 'uncertainty of management' (Streeck, 1987) has become a structural feature even in cases where firms have moved beyond the phase of the 'management of uncertainty'. There is no obvious reason why even similar firms in the same sector and country (without going into cross-sector or cross-country comparisons) should, as they do, continue to pursue divergent strategies of labour regulation. Some of them, in fact, adopt non-union personnel management, or human resource policies. Others follow a more traditional mixed policy of unilateral management and collective bargaining. In yet others, trade unions are given the status of consensual partners, of joint regulators of labour and of other production issues at the workplace level. These differences are not fully explained by either technological-economic factors or by the varying strength of labour movements. Institutional traditions and arrangements, as well as managerial cultural orientations, seem to play a more important role; but will they survive the tensions induced by the continuing process of international competition and of market integration, or is a trend towards greater convergence – though not necessarily towards the search for a new 'one best way' – more likely?

As far as Europe is concerned, the approach of the deadline for a Single Market in 1993 has induced various commentators to predict a convergence of this kind, viewing it as the consequence of the advent of a less regulated economy, in which the stronger trade unions enjoying greater institutional protection – as, for instance, in Germany – will be forced to 'level down' to the positions of the weaker ones. However, careful inspection of the present scope for trade-union action in various European countries yields a more cautious scenario. If greater convergence does effectively come about, it will probably lead to the emergence of more pragmatic and procedural forms of cooperative labour relations (which could be termed 'institutionally soft versions of the German model') stemming either from the more or less reluctant acceptance of common imperatives by previously adversarial-bargaining actors, as in Italy and partly in the United Kingdom, or from the creation of new forms of labour representation often under the impulse of management in situations of weak unionism, as in France. This is certainly not enough to prove the case for convergent trends; but, at least in Europe, institutional and not just economic developments – that is, the prevalence in the political arena of pressures which strengthen the 'social dimension' of the Single Market – may persuade labour-relations actors to abandon *ad hoc* arrangements and informality and to engage in the negotiation of new, presumably more similar, rules and institutions. A 'soft version of the German model', rather than an outright neo-liberal policy, might then, at the micro-level of the firm, take on the role of 'second-best solution' for all the actors involved that concertation performed during the 1970s at the macro-national level.

Another feature of labour–management relations in the 1980s may develop quite differently in the new decade. On the one hand, for many employers and workers aggregate labour cost is no longer the only focal issue for negotiation; various aspects of the use and reproduction of the labour force (organization of working time, internal mobility and career, incentives, vocational training) are becoming even more crucial. On the other, this is truer of some firms (the post-Fordist ones) and of some categories of workers than others; it is not entirely clear, however, how this dualism will work (Kern and Schumann, 1984). If employers respond to these new challenges by adopting personnel policies which apply to the whole of their work-forces, then a dualism between sectors and countries is going to open up, depending on the varying proportion of Fordist versus post-Fordist firms in each sector and country. To give a rough example, even in the European Single Market, the dualism in labour–management relations between Spain and Germany will grow. If, however, most employers differentiate their personnel policies by dealing differently with the various professional groups, then, paradoxically, we shall witness a new convergence among these countries: one based on a generalized segmentation of internal labour markets.

Turning to relationships between labour movements and the state, a further unanswered question concerns the kind of political role that labour will play in the new decade. Discussion may begin with the varying labour-market strength enjoyed by workers in advanced industrial democracies; a strength which in the 1970s was the major factor that led many governments to involve labour in social concertation or in various forms of incomes policy. Should workers become stronger in the labour market again, will new attempts at concertation emerge?

The problem is establishing what all the actors concerned have learned from the experience of the 1970s, and the extent to which they will avoid engaging in the forms of political bargaining discussed in section 2. More in general, we must ask ourselves whether European labour movements consider their relationship with governments to be the outcome of a phase now irremediably come to an end, or whether they still see this relationship as having some function to perform.

A first and plausible scenario is that some form of concertation will reappear, perhaps with a low degree of formalization. The scope of such concertation would be restricted, but this might force the actors – the labour movements, in particular – to examine its potential more carefully. There seem to be two main areas which could be fruitfully explored.

First, concertation can still allow certain goals of 'general interest' to workers, those in the mainstream of the North European tradition, to be pursued: measures designed to create jobs and to encourage mobility and retraining, greater distributive justice, economic and social policies less polluted by sectoral interests. These goals resemble those 'public goods' (Olson, 1965) which imply a cost that none of those potentially interested in acquiring them wish to pay, seeing that they will enjoy the benefits in any case. They are therefore goals that are extremely difficult to pursue either through the party mediation of interests or through collective bargaining, given that these traditional processes for articulating demands tend to be dominated by a sectoral definition of interests. Since the actors in concertation are instead forced to represent aggregate interests and since they enjoy an oligopolistic position – that is, they are relatively unconstrained by competition from other interest groups – they can aim at those results that in other forms of decision-making are so difficult to achieve (Lange and Regini, 1989). And in order to obtain them, they can also sustain the cost of a reduction in the wage dynamic.

Secondly, concertation can also be used for non-traditional purposes; that is, to create a basis and a coordinating framework that will give renewed vitality to decentralized bargaining. We know that diversification in the demand for labour can give rise to individual forms of bargaining which abort the functions of the trade unions. We also know that many new social and professional figures believe trade-union action to be incapable of representing their demands. From this point of view, there is no doubt that the road to the trade unions' recovery of representation lies through the development of new forms of flexible decentralized bargaining which match the heterogeneity of the occupational situation. Yet, for decentralized bargaining to fulfil the minimal criteria of coherence and fairness, for it to aim at shared objectives and not merely to reproduce market relationships, it will probably require the backing of a centralized political negotiation which fixes the rules and draws up the agenda. For example, flexible and finely tuned bargaining over part-time employment requires rules that have been centrally negotiated and established. And even those who propose increasing employment opportunities, not through a general reduction in working hours but through 'individual options for temporary withdrawal from work' (Offe, Hinrichs and Wiesenthal, 1984), obviously acknowledge the need for guaranteeing the effective temporariness and freedom of these individual choices by means of centrally decided rules.

However, a revival of concertation is not the only possible scenario for relationships between labour movements and the state. There is also what, in the context of the European Single Market, Schmitter and Streeck (1990) have termed 'Euro-pluralism and pressure politics'. Quite apart from their reasons for the emergence of such a pattern in a unified European polity, Schmitter and Streeck's scenario seems plausible also at the national level. Among the many reasons for this, there is one that seems outstanding: the greater fragmentation (not only professionally, but also politically and culturally) of what once could be politically defined as a homogeneous working class, and the consequent growing difficulty for labour movements to 'speak on its behalf'.

My last point concerns the relationship between labour movements and workers. I have already touched on the significance of the growing heterogeneity of the labour force, and especially of the emergence of new professional and social groups quite different from traditional wage earners. To be sure, this is no novelty in advanced capitalism, as much criticism of these views insistently tells us, but at least two points should be stressed in this regard. First, the proliferation of professional figures with an 'atypical' status in the labour market or with ambivalent positions in the labour process is, probably for the first time in history, seen by many of the workers involved as not necessarily negative; that is, as representing the spread of 'substandard' or ambiguous contracts. On the contrary, it often corresponds to rather vague but nevertheless diffuse attitudes towards work. More generally, far more than in the recent past, even when jobs appear to be relatively standard or similar, an apparently major preoccupation among workers is to differentiate one group's position from another's, rather than to find elements in common. Secondly, irrespective of how it is assessed, this heterogeneity has a more profound effect than in the recent past on the ability of workers' organizations to reconstruct aggregate interests and to unify demands around hegemonic professional figures (Accornero, 1984).

Here, the unresolved question concerns the new meaning and scope of solidarity among workers, or, to put it bluntly, the capacity itself of labour movements to pursue the social and political construction of solidarity. The only unequivocal point is that old socialist-egalitarian ideologies as 'identity incentives' have declined, even in countries where they best performed this role in the past. It is, however, difficult to predict whether or not new identity incentives will develop. Should they fail to do so, labour organizations will have to do without a unifying ideology, and their only recourse will be simply to try to convince their members that cooperation among individuals with interests in common may work to their advantage. This will probably lead to a situation rather similar to nineteenth-century craft unionism. In this event, one would be tempted to abandon the notion of labour movements altogether as by now clearly obsolete. However, the fact that periods in which craft unionism predominated have been followed by a resurgence of class-based movements; or, to put it otherwise, the awareness that labour movements are quasi-cyclical in nature should warn us against any such premature conclusion. There is still much work ahead for students of labour movements.

Note

1 Unfortunately, comparisons including other world areas where labour movements are important actors – such as Latin America, Australia, East Asia and Eastern Europe – have been rare and rather unsatisfactory. The generalizations set out in this introduction apply mainly to Western Europe and to some extent North America.

References

Accornero, A. (1984) 'Social Change and Trade Union Movement in the 1970s', in O. Jacobi, B. Jessop, H. Kanstendiek and M. Regini (eds), *Technological Change, Rationalisation and Industrial Relations*. London: Croom Helm.

Berger, S. (ed.) (1981) *Organizing Interests in Western Europe*. Cambridge: Cambridge University Press.

Blauner, R. (1964) *Alienation and Freedom*. Chicago: University of Chicago Press.

Boyer, R. (ed.) (1986) *La flexibilité du travail en Europe*. Paris: La Découverte.

Braverman, H. (1974) *Labor and Monopoly Capital: the Degradation of Work in the Twentieth Century*. New York: Monthly Review Press.

Crouch, C. (1977) *Class Conflict and the Industrial Relations Crisis*. London: Heinemann.

Crouch, C. and Pizzorno, A. (eds) (1978) *The Resurgence of Class Conflict in Western Europe since 1968*. London: Macmillan, 2 vols.

Dahrendorf, R. (1959) *Class and Class Conflict in Industrial Society*. London: Routledge & Kegan Paul.

Dore, R. (1986) *Flexible Rigidities: Industrial Policy and Structural Adjustment in the Japanese Economy 1970–1980*. Palo Alto, CA: Stanford University Press.

Goldthorpe, J. (ed.) (1984) *Order and Conflict in Contemporary Capitalism*. Oxford: Clarendon Press.

Goldthorpe, J., Lockwood, D., Bechhofer, F. and Platt, J. (1969) *The Affluent Worker in the Class Structure*. Cambridge: Cambridge University Press.

Hibbs, D. (1976) 'Industrial Conflict in Advanced Industrial Societies', *American Political Science Review*, 4: 1033–58.

Hyman, R. (1972) *Strikes*. London: Fontana/Collins.

Kern, H. and Schumann, M. (1984) *Das Ende der Arbeitsteilung? Rationalisierung in der Industriellen Produktion*. Munich: Beck.

Kerr, C., Dunlop, J., Harbison, F. and Myers, C. (1960) *Industrialism and Industrial Man*. Cambridge, MA: Harvard University Press.

Korpi, W. (1970) *Varför strejkar arbetarna*. Stockholm: Tiden.

Korpi, W. (1983) *The Democratic Class Struggle*. London: Routledge & Kegan Paul.

Korpi, W. and Shalev, M. (1980) 'Strikes, Power and Politics in the Western Nations, 1900–1976', in M. Zeitlin (ed.), *Political Power and Social Theory*, Vol. 1. Greenwich, CT: Jai Press.

Lange, P. and Regini, M. (eds) (1989) *State, Market and Social Regulation.* Cambridge: Cambridge University Press.

Lange, P., Ross, G. and Vannicelli, M. (1982) *Unions, Change and Crisis: French and Italian Union Strategy and the Political Economy 1945–1980.* London: Allen & Unwin.

Lehmbruch, G. (1982) 'Introduction: Neo-corporatism in Comparative Perspective', in G. Lehmbruch and P. Schmitter (eds), *Patterns of Corporatist Policy-making.* London: Sage.

Lehmbruch, G. and Schmitter, P. (eds) (1982) *Patterns of Corporatist Policy-making.* London: Sage.

Mallet, S. (1963) *La nouvelle classe ouvrière.* Paris: Editions du Seuil.

Müller-Jentsch, W. and Sperling, H.J. (1978) 'Economic Development, Labour Conflicts and the Industrial Relations System in West Germany', in C. Crouch and A. Pizzorno (eds), *The Resurgence of Class Conflict in Western Europe since 1968*, vol 1. London: Macmillan, 2 vols.

Offe, C., Hinrichs, K. and Wiesenthal, H. (1984) 'The Crisis of the Welfare State and Alternative Modes of Work Redistribution', Paper presented at conference on 'The future of the welfare state', Maastricht (19–21 Dec.).

Olson, M. (1965) *The Logic of Collective Action.* Cambridge, MA: Harvard University Press.

Panitch, L. (1977) 'The Development of Corporatism in Liberal Democracies', *Comparative Political Studies*, 10: 61–90.

Piore, M. and Sabel, C. (1984) *The Second Industrial Divide.* New York: Basic Books.

Pizzorno, A. (1978) 'Political Exchange and Collective Identity in Industrial Conflict', in C. Crouch and A. Pizzorno (eds), *The Resurgence of Class Conflict in Western Europe since 1968*, vol. 2. London: Macmillan, 2 vols.

Pizzorno, A., Reyneri, E., Regini, M. and Regalia, I. (1978) *Lotte operaie e sindacato: il ciclo 1968–1972 in Italia.* Bologna: Il Mulino.

Regalia, I., Regini, M. and Reyneri, E. (1978) 'Labour Conflicts and Industrial Relations in Italy', in C. Crouch and A. Pizzorno (eds), *The Resurgence of Class Conflict in Western Europe since 1968*, vol. 1. London: Macmillan, 2 vols.

Regini, M. (1984) 'The Conditions for Political Exchange: How Concertation Emerged and Collapsed in Italy and Great Britain', in J. Goldthorpe (ed.), *Order and Conflict in Contemporary Capitalism.* Oxford: Clarendon Press.

Regini, M. (1987) 'Industrial Relations in the Phase of Flexibility', *International Journal of Political Economy*, 17 (3): 88–107.

Regini, M. and Sabel, C. (eds) (1989) *Strategie di riaggiustamento industriale.* Bologna: Il Mulino.

Ross, A. and Hartman, P. (1960) *Changing Patterns of Industrial Conflict.* New York: Wiley & Sons.

Schmitter, P. (1974) 'Still the Century of Corporatism', *The Review of Politics*, XXXVI: 85–131.

Schmitter, P. and Lehmbruch, G. (eds) (1979) *Trends toward Corporatist Intermediation.* London: Sage.

Schmitter, P. and Streeck, W. (1990) 'Organized Interests and the Europe of 1992', Paper for a conference on 'The US and Europe in the 1990s', Washington, DC (6–8 March).

Shorter, E. and Tilly, C. (1974) *Strikes in France, 1830–1968.* Cambridge: Cambridge University Press.

Soskice, D. (1988) 'Reinterpreting the Economics of Corporatism: Cooperative and Non-Cooperative Market Economies', Paper presented at conference on 'Markets, Institutions and Cooperation', Venice (20–22 Oct.).

Streeck, W. (1982) 'Organisational Consequences of Corporatist Cooperation in West German Labour Unions', in G Lehmbruch and P. Schmitter (eds), *Patterns of Corporatist Policy-making*. London: Sage.

Streeck, W. (1984) 'Neo-corporatist Industrial Relations and the Economic Crisis in West Germany', in J. Goldthorpe (ed.), *Order and Conflict in Contemporary Capitalism*. Oxford: Clarendon Press.

Streeck, W. (1987) 'The Uncertainties of Management in the Management of Uncertainty', *International Journal of Political Economy*, 17 (3): 57–87.

Streeck, W. (1989) 'On the Social and Political Conditions of Diversified Quality Production', Paper for conference on 'No Way to Full Employment?', Berlin (5–7 July).

Tarantelli, E. (1978) *Il ruolo economico del sindacato*. Bari: Laterza.

Tarrow, S. (1988) *Democracy and Disorder: Protest and Politics in Italy, 1965–1975*. Oxford: Oxford University Press.

Touraine, A. (1972) *Le communisme utopique. Le mouvement de mai 1968*. Paris: Editions du Seuil.

1

The Strength of Union Movements in Advanced Capital Democracies:

Social and Organizational Variations

Jelle Visser

In which direction are trade-union movements in advanced capitalist democracies moving? Have trade unions recovered from the membership losses of the early 1980s? Is membership still a relevant indicator? Do unions need members? In what ways has the social and organizational outlook of trade-union movements altered? Do trade unions still combine in encompassing labour movements? These are among the questions to be addressed in this chapter.

Starting with a discussion of union membership, union representation, and problems of cross-national comparison, I shall consider several measures of union strength: union density; membership composition; unity, organizational concentration; centralization; bargaining extension; and work-place representation. I define the strength of trade unions in a given (national or international) community as the degree to which they combine in representative, comprehensive, and inclusive movements. This goes beyond mere union power defined as the capacity of trade unions to apply sanctions against others by organizing strikes, inflicting damage, or withholding political support.

Trade unions may be characterized as oppositions that never become governments. But there are oppositions of sorts. Unions may behave as mere 'distributional coalitions' (Olson, 1982) or help to ally worker interests to policies that promote the production of wealth and a more efficient use of scarce resources (Freeman and Medoff, 1984; Swenson, 1989; Streeck, forthcoming). Trade unions may or may not be 'inclusive'; they may or may not give extra weight to the unspoken claims and rights of future generations or foreign constituencies (Visser, 1990a). The objectives for which trade unions amass power and mobilize workers, and the productive or distributive implications of these objectives are as interesting and probably vary as much as union power itself.

Cross-national Variation in Unionization and Union Decline

The fastest way to compare the state and development of trade union representation across the world is by looking at union density rates. Table 1.1 presents the available data on union membership and unionization levels for eighteen countries between 1970 and 1990.[1] We observe that there are *sizeable differences* in the level of union organization across advanced capitalist democracies. Not only between the extremes, Sweden and France, but also within the same region, between the United States and Canada, France and Italy, the Netherlands and Belgium, Norway and Sweden, Germany and Switzerland, the differences in levels of unionization are much larger than warranted by differences in economic development, industrialization, social structure, or public spending (Lipset, 1986; Visser, 1985; Wallerstein, 1989; Stephens, 1990).

A second feature of Table 1.1 is that in fourteen of the eighteen countries *unionization levels fell in the 1980s.* Judged by its size and length, this decline was unprecedented as far as post-war trends go. Just as much as the 1970s appeared to be the 'decade of trade unions', with most union movements, especially in Western Europe, expanding their membership, in the 1980s employers seem to have regained the initiative in industrial relations (Kochan et al., 1986; Rojot, 1992). High and rising levels of unemployment are one reason for the growing difficulties of unions. The associated shift to neo-liberal supply-side policies of governments, combined with the greater capacity and willingness of employers to resist union demands, expose trade unions to a chillier market place.

Only in Denmark, Finland, Sweden, Norway and Belgium unions seemed at first undeterred by the recession. With the exception of Norway these are countries in which unions continue to administer unemployment benefits (Flora, 1986; Pedersen, 1989). In Norway, unemployment levels remained comparatively low, as in Sweden. However, for the first time since 1911 the membership in the Swedish confederation of trade unions, the LO, declined in 1988 and 1989. After 1986 there was also union decline in Denmark and Belgium. Small falls in membership occurred in West Germany, Austria and Switzerland, leading to a slowly declining unionization rate. Outside Europe, labour unions expanded their membership in Canada, and the union density rate appears to be holding at about one-third of the employed dependent labour force. Like the German unions (Streeck, 1987), Canadian unions

Table 1.1 *Union membership and union density in eighteen advanced capitalist democracies, 1970–89**

Country	Total union membership (in 000s)			Aggregate union density rates (%)				
				Employed only		Unemployed		
	1970	1980	1989	'80	'89	'70	'80	'89
Sweden	2,546	3,486	3,855	80	85	68	80	85
Denmark	1,143	1,796	2,034(a)	77	73(a)	60	78	74(a)
Finland	950	1,646	1,895	70	71	51	71	72
Norway	760	1,049	1,204	57	57	51	56	56
Belgium	1,606	2,310	2,291	57	53	46	59	56
Luxembourg	52	72	75	52	50	47	52	50
Ireland	423	544	474(b)	57	52(b)	53	52	47(b)
Austria	1,530	1,661	1,644	54	46	60	53	45
Australia	2,331	2,956	3,410	49	42	50	47	40
UK	11,187	12,947	10,238(a)	51	42(a)	45	49	39(a)
Italy	5,225	8,772	9,568	49	40	36	45	35
W. Germany	8,251	9,646	9,637	37	34	33	36	32
Canada	2,231	3,487	4,031	35	35	31	32	32
Japan	11,605	12,369	12,230	31	27	35	30	26
Switzerland	843	954	900	31	26	31	31	26
Netherlands	1,585	1,741	1,636	35	25	37	32	23
USA	21,248	20,095	16,960	23	16	30	22	15
France	3,549	3,374	1,970	19	12	22	18	10

Notes: * Membership data include unemployed and retired workers, but exclude self-employed persons; labour-force data include all wage earners and salaried persons in employment. (OECD *Labour Force Statistics* data). For further notes, see Visser (1991); in particular, Appendix 4A, on sources and methods. (a) = 1988; (b) = 1987.

Source: Visser (1991)

demonstrate a remarkable resilience, especially considering the relatively low level of overall representation. In the Canadian context this has been labelled the 'comfortable stability of trade unions' (Kumar, 1986).

No comfort, but only adversity and turbulence was experienced by unions in the United Kingdom, France, Ireland, Italy, the Netherlands, Australia, Japan, and the United States. A sharp fall in membership and unionization occurred in France, where union membership in 1988 is estimated at half the number in 1976, and union density dropped to around an estimated 10 per cent of the dependent labour force (Rosanvallon, 1988; de Noblecourt, 1989; Groux and Mouriaux, 1990);[2] in the USA, where unions have been losing ground ever since the mid-fifties; following a particularly large drop in membership between 1980 and 1983, union density is at a current low of 16 per cent (Kochan and Verma, 1992; BLS, 1990); in the United Kingdom, where unions lost one-quarter of their membership since 1979 and union density, which had risen from 45 per cent in 1969 to 55 per cent in 1979, was down to 45 per cent in 1983, and slipped further to 41 per cent by 1989 (Stevens and Wareing, 1990); in Italy, where the growing number of pensioners in the unions conceals a loss of over 1 million members between 1980 and 1988, and most of the 1970s gains in unionization have evaporated, though overall losses might be less severe if 'autonomous unions' are taken into account (Squarzon, 1991; de Nicola, 1991); in Ireland, where the fall in membership and density in the first half of the 1980s was described as the largest since the 1930s (Roche and Larragy, 1990); in the Netherlands, where unions lost over one-quarter of their members between 1980 and 1986, and union density fell to its lowest level since the 1920s (Visser, 1990b); in Australia, where the brunt of the ten points' drop in union density between 1976 and 1988 occurred after the early 1980s (ABS, 1988; Peetz, 1990); and in Japan, where stagnating or slowly declining membership numbers in the 1980s came on top of a long-term downward trend in unionization (Shimada, 1988; JIL, 1990). France, the United States, Japan and, since the early 1980s, the Netherlands have been weakly unionized, while the level of union organization in Britain, Australia, Ireland, and Italy is above average. The downturn in membership, but not in unionization, was reversed in the later 1980s in the Netherlands, but there was no turnaround in France, the United States, Japan, the United Kingdom or Ireland. We also note that membership continues to stagnate in Italy, Norway, West Germany, Switzerland, and Austria – all this despite the economic boom in the second half of the 1980s.

Unions in all countries found it less easy than in previous decades to attract or hold on to members. Unions with an extended basis of representation fared better (the Scandinavian countries, Belgium, Australia), although Britain is an awkward exception. In the 1980s the gap between highly and weakly unionized countries widened. The coefficient of variation is larger in 1988–89 than in 1970 or in 1950. Differences have grown larger between Western Europe, Japan, and North America, but also between countries in the same region and with ever more integrated economies like France and Germany, the Netherlands and Belgium, or Canada and the United States. The question arises, therefore, what consequences do such large differences in union representation have for the economic performance and social welfare in these countries? Will European economic integration trigger a process of convergence in union representation? Or will we instead see a bifurcation between highly unionized countries (areas, regions) and ill-organized ones, combined with social dumping and wage competition? Before deciding on how to answer these questions, we must consider the possibility that membership and density are poor indicators of the roles and activities of trade unions. Maybe the figures on unionization shown in Table 1.1, with their semblance of quantified precision, overstate the real differences between unions in these countries?

Is Comparison of Unionization Rates Meaningful?

Comparing unionization levels across countries is fraught with problems. Over time and across countries trade unions hold their members to different rights and obligations, and they administrate membership statistics with a differing degree of accuracy. Statistical coverage by government agencies, federations, or statistical bureaus is also variable. Inevitably, differences remain with regard to the definition and recognition of trade unions (should one include staff associations and professional bodies?), statistical coverage (are independent and non-affiliated unions included?), membership (full-paying members only? self-employed and retired members?), and the labour force (unemployed workers and first-time job-seekers? domestic services? agriculture?). Finally, in some countries (France, Greece, Spain, Portugal, Italy in the 1950s and 1960s) membership numbers may be a secret even for union leaders.

Precision can be misleading (Clegg, 1976: 13) if we ignore the conceptual, methodological, and practical problems involved or if we fail to detail which definitions of unions, union membership and employment we apply. Once we do that, it would be 'equally wrong, however, to overemphasize these problems and to suggest that the margin of error is so great as to inhibit their use' (Bain and Price, 1980: 9). Indeed, in contrast to Bamber and Lansbury (1987: 256), I see no reason why unionization data should be less reliable than data on unemployment, wages, unit labour costs, strikes, or productivity. In all these fields we need standards and caution in the use of statistics.

Precision would turn into blindness if we were to suggest that union membership, or union density, provides a ready-made yardstick for union strength. To make that translation we need to know more about the composition of the membership, the structure and government of unions, their accumulated resources and contracts, and the commitments of members. We cannot make the equation union density = union strength without studying labour and association laws, collective bargaining practices, organizational charters, public roles of labour, and understanding how members are recruited, how they are convinced to stay, to pay, and, if needed, to act – in short, unless we understand how numbers become occasionally compelling arguments for employers, governments, agencies, competing unions, politicians, and other interlocutors. Thus, our comparison of figures, such as presented in Table 1.1, must be enriched with institutional, organizational, and political detail.

Students of French unions have questioned the comparability of unionization rates across countries on the ground that such rates reflect various degrees of coercion and public support (Mouriaux, 1983, 1986; Rosanvallon, 1988). Thus, while taking a membership card in French unions is held to be a commitment to militancy, across its borders (for instance, in Britain or Belgium) membership is believed to be propped up with administrative measures (social insurance check-off, closed shop). In Britain as many as 80 per cent of union members in establishments where unions are recognized have their dues deducted from their payroll (Milward and Stevens, 1986). Such a 'check-off' would be unlawful in France.[3] Are, perhaps, union members in France better compared to unpaid union organizers and shop stewards in Britain? Is the French equivalent of the British union member the worker who gives her vote to the union in works council elections (Adam, 1983; Rosanvallon, 1988; Caire, 1990)?[4]

Perhaps, the answer is 'yes', following empirical study of the roles and activities of union sympathizers, members, and activists in Britain and France (and in other countries). It is only reasonable to assume that our understanding of union membership, and its significance today, would improve if we knew more about the costs and commitments it implies (see also Regalia, 1987). We need not doubt that social pressure, administrative coercion, and public supports of various kinds do play a role in union organizing, and that there are members in unions, as in most other 'voluntary associations', who would not be there but for coercion or selective benefits.[5] Closed shops are rare in Europe, except in Britain, but elsewhere there may be 'soft' functional equivalents which operate through union-influenced policies of hiring, firing, redeployment, training, and promotion (Hansen, Jackson and Miller, 1982). French unions *are* incomparable, since – as Flanagan, Soskice and Ulman (1983: 585) drily note in their overview of European wage policies – 'no benefits accrued in France from union activity, and most of those that did offered no privatisation'.

Union Membership and Worker Mobilization

We do not have to assume that union membership is completely voluntary, least of all that it is unselfish, in order to accept the notion that in a broad sense unionization does mean a *collective rather than individualistic definition of interests*, and indicates a *collective capacity to act* (Shorter and Tilly, 1974; Korpi, 1983). There is no automatic link with militancy. High levels of militancy are found in countries with low and high unionization rates (Korpi and Shalev, 1979; Korpi, 1983; Poole, 1986; Visser, 1990a). Unions are capable of mobilizing considerable energies and exerting significant pressure even with small fluctuating memberships when they are seen as crucial intermediaries for public policies or important contributors to political and social equilibria. Spain in the 1980s is a case in point. Despite a small and apparently declining membership, Spanish unions have in recent years shown a remarkable capacity for general worker mobilization (Aguilar and Roca, 1990).

Does it follow that unions do not need (many) members? Apart from three brief episodes (1919, 1936, and 1945), French unions have never been a mass phenomenon (Shorter and Tilly, 1974; Visser, 1989). Occasionally, syndicalist or communist leaders have cherished a notion of *elite unionism*. I like to quote Albert Levy, who was CGT treasurer before World War I. This did not prevent him from arguing against a large membership, 'car la lourde modération entre avec le grand nombre' (cited in Birien, 1978: 88). The French sociologist Rosanvallon argues against the need for massive membership for opposite reasons:

> The role and influence of trade unions derives more from their institutional status, and less and less from their sociological quality. Membership does not manifest itself directly as a means of strengthening trade unionism. Thrust from fellow workers, and support from the law seem sufficient for a small number of militants to play their role as interlocutors of company management. (Rosanvallon, 1988: 39–40)

In this view, trade unions need more electoral tests, to give credibility to their claim of representation. Like political parties they need committed activists and well-trained functionaries to win elections.

Unlike Rosanvallon I believe that membership still is a critical resource. Political parties derive their power from winning elections. Unions often benefit and sometimes suffer badly from their proximity to political parties and the state. But in the last resort they are valued by their capacity to represent, to express, and to defend what Piore (1985) has called a 'social vision' – of professional competence, equity, fairness, justice. This vision changes with the sociological quality of unions, as much as the capacity of unions to influence other changes with their organizational quality. For instance, union militancy becomes only a strategic resource, expendable for chosen ends at chosen times, when the union leadership commands sufficient authority over workers' decisions when to strike (demonstrate, deny electoral support, and so on), what for, and how long. That condition will probably fail when union leaders have estranged themselves from their following (Britain, in the early 1980s) or when membership is forced upon workers (as in Eastern Europe before 1989). It certainly fails when unions have no members or have not accumulated trust and resources which can be offered as selective incentives to members in order to influence workers' decisions to come out on strike or go back to work. It has long been argued that this is the case in France, where for lack of members and dire finances unions have no strike monopoly (Reynaud, 1975; Delamotte, 1982). In Sweden or Germany, on the other hand, trade unions have effectively monopolized the strike weapon, which means that they can plan and calculate its use.

My conclusion is, therefore, that unionization data serve as a useful starting point for the study of trade unionism. Across countries, union density rates offer a short-hand though incomplete picture of the overall strength of unions. Over time they present an indicator of the direction in which labour relations are moving. Unionization data are more readily used as a measure of developments over time than as a measure of the position of union movements across countries.

Institutional Detail

If one compares the sharp fall in unionization in the Netherlands with the apparent stability in Belgium – adjacent small countries with soaring unemployment in the 1980s – it is helpful to know that Belgium is among the few countries (with Sweden, Denmark, and Finland) in which the relationship between union membership and unemployment insurance funds was maintained or reestablished after 1945. In the Netherlands unemployed workers are likely to let their membership lapse, while in Belgium they have the good reason of a highly selective benefit to retain their membership card.[6] Here, we stumble on a tiny institutional detail which appears to matter a great deal both for the explanation and interpretation of unionization trends.

However, unionization trends in Belgium and the Netherlands diverged as early as the 1950s. This divergence in collective worker organization between two countries of roughly the same size, similar post-war (but not pre-war) employment structures, high dependence on export and foreign competition, importance of transnational firms, (French) legal-administrative traditions, deep-seated ideological splits between unions, 'segmented politics', and the political dominance of Christian parties would be hard to explain without taking into account the fact that Belgian unions are workplace based and run a reasonably effective grievance-handling system in firms. Mok (1985) calls it the 'small difference with the large effects'. Dutch unions are absent from the workplace. Unlike Belgium, the statutory works council came prior to and takes precedence over union attempts to 'conquer the workplace'. Highly centralized union movements contribute to a wide coverage of collective agreements, but, not having access to the workplace, they often lack bargaining depth (Clegg, 1976). They usually find it difficult to convince workers to join despite considerable institutional protection (see also Kjellberg, 1983). Windmuller (1969) stressed this repeatedly in his study of Dutch labour relations.

Finally, from the steep decline in unionization in the Netherlands in the 1980s one might infer that Dutch unions lost a great deal of power, and as a matter of fact they did (Albeda, 1985; Reynaerts, 1985; Visser, 1990b). But contrary to what happened in the 1930s, the fall in union representation did not greatly diminish multi-employer bargaining or reduce bargaining coverage in the private sector. Elsewhere I have argued that the reasons for that non-event are to be found in the prevailing legislation, the high degree of collective employer organization, and the apparent choice of the large majority of Dutch employers not to add insult to injury and unsettle what after all was a tradition of forty years' peaceful, cooperative, and moderate labour relations (Visser, 1988). This is a fragile balance, which can easily become unsettled. Membership may decline further and unions may lose their (monopoly) claim of representation in national and industrial fora, the present legislation in favour of collective bargaining extension may be reviewed, national and sectoral employers' associations may destabilize in the process of further European integration, and highly visible union replacement strategies of large companies may find imitators. Unions in Belgium seem in a much better position if they are only judged by membership numbers. On the other hand, with a sizeable portion of their membership out of work or otherwise dependent on social assistance, Belgian unions are severely challenged by a labour market which, for almost a decade, has exhibited one of the highest youth and long-term unemployment rates in Western Europe. There is little doubt that union bargaining power has been eroded following several painful government diktats which register the enhanced power of employers in such a labour market (de Broek, 1989; Spineux, 1990).

The Social and Organizational Fragmentation of Union Movements

The decline of employment in manufacturing industry and manual labour, together with the sharp increase in unemployment in many countries, have often been cited as the causes of the current union decline. There is little doubt that the continuing shift of production and employment from manufacturing to services, as it is accompanied by a process of deconcentration of employment and more white-collar, female, and part-time jobs, challenges the recruitment and organizing methods of trade unions. But will it, as suggested in many popular discussions of the topic, inevitably set the stage for union decline?

Structural employment shifts and unemployment did play a significant role in the 1980s decline. Up to 50 per cent of the decline can be accounted for by these factors alone in countries like Britain and the Netherlands (Visser, 1990a: ch. 3). Another way of putting this point is as follows: if, for instance, the British or Dutch employment structure in 1985 had been similar to that of West Germany, with its strong base in manufacturing industry, the 1985 union density rate would have been 47 per cent rather than the actual 42 per cent in Britain, and 30 per cent rather than 25 per cent in the Netherlands. There would still have been a decline, though.

Table 1.2 *Union density rates in manufacturing (ISIC 3), financial services (ISIC 8), public services, and among males and females*

Country	Manufacturing		Financial services		Public services		Males		Females	
	1970	1988	1970	1988	1970	1988	1970	1988	1970	1988
Sweden	84	100	70	72	–	81	77	82	54	88
Denmark	80[b]	100	37[b]	36	–	70	–	78	–	72
Norway	67	87	51	33	68	75	–	–	–	–
Belgium	60	95	20	23	–	–	–	–	–	–
Austria	68	53	37	28	78	57	73	57	45	37
Britain	52	41	21	25	60	55	54	44	29	33
Italy	40	47	33	22	47[a]	54[a]	–	–	–	–
Germany	36	48[f]	15	17[f]	61	45	42	47	15	22
Switzerland	27	34	26	14	75	71[f]	42	34	11	13
Netherlands	41	25	8	9	64	49	44	35	14	13
Australia	54[e]	48	42[e]	28	73[e]	68	56[g]	46	43[g]	35
Canada	44	38	3[d]	6	–	63[f]	36	39	21	30
Japan	35[d]	32	52[d]	50	78	56	37[g]	30	29[g]	19
USA	41[c]	22	5[c]	2	29[c]	37	28[c]	20	16[c]	13

Notes: [a] Probably much higher if independent unions are taken into account; [b] = 1972; [c] = 1973; [d] = 1980; [e] = 1982; [f] = 1986; [g] = 1976.

Source: Visser (1991)

It is impossible to say where the contraction of the manufacturing industry will end. Presumably, each country will retain some manufacturing – at 20 per cent of total dependent employment, as in Norway, Denmark or the Netherlands now, or at 10 or even 5 per cent? Given its greater efficiency and specialization, manufacturing industry will probably remain more important in Germany than in Britain, more viable in Switzerland than in the Netherlands. Further European integration is likely to intensify cross-border specialization. There is, however, nothing inevitable about structural employment shifts and union decline.

American unions suffered their biggest losses in manufacturing; in most European countries, trade unions advanced in manufacturing, though the overall number of unionists often declined. The decline of unions in US manufacturing enterprises is presumably related to the capacity of employers to create a union-free environment or relocate investment and labour to a non-union environment; the decline in unionization in manufacturing in Britain and the Netherlands was related to the crisis in old industries, large firms, and firms or sectors from which support with the public purse was withdrawn. The examples of Sweden and Denmark show that unions still have a growth potential if they succeed in organizing related commercial and financial services, as well as the so-called 'knowledge workers'. In most countries, unions have yet to make a breakthrough in the financial sector and among salaried white-collar employees outside the public sector. They also have much ground to make up among female workers (see Table 1.2). In Europe in particular, union growth in the past two decades has depended heavily upon the expansion of government employment and communal services.

Whatever the consequences for union growth, changes in the occupational and industrial structure of employment will have a lasting impact on the sociological and organizational quality of trade unions. The most likely effect is a further *social and organizational fragmentation* of union movements, a decline of trade unions as movements. Blue-collar workers and members in manufacturing establishments and sectors exposed to international competition will become an ever smaller minority within the labour movements of which they were once the proud founders. Inevitably, their voice will carry less weight in general councils, national confederations, and bargaining fora. They had already lost their dominant position in the 1970s, when relative decline turned absolute. In many countries the largest unions, or cartels of unions, are now in the public sector. In 1985, metalworkers' unions retained their traditional first place only in Germany, Switzerland,

Table 1.3 *The changing social composition of labour movements, 1950–89*

Country		Private sector — Manual		Private sector — Non-manual		Public sector		Industry		Females	
		1950	1989	1950	1989	1950	1989	1950	1989	1950	1989
Germany	DGB	65	49	10	18	25	33	68	57	18	25
		71	57	6	14	23	29	73	63	17	23
Austria	ÖGB	59	43	12	22	29	36	53	48	26	31
		59	43	18	22	30	36	53	48	26	31
Switzerland	SGB	58	43	18	27	24	31	57	52	–	19
		68	63	1	2	25	26	68	61	11	12
Britain	TUC	62	41	10	20	28	39	57	35	18	38
		72	47	6	18	22	35	63	39	17	37
Denmark	LO	–	40	–	24	–	36	68	38	–	46
		82	57	10	16	–	27	77	47	20	45
Sweden	LO	64	36	13	23	23	42	55	37	22	50
		80	62	4	9	16	28	61	40	19	47
Norway	LO	75	31	8	17	18	53	56	36	–	–
		75	51	8	10	18	39	56	47	17	35
Netherlands	FNV	65	34	9	16	26	50	55	36	6	18
		72	53	9	14	19	33	61	38	3	16
Italy	CGIL	–	–	–	–	14[a]	33	49[a]	42	–	–
		–	–	–	–	11	26	51	49	–	–

Notes: [a] 1950 data without UIL
Source: Visser (1989, 1990), and updates from DUES database

and one of the two Belgian federations. In Austria, they were outnumbered by a general white-collar union; in Denmark, Ireland, and Britain by large, general unions straddling all industries; in Sweden, Norway, the Netherlands, and France by public employee unions; in Italy by pensioners. These shifts in the social, occupational, and industrial composition – stylized in Table 1.3 – will only accelerate if unions succeeded in their attempts to organize larger numbers of salaried white-collar employees.

The second point is that the major union confederations will increasingly be challenged by new, emergent groups, especially among professional employees and in the (semi-)public sector: staff and departmental unions, *Comitati di Base, les coordinations, categorale bonden*, vocational unions. These groups tend to copy the methods of collective action of skilled blue-collar workers but often prefer organizations and temporary alliances of their own, the archetypical 'distributional coalitions' of Olson (1982), which owe great power to their position in the labour market (skill scarcity) or to political protection (power to upset political balances or withhold votes). Not important in quantitative terms, these groups tend to undermine the intraclass compromises negotiated by encompassing organizations such as the general confederations of trade unions.

Table 1.4 documents the decline in associational monopoly of the major (still dominant) confederations in Western Europe. This decline is entirely due to the inability to integrate white-collar employees. Among blue-collar workers the monopoly of representation – though shared with religiously or ideologically rival organizations in Belgium, the Netherlands, Switzerland, Italy, and France – is nearly complete and remains stable. The communist CGT in France is the most dramatic instance of decline – from three-quarters to less than one-third of all union members. The Italian CGIL also lost its dominant position, but in the 1970s and 1980s it stabilized its majority share. We also note the continuing decline in associational monopoly of the confederations which are 'blue-collar only (or mainly)': the LOs in the three Scandinavian countries, and the socialist organizations in Switzerland and Belgium. The position of the Austrian confederation of trade unions (ÖGB) is unique, and the success of its German sister organization, DGB, remarkable. The fall in associational monopoly, from 90 to 80 per cent, occurred in the 1950s but has since stopped. The coherent internal structure of the DGB – one union per sector – has not prevented it from rallying seven out of ten organized white-collar employees and almost six out of ten organized civil servants. In this sense, its accomplishment is far

Table 1.4 *The representativeness of central union organizations, 1950–89*

Country/Confederations			All members		Associational monopolies			
					Manual members		Non-manual members	
	Name	Orientation	1950	1989	1950	1985	1950	1985
Austria	ÖGB	socialist	100	100	100	100	100	100
Germany	DGB	socialist	92	81	99	97	62	62
UK	TUC	labour	84	88	93	97	54	84
Sweden	LO	socialist	79	59	98	99	27	18
	TCO	white-colar	17	33			64	69
Denmark	LO	socialist	85	70	98	98	43	49
	FTF	white-collar	12[a]	16			34[a]	28
Norway	LO	socialist	82[a]	67	99[a]	99	44[a]	43
	YS	occupational	9[c]	11			16[c]	18
Belgium	FGTB	socialist	49	38	63	50	26	37
	CSC	Catholic	44	54	35	48	74	56
Netherlands	NVV	socialist	33	43[d]	34	46[d]	24	36[d]
	NKV	Catholic	26	18[d]	28	35[d]	12	8[d]
	FNV	general		60		81		43
	CNV	Protestant	14	20	13	16	12	21
Switzerland	SGB	socialist	60	51	76	75	19	16
	CNG	Catholic	8	12	11	20	2	4
	VSA	white-collar	16	17			41	42
Italy	CGIL	communist	67[a]	42				
	CISL	Catholic	20[a]	27				
	UIL	socialist	13[a]	14				
France	CGT	communist	76	29				
	FO	reformist	9	22				
	CFDT	radical	16[b]	23				

Notes: [a] = 1960; [b] = 1964; [c] = 1976; [d] = 1980
Source: Visser (1989; 1990, tables 19–21); extended for Belgium and updated to 1989 from DUES database

more remarkable than that of the British TUC, where there is no such integration of white-collar and blue-collar employees in common sectoral unions. And in this particular sense the position of the DGB and its industrial affiliates is stronger and more promising than that of its sister organizations in Austria, Sweden, Switzerland, or Belgium. In each of these cases white-collar workers organize separate from blue-collar workers. In the Netherlands, Norway, and Italy industrial unions try to follow the German example, but do so with less success. Industrial and general blue-collar unions in Austria, Belgium, Britain, Denmark, the Netherlands, Norway, Sweden, and Switzerland are severely disadvantaged by being confined to a declining segment of the labour market.

The social and organizational fragmentation of labour movements has made the search for responsible wage policies more difficult. The leading role of the unions in manufacturing, and in metal engineering in particular, has become less self-evident or has been openly challenged (Visser, 1990a). Models of incomes policies, as practised in the 1970s in Britain, Scandinavia, the Netherlands, or Belgium, became increasingly strained by the divide between public and private sector unions (Flanagan, Soskice and Ulman, 1983; Rehn and Viklund, 1990). The rise of independent unionism was accelerated by excessive claims of general representation in the context of centralized policies of pay control in Norway and the Netherlands, both in the 1950s and 1970s, in Denmark in the 1970s, and in Italy in the 1980s. Interest aggregation within central organizations of labour became a more strenuous task, and central control of pay policies was often impossible. Unilateral adjustment, without prior agreement, by other unions to the wage leadership of the metalworkers (or a similar strong group in the exposed sector) has little chance of success outside Germany and, perhaps, Austria and Switzerland.

Exclusive jurisdiction, as it exists in the United States or Japan, is exceptional in Western Europe, though Japanese firms in Britain have pressed for single union deals, just as American firms in Britain tend to practise union avoidance. The German union system comes closest to one firm/one union, or rather, one industry/one union. There is some competition from an independent white-collar union in manufacturing and commercial services and from an independent civil servants' centre in the public sector,[7] but the DGB affiliates tend to monopolize representation at bargaining tables, as regards co-determination and in the elected works council (Müller-Jentsch, 1987). Thus, in a leading sector such as metal there will be only one union in Germany, while there

Table 1.5 Number of affiliates, major unions, and membership shares in European union confederations, 1950 and 1989 (percentages)

Country/ Confederation	No. of affiliates 1950	Largest	%	Second	%	No. of affiliates 1989	Largest	%	Second	%
Austria ÖGB	16	metal	(16)	build	(11)	15	gen[d]	(21)	metal	(15)
Germany DGB	16	metal	(26)	govt	(13)	17	metal	(33)	govt	(15)
UK TUC	186	manual[c]	(16)	metal	(14)	84	manual[c]	(14)	gen/govt	(11)
Sweden LO	45	metal	(17)	build	(9)	24	govt	(28)	metal	(20)
TCO	42	indust	(24)	superv	(11)	21	indust	(24)	govt	(15)
Denmark LO	70	manual[c]	(37)	trade	(8)	30	manual[c]	(23)	trade	(22)
FTF	11[a]	govt	(19)	govt	(16)	56	govt	(21)	govt	(13)
Norway LO	39[a]	metal	(11)	build	(11)	33	govt	(22)	metal	(13)
YS							finance	(25)	health	(22)
Belgium FGTB	21	metal	(26)	manual[c]	(25)	12	govt	(23)	manual[c]	(22)
CSC	17	textile	(25)	build	(21)	21	metal	(17)	build	(14)
Netherlands NVV	28	metal	(18)	govt	(14)	16[b]	govt	(22)	indust	(18)
NKV	24	build	(14)	metal	(14)	9[b]	indust	(24)	build	(19)
FNV						16	govt	(27)	indust	(23)
CNV	26	govt	(17)	metal	(17)	15	govt	(27)	indust	(17)
Switzerland SGB	15	metal	(27)	build	(27)	15	metal	(27)	build	(26)
CNG	9	metal	(29)	build	(28)	12	build	(34)	metal	(26)
VSA	8	trade	(70)	metal	(13)	10	trade	(52)	metal	(17)
Italy CGIL	–					17	retired	(35)	metal	(10)
CISL	–					17	retired	(25)	agric	(10)
UIL	–					27	retired	(11)	metal	(9)

Notes: [a] = 1960; [b] = 1980; [c] = general union of mainly manual workers in mainly private sector; [d] = general union of non-manual workers in private sector. % = membership of union as proportion of total confederal membership (in brackets); extended for Belgium and updated till 1989 from DUES database.
Source: Visser (1989; 1990, tables 18 and 25).

will be always two in Austria, three in Sweden, Norway, Italy, and the Netherlands, four in Belgium, Denmark, and Switzerland, five in France, and six or more in Britain.

Inter-union rivalry adds to the difficulties of interest aggregation. Table 1.5 documents a large variation in the number of affiliates of the major union confederation. Not shown in the table are the many small unions which exist outside these confederations. Their number has not declined very much in the past twenty years; rather, old craft unions have been replaced by a new generation of professional and staff associations.

The organizational fragmentation of unions is quite simply the expression of three failures: (1) the failure *to rationalize* union structure along industrial lines, (2) the failure *to integrate* white-collar employees, and (3) the failure *to unite* workers of different religious or ideological persuasions. Its consequences are also simple: whatever is added to the choice of workers is lost in union strength and the capacity of intra- and inter-class coordination of union action. Differences across countries along this dimension are substantial. Thus, whereas in Austria and Germany fifteen to seventeen unions exist, and only ten to twelve are significant in collective bargaining, we find always two or three times that number in Sweden, Switzerland, the Netherlands, or Belgium, and six to ten times that many independent actors in Britain. Paradoxically, the larger the number of unions, the more intra- and inter-class coordination of policies will depend on the presence of a comprehensive and powerful central organization, and the less likely will it be that such a centre will emerge and persist. Only in Germany, or in Austria, is it feasible to convene with the ten or so more important union leaders; this is already much more difficult in Sweden, Italy, or the Netherlands, and a sheer impossibility in Britain. In recent years, provoked by industrial decline and membership losses, there has been a reduction in the number of affiliates as a consequence of failures, of mergers, or – more rare – of conscious attempts to rationalize union structure, prevent double representation or prepare for European integration. For instance, the number of affiliates of the TUC has further declined to eighty-eight, twenty unions fewer than in 1979, but the erratic pattern of mergers has left the British union system just as 'uneven, illogically structured and excessively decentralized as always' (Crouch, 1990: 354). Recent attempts of the Danish LO to concentrate its affiliates in five main unions have met with severe opposition from its union of skilled metalworkers. In the Netherlands, the two largest affiliates vetoed in 1987 a further discussion of reorganization in the FNV; one more testimony to its rapidly dwindling authority (Visser, 1990a).

Union Structure and Multi-employer Bargaining

Germany and Britain can be seen as polar cases in terms of union structure, union government, and industry-wide collective bargaining (Windmuller, 1981; Streeck, 1984). British unions developed over a long period of time, establishing small but solid craft organizations and then only later large general unions that, rather than eliminating the craft unions, occupied the possible space for industrial unions to develop (Fulcher, 1988). In Germany, industrial unions came soon after the first established craft unions, which they replaced or enveloped in the main industrial sectors; the redesign of German unions after 1945, with the help of British and American advisers, further rationalized a comprehensive structure of interest representation in that country. The other influence that helped to shape unions in Germany and elsewhere on the continent was socialism and the socialist vision of a common and undivided worker organization confronting employers. Socialism also helps explain the relative centralization of trade unions on the European continent.

Multi-employer bargaining, by industry and region, has remained the norm in Germany. Its conduct is under the control of national union headquarters. Additional bargaining activities at the level of companies, and with the involvement of the statutory works councils, have increased in intensity and importance during the 1980s. The increased involvement in bargaining over working hours and training, together with their statutory consultation rights and increased role in handling grievances, tend to elevate the role of works councils to that of 'company unions'. There is evidence that the current pressure to customize labour relations according to local conditions – for instance, in the context of flexible working hours and multi-skilling – has created tensions in German trade unions (Jacobi and Müller-Jentsch, 1990). Yet the increased bargaining activities in firms have not replaced the industry-wide agreement. The legal restrictions on works council involvement in collective bargaining and strike action help to explain the continued integrity of industry-wide agreements. Streeck (1984: ch. 3) has stressed a more positive function as well. Elected by union members and non-union members alike but dominated by local union representatives, works councils are instrumental in adapting industry-wide agreements to local environments and extending identical conditions to unionized and non-unionized workers. It helps to sustain 'inclusive unionism' within firms, whereas sectoral multi-employer agreements are instrumental in maintaining a common 'level-ground playing field' in labour relations between firms who face the same product market constraints. With the benefit of hindsight, it is no surprise that, of all European countries, multi-employer bargaining should have disappeared, or receded, during the 1980s in Britain, France, and Italy. Brown gives a forceful, if sarcastic, summary of three decades of British collective bargaining: 'The undue reliance placed by unions on shop stewards in the 1960s and 1970s appears to be producing a parochial, fragmented, and more managerially malleable form of unionism in the 1980s' (Brown, 1985: 170). Rubery (1986: 87) and Lash and Urry (1987: 270), from a leftist point of view, arrive at a similar conclusion. In the 1960s and 1970s pay bargaining at intermediary and local levels typically involved shop stewards. Given the fragmentation in national organization and the extent of inter-union rivalry, poor communication between unions and local bargainers developed. As a result, a closer relation between stewards and their single worker constituency, and likewise a fragmentation between local bargainers and the national union, existed. This development, first in manufacturing, then elsewhere in the private sector, weakened industry-wide collective bargaining long before management felt the pressure of global competition and seized the opportunity of a slack labour market and an anti-union government to establish greater control over industrial relations and labour management. In Britain in the late 1980s 90 per cent of all private sector pay, and 65 per cent of working hours, were decided at the company level (Milward and Stevens, 1986). National-level bargaining outside the public sector was rare in Britain in the late 1980s. Voluntary policies of wage moderation that assume central guidance, rather than the squeeze of credits and bankruptcies, are now a thing of the past. So there is one less strategic option for labour, and a real danger of a growing disparity, and dualism (Goldthorpe, 1984), between conditions of employment in a union and non-union sector.

In France collective bargaining has a troubled history, largely for ideological reasons connected with employer paternalism *cum* revolutionary syndicalism. With collective bargaining playing a modest and unstable role in the regulation of the terms and conditions of employment, direct intervention of the state in establishing minimum conditions and standards was much relied upon. In the 1970s, following the changing political climate and industrial balance of power in the aftermath of 1968, a number of inter-confederal agreements over non-pay issues such as minimum wage standards, working time, job classification, collective dismissal protection, and social security issues were reached. In the second half of the 1970s governments had little success with their attempts to promote the negotiation of sectoral multi-employer agreements. The 1982 reforms introduced by the socialist government made it obligatory for French employers to negotiate collective terms of employment in firms and legalized a worker's right of expression in firms. Together with the inducements for working time reduction and training and employment of young workers, these reforms have boosted the number of company agreements and further narrowed the space for industry agreements (CGP, 1988). It appears that the reforms of the early 1980s have exposed the weaknesses of French unions beyond repair. The extraordinary degree of ideological division in the French movement,[8] and the traditional reliance of French unions on political pressure instead of industrial bargaining, help to understand the debilitating impact of these new bargaining rights on French unions.

Developments in Italy are more difficult to understand. There was a decline in union representation, though less so than in Britain or France. In the early 1980s, some of the old ideological and political divisions in the Italian union movement were reopened, but there is still a high degree of inter-union cooperation when compared to the 1950s or 1960s, or indeed when compared to France. Industry-wide collective bargaining in the private sector has not disappeared, but it is certainly under threat and less important than in Northern Europe. In Italy much of the travail of multi-employer bargaining presumably corresponds with the regional variation in labour markets and industrial development, and with weak sectoral organization of employers. In the 1970s, bargaining at the level of industries was first squeezed by the resurgence of local shop-floor militancy and then by the growing emphasis on political bargaining through central confederations. This ended in 1983–84 in controversy; developments since have been characterized as 'division and impasse at the centre and innovation at the periphery' (Mershon, 1990: 38).

Still a Role for Peak Federations?

In the 1970s it was generally accepted that some degree of centralization in collective bargaining above the level of companies, occupations, or even industries was needed so as to involve trade unions successfully in macroeconomic management (Headey, 1970; Blyth, 1979; Schmitter, 1979, 1981; Schmidt, 1982; Flanagan, Soskice and Ulman, 1983; Regini, 1984; Crouch, 1985; Tarantelli, 1986; Scharpf, 1987; Visser, 1990a). Where national unions or employers' associations had lost control over timing, terms, and methods of collective bargaining to local representatives or firms there was little point in fine tuning. This was the bitter lesson of British labour in the late 1970s.

According to Windmuller (1975), peak federations usually fulfil three main functions within the union movement: (1) representing the movement before government bodies, joint councils, and sometimes political parties; (2) rendering services to the movement as a whole (training and education; legal advice; research); and (3) adjudicating inter-union relations. In some countries (Sweden after 1938; Norway and Austria after the war; the Netherlands from 1945 to 1968; Belgium and Denmark more intermittently) central organizations acquired a fourth role: negotiating the basic terms of employment with central employers' organizations or governments. In the 1970s and early 1980s there were attempts, and occasionally small successes, at bipartite or tripartite agreements in Belgium, Britain, Denmark, Ireland, Italy, the Netherlands, Portugal, and Spain (Flanagan, Soskice and Ulman, 1983; Regini, 1984; ILO, 1987; Baglioni and Crouch, 1990). Economy-wide bargaining through central organizations presupposes confederal authority over affiliates. However, only where central bargaining has become a repeated practice over a considerable period of time is it likely that 'authority gravitates from national unions to national centres' (Windmuller, 1975: 98).

One of the changes of the 1980s, observable in all European countries, was 'the very widespread diminution of the role played by central organisations' (Baglioni and Crouch, 1990: 10). It is not quite clear when, and why, it started. I have, for instance, emphasized the growing strains in confederal structures and policies which surfaced in the 1970s and were caused by the increasing social and organizational fragmentation. Once the exposed sector unions lost their dominant position, it became simply more difficult to define, negotiate, and implement a common policy of wage restraint (Visser, 1990a). But in the 1980s the shift in employers' priorities was probably the main casual factor. The empty hands of governments and, later, the shift from incomes policies to policies focusing on existing or perceived supply-side constraints (unemployment relief, mobility, training, flexibility, hours) added to the erosion of the authority of central organizations. What could they offer to their affiliates that these affiliates, especially the strongest among them, could not do themselves, and better, with greater knowledge and articulation of local bargaining practices?

The future of national peak federations of trade unions is more uncertain than it ever was in the past fifty years. In Europe further steps towards social and economic integration after 1992 will further diminish the importance of national fora in which confederations are represented. General and political representation of the union movement will increasingly have to be addressed to Brussels or other international centres of law- and policy-making. One among the many problems of the European Trade Union Confederation (ETUC) is that its mandate is derived from peak federations which are themselves in the process of weakening. At the time of writing it does not seem likely that the ETUC will develop into a strong federation with direct affiliation of national and international industry or sector unions. The extreme diversity of European union confederations, their internal rivalries, differences in organization and ideology, the absence of a dominant union centre able and trusted to fulfil a leadership role, and the non-availability of a European target organization of employers whose coordination abilities must be paralleled, are as many obstacles on the road to transnational unionism in Europe (Visser and Ebbinghaus, 1992).

The Future: Can US-style Union Decline be Avoided?

In considering the future of trade unions in advanced capitalist societies we may ask ourselves whether the dramatic decline of unionization in the largest capitalist economy, the United States, will remain an isolated phenomenon. Or is the United States ahead of other countries, and are we at the initial stage of a convergence towards the American pattern of industrial relations and human resource management without unions?

There is no dispute over the depth of the crisis of unionism in the United States (see Lipset, 1986; Troy, 1986; Edwards, Garonna and Tödtling, 1986; Kochan, Katz and McKersie, 1986; Goldfield, 1987; Kochan, 1988; Freeman, 1990). Since the mid-1950s union representation has continued to fall from just one-third of all wage and salary earners to 15 or 16 per cent at the time of writing. Kochan and Verma (1992: 88) observe that 'even these numbers understate the extent of the crisis facing the American labour movement'. For US unions are now more than ever encapsulated in old and declining industries, and some public services. They continue to fail in their organizing efforts to recruit new members in expanding occupations and industries. Weakness breeds weakness.[9] Despite pockets of considerable worker organization (cars, steel, aerospace, communications, some public services), in large areas of the United States the weakening of trade unions may have gone too far. Finally, nowhere in the world is the labour movement so isolated and without political allies.

The main reason for believing that US-style union decline is unique is that in no other advanced capitalist democracy has capital gone so far in rejecting trade unions and collective worker representation. In Western Europe, while it was found that in the 1980s employers had achieved greater control over employment relations and labour management within firms, unions are still accepted as a legitimate voice of workers. Probably, unions are considered a nuisance, a cause or sign of economic malfunctioning, rather than a valuable co-manager of economic progress, as was believed back in the 1940s and 1950s. But in none of the European countries have mainstream organizations of employers staged a fundamental attack on unions aiming at 'eliminating the principle of collective contracts in governing employment relations', and nowhere in Europe 'do we find a determination to cancel the legitimacy of the unions as representatives of the collective interests of working people' (Baglioni and Crouch, 1990: 13). Can we confidently predict that no such attack will be attempted – for instance, after a further decline in unionization or after changes in labour, association, and strike laws styled after the US experience?

Mitchell and Zaidi (1989) argue that those (Europeans) who say 'it can't happen here' need to think twice. They list five reasons why American-style erosion of collective bargaining and unionism has not yet occurred elsewhere: (1) legal and institutional rules, (2) social and cultural pressures, (3) initial conditions (the United States started at a low level of unionization), (4) wage-setting structures which prevent the emergence of a gap between productivity and real wages, and (5) the accommodation of capital interests in flexibility through company bargaining.

The point about the legal and institutional environment has been emphasized before. Its importance is evident, for instance, in the comparison between Canada and the United States (Meltz, 1985; Lipset, 1986; Kochan and Verma, 1992). Union membership in Canada has grown during the same thirty years as US unions have declined. Overall membership has increased, and union density is now twice the US rate. Both countries have more or less the same social and economic structure, host the same (multinational) firms with managers who have been trained in similar business schools, and labour unions which often are branches of the same international organizations or otherwise much like one another. Kochan and Verma (1992) argue that Canadian and American unions also share common weaknesses, such as fragmented unionism, company bargaining, and a sharp distinction between the union and non-union sector. We should note that, with 32 per cent union density, Canada is as low as union density was when the erosion of union representation in the United States began. Fewer than two out of every five Canadian workers are represented in collective bargaining – a high proportion compared to the 20–25 per cent in the United States, but low by European standards. Yet, 'Canadian managers appear to be less aggressive in seeking non-union options over this period of time' (Kochan and Verma, 1992: 90). The reason is seen in the fact that Canadian labour law has been strengthened rather than weakened in the past decades, and has constrained management from pursuing a vigorous non-union strategy.[10]

Union decline in Britain also evidences the impact of the legal and political environment, but there are further lessons. Of all the European union movements the British movement took a particularly bad beating in the 1980s. Not a dramatic shift in employer's attitudes and behaviour but government hostility, combined with perennial weaknesses of its own, have been cited as its proximate cause. Most observers are in agreement that British management have been quite cautious in exploiting the new opportunities which initially a slack labour market, a weakened and badly fragmented labour movement, and an aggressive anti-union government offered them (Brown, 1985; Edwards, 1986; Beaumont, 1992; Crouch 1990). Brown argues that the decline in membership must be explained by the contraction of the highly unionized manufacturing and public-sector industries rather than by employer hostility or employee dissatisfaction with unions. Despite the curtailment of union rights, British unions still have a fair number of 'securities',[11] and there is no 'right to work' legislation, American-style in Kent, Sussex, or East Anglia.

Why did British managers not join the *jihad* against unions of their American counterparts? They could have counted on the backing of 'the first government this century to be explicitly hostile to collective bargaining' (Brown, 1985: 151). Do British managers hold different values? Beaumont correctly exposes the weakness of arguments which use values and traditions among managers in different countries as the main explanation for differing behaviour towards unions. British (or Dutch and German) employers may behave just like American employers in the United States but not at home. There may be social and cultural inhibitions which prevent employers from attempts to bust, eliminate, or bypass trade unions, but it is difficult to say whether these inhibitions will survive the erosion of legal obstacles or a further retrenchment of trade unions. Clearly, there are international differences in the opportunity costs of a union-replacement strategy. In the British case these costs include a real fight with unions such as could have been witnessed in recent years in mining or printing. Even after the severe decline of the 1980s, British unions are still a force to reckon with – the third point in the list of Mitchell and Zaidi. And where British employers do succeed in marginalizing the unions they must still come to terms with a deeply entrenched form of work-place unionism.

What could have been the gain? Freeman and Medoff (1984) and Kochan and his associates (1986) have quoted the size and the growth of the *wage mark-up* as an incentive for employer opposition against unions in the United States. In Britain the size of this mark-up, of union over non-union wages, was larger than in for instance, Sweden, West Germany, Belgium, or the Netherlands given the prevalence of multi-employer bargaining and the widespread practice of extending collective agreements in these countries, but it was still only between 7 per cent in the late 1970s and 11 per cent in the early 1980s, while in the United States in the same period a figure of between 25 and 30 per cent was reported (see also Blanchflower and Freeman, 1990).

Developments in collective bargaining and decentralization in Britain suggest that managers in Britain have obtained a much more malleable form of unionism, at least in the private sector. This does not mean that workers have become more docile, or that shop-steward power has waned (Batstone, 1984; Edwards, 1986; Milward and Stevens, 1986), though the evidence does suggest that managers have it more often their way (Metcalf, 1989; Kelly and Richardson, 1989). Capital interests in flexibility appear to be better accommodated in the context of company bargaining, but the price is a further isolation and fragmentation of British unions. If the lesson from the United States is that trade unions should defuse the always present employer temptation to create a non-union environment by being adaptable and flexible at local levels, then the pragmatism of 1980s-style company bargaining may have relieved some of the pressure on British unions. If the lesson is that unions should defend the integrity of national collective structures of interest representation so as to prevent the very existence of a relevant non-union territory, then the response of British unions may prove a particularly poor one.

Conclusion

Colin Crouch writes in his Afterword to *European Industrial Relations: the Challenge of Flexibility* that '[U]nions may have a long-term future, but do union *movements*?' (1990: 359, his italics). Undoubtedly, most trade unions will in some way or another survive the membership crisis of the 1980s as most of them did in the past. Some unions may even grow larger and stronger than ever before. However, we can be less confident that *encompassing* union movements – as we have known them for much of the past century in the democratic part of Europe – will make it into the next century.

In my view, European trade-union movements have a heritage to defend of collective structures of representation within and between industries, firms and occupations. They should be extremely reluctant to abandon supra-firm collective bargaining structures and institutions where such structures exist. At the same time, they are challenged to find new methods of application and variation in response to changing needs and pressures of capital and a more heterogeneous labour force. Unions should try to carry the banner of 'flexibility' rather than be seen, and be scorned, as its main enemy. This is no easy task, since it is also a vital task of unions to defend, raise, and extend the minimum conditions and standards of civilized labour. Without the strong countervailing power of trade unions, capital is given to abuse its power and freedom. For the future of *civilized* capitalism it is essential that union movements and legislators prevent the emergence of relevant non-union sectors as a viable option for individual capitalists. In Europe after 1992 this will become a problem of great importance, since regional economies and labour markets differ widely as regards the presence and quality of union organization and union action.

Notes

1 I have not been able to find figures with similar precision for Israel, Iceland, New Zealand, Greece, Portugal, Spain, or Turkey (but see also Visser, 1991, for additional data). Union density in Israel is believed to be very high, around 80 per cent; density in New Zealand was just under 50 per cent in the late 1970s but declined to 42 per cent in the late 1980s. Unionization in the new democracies of Southern Europe is probably low (between 10 and 30 per cent), and has declined in recent years in Portugal and Spain (see Pinto, 1990, Stolaroff, 1990, and de Lima and Oliveira, 1990, for Portugal; Estivill and de la Hoz, 1990, and Aguilar and Roca, 1990, for Spain). Aguilar and Roca, for instance, put the density rate in Spain at no more than 15 per cent. The European Trade Union Institute (ETUI) in Brussels gives the following figures for 1988: Greece (35 per cent), Portugal (35 per cent), Turkey (25 per cent), Spain (20–25 per cent), but recommends a cautionary use of these estimates.

2 Rosanvallon's estimate is 9 per cent, whereas the group *réflexion syndicale*, founded in Lyon in July 1989, put union density at 7 per cent (cited in Groux and Mouriaux, 1990: 51). This dramatic decline was corroborated by a representative survey of the French population of 18 years and older in October 1989. Only 12

per cent of blue-collar and 7 per cent of white-collar workers responded 'yes' to the question 'are you a union member?', compared to 25 and 22 per cent in a similar survey of April 1981 (*Espace Social Européen*, 16 and 23 Feb. 1990). The assertion of the French employers' association in metal engineering (UIMM) that density in their sector was down to 5 per cent in 1985 is not improbable, given the concentration of French unions in the public and nationalized sector (Visser, 1989: ch. 3).

3 According to one well-known labour lawyer this is 'a prohibition to which, for obvious reasons (sic!), the unions have no objection' (Blanc-Jouvan, 1989: 12). None of the French union federations have ever sought to change the law, despite the fact that they all find it extremely hard to collect dues. In France unions appear to depend much more strongly on the state for their finances than elsewhere. As much as 40 per cent of annual union revenues of the CGT and CFDT comes from direct and indirect state sources.

4 Given the absence of reliable membership data in France, electoral data are especially useful for measuring the relative position of the union currents. The story these data tell is not very different. Participation in social security or works-council elections is, of course, wider than union membership, but it has fallen too – dramatically in the case of the Communist CGT, slightly but steadily in the case of the CFDT. In the late 1960s the CGT attracted over 50 per cent of the votes, in 1979–80 it was down to 36 per cent, in 1987–88 to 27 per cent (compare with Table 1.4). The two really growing 'parties' in these elections have been the non-union lists (21 per cent) and those abstaining from voting (30 per cent), while it should be noted that the growing number of workers in the small-firm sector or employed on non-standard labour contracts are not eligible to vote (see Labbé, 1991).

5 It is, of course, extremely difficult to estimate the proportion of 'reluctant members' in unions. Korpi, after considering the issue of social pressure from workmates in Sweden and after citing surveys which show that Swedish workers perceive their membership as voluntary, argues in favour of the 'safe hypothesis that variations in the level of unionization between the Western nations cannot be accounted for in terms of differences in the extent to which unions have been able to compel or to force workers to join' (Korpi, 1983: 33). Savery and Soutar (1989) consider the issue in Australia, where pay awards often include clauses for preferential treatment of union members. They found that 55 per cent of those who were or had been members in 1985 joined because they believed that they were required to do so; 18 per cent held the same belief but said that they would have joined anyway; and 26 per cent said they were a 'voluntary member'. Hill, Howard and Lansbury (1982: 85), while reviewing earlier surveys, agree that in the Australian case there are 'probably a number of workers who would not have joined their union in the absence of coercion', but suggest that this is probably not much different in other countries.

6 According to Martens (1985), about one-fifth of Belgium union members were on unemployment benefits in the early 1980s. According to Hancké (1989), 80 per cent of the unemployed in Belgium are unionized, compared to 60–65 per cent of the employed. In Dutch unions less than 5 per cent of all union members were unemployed in 1985 while the unemployment rate stood near 15 per cent. In the 1930s when Dutch unions still ran their own government-subsidized unemployment funds, they were able to fend off membership losses at the onset of the recession (membership increased until 1932–33), but inevitably lost unemployed members whose insurance had ended (Harmsen and Reinalda, 1975). See also Pedersen (1982) for the relation between unionization and unemployment in Denmark between the

wars, and Bain and Elsheikh (1976) for a general model of cyclical economic influences on union growth and decline.

7 There is also a Christian union confederation, founded in 1959, but the overlarge majority of Christian unionists and members of the Christian Democratic parties in Germany are in DGB unions. The fifty or so independent unions that exist in Germany are mainly professional associations (journalists, air pilots, writers, doctors, and so on) in the public sector, and attract only a very small percentage of the total membership (1–3 per cent) and play no significant role in collective bargaining (Armingeon, 1988; Visser, 1989).

8 According to Segrestin in the 1980s these divisions 'appeared deeper than ever, involving [. . .] fundamental, long-term differences over [. . .] the concept of trade unionism and the relationships with the rank and file, the definition of the "working class", and relations between organized labour and government' (Segrestin, 1990: 98).

9 One reason for this is the 'virtuous cycle of decline' described by organizational sociologists such as Cyert, Meyer, Zucker, or Whetten. Stagnating and declining organizations have greater difficulty in attracting quality leaders, staff, or members, and frequently develop legitimacy deficits. Collective action researchers (Elster, Hardin, Hechter, Klandermans, Oliver) emphasize that declining membership implies that networks are destroyed and recruitment links between generations broken; they also show that some threshold must be reached before rewards can be secured and 'free-riders' are discouraged or socially punished. For all these reasons it is much easier to defend or expand a density rate of 40 per cent than to defend or expand a density rate of 10 per cent.

10 Panitch and Schwartz suggest, however, that a new era of state policies towards labour is emerging, marked by a 'shift away from the generalized rule-of-law form of coercion (whereby an overall legal framework both establishes and constrains the rights and powers of all unions), towards a form of selective *ad hoc*, discretionary state coercion (whereby the state removes for a specific purpose the rights contained in labour legislation' (1988: 31). In two provinces (British Columbia and Alberta), stricter requirements for determining union representation have been introduced which may have helped employers' ability to thwart union attempts to move into new areas and thereby hasten their decline (Reshef, 1990).

11 In 1986 only 20 of the 116 known employee ballots concerning the continuation of a closed shop – a legal requirement under the 1984 Act – were in favour of their removal. However, in 1984 a larger proportion of manual workers worked in establishments where unions are either not present (20.6 per cent) or not recognized (9.1 per cent) than in 1980, when the percentages were 10.8 and 5.5. There is a clear North–South pattern in non-recognition or union absence (Beaumont and Harris, 1988).

References

ABS (Australian Bureau of Statistics) (1988) *Trade Union Members: Australia*. Canberra: ABS.

Adam, Gérard (1983) *Le pouvoir syndical*. Paris: Dunod.

Aguilar, Salvador and Roca, Jordi (1990) '14 décembre: économie politique d'une grève', in J. Goetschy and D. Linhart (eds), *La crise des syndicats en Europe occidentale*. Paris: La documentation française (dossiers d'actualité mondiale), pp. 28–37.

Albeda, Wil (1985) 'Recent Trends in Collective Bargaining in the Netherlands', *International Labour Review*, 124.

Arcq, Etienne and Neuville, Jean (1989) 'L'évolution du taux de syndicalisation 1972-1981', *Cahier Hebdomadaire*, 1147, Brussels: CRISP.

Armingeon, Klaus (1988) *Die Entwicklung der deutschen Gewerkschaften 1950-1985*. Frankfurt: Campus.

Baglioni, Guido and Crouch, Colin (eds) (1990) *Industrial Relations in Europe: the Challenge of Flexibility*. London: Sage.

Bain, George S. and Elsheikh, Farouk (1976) *Union Growth and the Business Cycle*. Oxford: Basil Blackwell.

Bain, George S. and Price, Robert (1980) *Profiles of Union Growth: a Comparative Statistical Portrait of Eight Countries*. Oxford: Basil Blackwell.

Bamber, Greg J. and Lansbury, Russell D. (1987) *International and Comparative Industrial Relations*. London: Allen & Unwin.

Batstone, Eric (1984) *Working Order: Workplace Industrial Relations over Two Decades*. Oxford: Basil Blackwell.

Beaumont, P.B. (1992) 'Structural Change and Industrial Relations: the United Kingdom', in A. Gladstone, H. Wheeler, J. Rojot, F. Eyraud and R. Ben-Israel (eds), *Labour Relations in a Changing Environment*. Berlin/New York: de Gruyter, pp. 203-14.

Beaumont, P.B. and Harris R. (1988) 'The Organising Process: Contemporary Changes and Union Responses in Britain', in *Proceedings of the Forty-Second Annual Meeting*, IRRA series, Atlanta (24-30 Dec.), pp. 91-100.

Birien, Jean-Louis (1978) *Le fait syndical en France*. Paris: Publi-Union.

Blanc-Jouvan, Xavier (1989) 'France', in M. Biagi (ed.), *Trade Union Democracy and Industrial Relations*. Deventer and Boston: Kluwer Law and Taxation (*Bulletin of Comparative Labour Relations*, no. 17).

Blanchflower, Daniel G. and Freeman, Richard B. (1990) 'Going Different Ways: Unionism in the US and Other Advanced OECD Countries', London: LSE, Centre for Economic Performance, Discussion Paper no. 5.

BLS (Bureau of Labor Statistics) (1990) 'Union members 1930-1989', Washington DC, mimeo.

Blyth, Cornelis (1979) 'The Interaction between Collective Bargaining and Government Policies in Selected Member Countries', in OECD, *Collective Bargaining and Government Policies*. Paris: Organization for Economic Cooperation and Development.

de Broek, Gilbert (1989) 'De overheid en het sociale overleg', in T. Beaupain et al., *50 Jaar Arbeidsverhoudingen*. Brueghes: de Keure/Belgische Vereniging voor Arbeidsverhoudingen, pp. 49-70.

Brown, Wilfred (1985) 'The Effect of Recent Changes in the World Economy on British Industrial Relations', in H. Juris et al. (eds), *Industrial Relations in a Decade of Economic Change*. Madison, WI: IRRA, pp. 151-75.

Caire, Guy (1990) 'La fin d'un "syndicalisme de militants"?', in J. Goetschy and D. Linhart (eds), *La crise des syndicats en Europe occidentale*. Paris: La documentation française (dossiers d'actualité mondiale), pp. 7-9.

CESOS/Centro di Studi Sociali e Sindacali (1990) *Le relazioni sindicali in Italia. Rapporto 1988/89*. Rome: Edizione Lavoro.

CGP/Commissariat Général du Plan (1988) *Négociation collective. Quels enjeux?* Report edited by Germain Férec and Jocelyne Loos, Paris: La documentation française.

Clegg, Hugh A. (1976) *Trade Unionism under Collective Bargaining: a Theory Based on Comparisons of Six Countries*. Oxford: Basil Blackwell.

Crouch, Colin J. (1985) 'Conditions for Trade Union Wage Restraint', in L.N. Lindberg and C.S. Maier (eds), *The Politics of Inflation and Economic Stagnation*. Washington DC: The Brookings Institute, pp. 103-39.

Crouch, Colin J. (1990) 'United Kingdom: the Rejection of Compromise', in G. Baglioni and C.J. Crouch (eds), *Industrial Relations in Europe: the Challenge of Flexibility*. London: Sage, pp. 326-55.

Delamotte, Yves (1982) 'Conflict Management in French Industrial Relations: Recent Developments and Trends', in G.B.J. Somers and R.B. Peters (eds), *Conflict Management and Industrial Relations*. Boston: MIT Press.

Ebbinghaus, B.O., Visser, J. and Pfenning W. (1992) *Trade Union Systems in Western Europe: a Data-handbook*, vol. 1, Frankfurt and New York: Campus.

Edwards, Paul K. (1986) 'Managing Labour Relations Through the Recession', *Employment Relations*, 7 (2).

Edwards, Richard, Garonna, Paolo and Tödtling, Franz (1986) *Unions in Crisis and Beyond: Perspectives from Six Countries*. Dover, MA: Auburn House.

Estivill, Jordi and de la Hoz, Josep M. (1990) 'Transition and Crisis: the Complexity of Spanish Industrial Relations', in G. Baglioni and C.J. Crouch (eds), *Industrial Relations in Europe: the Challenge of Flexibility*. London: Sage, pp. 265-99.

Farber, Henry S. (1985) 'The Extent of Unionization in the United States', in Th.A. Kochan (ed.), *Challenges and Choices Facing American Labor*. Cambridge, MA: MIT Press, pp. 14-44.

Farber, Henry S. (1987) 'The Decline of Unionization in the United States: What can be Learned from Recent Experience?' Cambridge MA: NBER Working Paper 2267.

Flanagan, Robert J., Soskice, David W. and Ulman, Lloyd (1983) *Unionism, Economic Stabilization and Incomes Policies: European Experience*. Washington, DC: The Brookings Institute.

Flora, Peter (ed.) (1986) *Growth to Limits*, vol 4. Berlin/New York: de Gruyter.

Freeman, Richard B. (1990) 'On the Divergence in Unionism among Developed Countries', in R. Brunetta and C. Dell'Aringa (eds), *Labour Relations and Economic Performance*. London: Macmillan, pp. 304-24.

Freeman, Richard B. and Medoff, James L. (1984) *What do Unions Do?* New York: Basic Books.

Fulcher, James (1988) 'On the Explanation of Industrial Relations Diversity: Labour Movements, Employers and the State in Britain and Sweden', *British Journal of Industrial Relations*, 26: 246-74.

Goetschy, Jeanine and Linhart, Danielle (eds) (1990) *La crise des syndicats en Europe occidentale*. Paris: La documentation française (dossiers d'actualité mondiale).

Goldfield, Michael (1987) *The Decline of Organized Labor in the United States*. Chicago: University of Chicago Press.

Goldthorpe, John T. (1984) 'The End of Convergence: Corporatist and Dualist Tendencies in Modern Western Societies', in J.H. Goldthorpe (ed.), *Order and Conflict in Contemporary Capitalism*. Oxford: Clarendon Press, pp. 315-44.

Groux, Guy, and Mouriaux, René (1990) 'Le cas français', in G. Bibes and R. Mouriaux (eds), *Les syndicats européens à l'épreuve*. Paris: Presses de la Fondation Nationale des Sciences Politiques, pp. 49-68.

Hancké, Bob (1989) 'François et les autres', *Socialistische Standpunkten*, 36 (5): 50–61.

Hansen, Charles, Jackson, Sheila and Miller, Douglas (1982) *The Closed Shop: a Comparative Study in Public Policy and Trade Union Security in Britain, the USA and West Germany*. Aldershot: Gower.

Harmsen, Ger and Reinalda, Bob (1975) *Voor de bevrijding van de arbeid*. Nijmegen: SUN.

Headey, Bruce W. (1970) 'Trade Unions and National Wage Policies', *Journal of Politics*, 32: 407–38.

Hill J.D., Howard, W.A. and Lansbury, R.D. (1982) *Industrial Relations: an Australian Introduction*. Melbourne: Longman Cheshire.

ILO (1987) *Collective Bargaining in Industrialised Market Economies: a Reappraisal*. Geneva.

Jacobi, Otto and Müller-Jentsch, Walther (1990) 'West Germany: Continuity and Structural Change', in G. Baglioni and C.J. Crouch (eds), *Industrial Relations in Europe: the Challenge of Flexibility*. London: Sage, pp. 127–53.

JIL/The Japanese Institute of Labour (1990) *Labor–Management Relations in Japan 1989*. Tokyo: Industrial Relations Series.

Kelly, John and Richardson, Ray (1989) 'Annual Review Article 1988', *British Journal of Industrial Relations*, 27 (1): 133–58.

Kjellberg, Anders (1983) *Fackling organisering i tolv lander*. Lund: Archiv.

Kochan, Thomas A. (1988) 'The Future of Worker Representation: an American Perspective', *Labour and Society*, 13 (2): 183–201.

Kochan, Thomas A., Capelli, Peter and McKersie, Robert B. (1984) 'Strategic Choice and Industrial Relations Theory', *Industrial Relations*, 23 (1): 16–39.

Kochan, Thomas A., Katz, Harry C. and McKersie, Robert B. (1986) *The Transformation of American Industrial Relations*. New York: Basic Books.

Kochan, Thomas A. and Verma, Anil (1992) 'A Comparative View of United States and Canadian Industrial Relations: a Strategic Choice Perspective', in A. Gladstone, H. Wheeler, J. Rojot, F. Eyraud and R. Ben-Israel (eds), *Labour Relations in a Changing Environment*. Berlin/New York: de Gruyter, pp. 187–202.

Korpi, Walter (1983) *The Democratic Class Struggle*. London: Routledge & Kegan Paul.

Korpi, Walter and Shalev, Michael (1979) 'Strikes, Industrial Relations and Class Conflict in Capitalist Societies', *British Journal of Sociology*, 30: 164–97.

Kumar, Pradeep (1986) 'Union Growth in Canada: Retrospect and Prospect', in W. Craig Ridell (ed.), *Canadian Labor Relations*. Ottawa, ONT: Minister of Supply and Services.

Labbé, Dominique (1991) 'Vingt-deux ans d'élections aux comités d'entreprise (1966–67, 1987–88)', Grenoble: CERAT (Centre de recherche sur le politique, l'administration et le territoire) (March).

Lash, Scott and Urry, John (1987) *The End of Organized Capitalism*. Oxford: Basil Blackwell.

de Lima, Marinus Pires and Oliveira, Luisa (1990) 'Portugal', in J. Goetschy and D. Linhart (eds), *La crise des syndicats en Europe occidentale*. Paris: La documentation française (dossiers d'actualité mondiale), pp. 28–37.

Lipset, Seymour Martin (1986) 'North American Labor Movements: a Comparative Perspective', in S.M. Lipset (ed.), *Unions in Transition: Entering the Second Century*. San Francisco, CA: ICS Press, pp. 221–38.

Martens, Albert (1985) 'Vakbondsgroei en vakbondsmacht in België', *Tijdschrift voor Arbeidsvraagstukken*, 1 (3): 35-41.

Meltz, Noah (1985) 'Labor Movements in Canada and the United States', in Th. A. Kochan (ed.), *Challenges and Choices Facing American Labor*. Cambridge, MA: MIT Press, pp. 315-34.

Mershon, Caron A. (1990) 'Relationships Among Union Actors After The Hot Autumn', *Labour*, 4 (1): 35-58.

Metcalf, David (1989) 'Water Notes Dry up: the Impact of the Donovan Reform Proposals and Thatcherism at Work on Labour Productivity in the British Manufacturing Industry', *British Journal of Industrial Relations*, 27 (1): 1-31.

Milward, N. and Stevens, M. (1986) *British Workplace Industrial Relations 1980-1984*. Aldershot: Gower.

Mitchell, Daniel J.A. and Zaidi, Mahmood A. (1989) 'International Pressures on Industrial Relations', Los Angeles, CA: Institute of Industrial Relations, UCLA Working Paper Series no. 175.

Mok, Albert (1985) 'Arbeidsverhoudingen in België en Nederland', in *Tijdschrift voor Arbeidsvraagstukken*. 1 (1): 1-17.

Mouriaux, René (1983) *Les syndicats dans la société française*. Paris: Presse de la Fondation Nationale des Sciences Politiques.

Mouriaux, René (1986) *La syndicalisme face à la crise*. Paris: Editions La Découverte.

Müller-Jentsch, Walther (1987) *Arbeitsbeziehungen in der Bundesrepublik*. Frankfurt: Campus.

de Nicola, Patrizio (1991) 'Confederali, autonomi, cobas: la sindicalizzazione nel terziaro', *Politica ed Economia*, 2 (Feb.).

de Noblecourt, Philippe (1989) *Les syndicats en questions*. Paris: Edition Ouvrières.

Olson, Mancur (1982) *The Rise and Decline of Nations: Economic growth, Stagflation, and Social Rigidities*. New Haven, CT: Yale University Press.

Panitch, Leo V. and Schwartz, Donald (1988) *The Assault on Trade Union Freedoms*. Toronto, ONT: Garamond.

Pedersen, Peder J. (1982) 'Union Growth in Denmark: 1911-1939', *Scandinavian Journal of Economics*, 84.

Pedersen, Peder J. (1989) 'Langsigtede internationale tendenser i den faglige organisering of den politiske venstrefløj' *Økonomie e Politik*, 62 (2): 91-9.

Peetz, D. (1990) 'Declining Union Density?', *Journal of Industrial Relations*, 32 (2): 197-223.

Pinto, Mario (1990) 'Trade Union Action and Industrial Relations in Portugal', in G. Baglioni and C.J. Crouch (eds), *Industrial Relations in Europe: the Challenge of Flexibility*. London: Sage, pp. 243-64.

Piore, Michael J. (1985) 'The Decline of Mass Production and the Challenge to Union Survival', *Industrial Relations Journal*, 16: 207-13.

Poole, Michael (1986) *Industrial Relations: Origins and Patterns of National Diversity*. London: Routledge & Kegan Paul.

Regalia, Ida (1987) 'Participare al sindacato. Forme, modelli, ipotesi di lavoro', *Quaderni di Sociologia*, 33 (9): 43-72.

Regini, Marino (1984) 'The Conditions for Political Exchange: How Concertation Emerged and Collapsed in Italy and Great Britain', in J.H. Goldthorpe (ed.), *Order and Conflict in Contemporary Capitalism*. Oxford: Clarendon Press, pp. 124-42.

Rehn, Gösta and Viklund, Birger (1990) 'Changes in the Swedish Model', in G. Baglioni and C.J. Crouch (eds), *Industrial Relations in Europe: the Challenge of Flexibility*. London: Sage, pp. 300-25.

Reshef, Yonathan (1990) 'Union Decline: a View from Canada', *Journal of Labor Research*, 11 (1): 25–39.

Reynaerts, Wim H.J. (1985) 'Kantelende posities: arbeidsverhoudingen in een keertÿd', in *Bespiegelingen over de toekomst van de sociale partners*. The Hague: OSA-Voorstudie no. 5.

Reynaud, Jean-Daniel (1975) *Les syndicats en France*, 2 vols. Paris: PUF.

Roche, William K. and Larragy, Joe (1990) 'Cyclical and Institutional Determinants of Annual Trade Unions' Growth and Decline in Ireland: Evidence from the DUES Data Series', *European Sociological Review*, 6 (1): 49–72.

Rojot, Jacques (1992) 'Structural Change and Industrial Relations Strategies. Introduction', in A. Gladstone, H. Wheeler, J. Rojot, F. Eyraud and R. Ben-Israel (eds) *Labour Relations in a Changing Environment*. Berlin/New York: de Gruyter, pp. 173–86.

Rosanvallon, Pierre (1988) *La question syndicale. Histoire et avenir d'une forme sociale*. Paris: Calman-Lévy.

Rubery, Jil (1986) 'Trade Unions in the 1980s: the Case of the United Kingdom', in R. Edwards, P. Garonna and F. Tödtling (eds), *Unions in Crisis and Beyond: Perspectives from Six Countries*. Dover, MA: Auburn House, pp. 66–113.

Savery, Lawson K. and Soutar, Geoffrey N. (1989) 'Community Attitudes on Trade Union Effectiveness', Brussels: Paper presented at Eighth IIRA World Congress, mimeo.

Scharpf, Fritz W. (1987) *Sozialdemokratische Krisenpolitik in Europa*. Frankfurt: Campus.

Scheuer, Steen (1990) 'Faglig organisering 1966 til 1987 – del 2: Vaeksten i funktionaer- og servicesektoren og i saerlige grupper med lav faglig organisering', *Ekonomi og politik*, 62 (1): 33 ff.

Schmidt, Manfred G. (1982) 'Does Corporatism Matter?' in G. Lehmbruch and P.C. Schmitter (eds), *Patterns of Corporatist Policy-making*. London and Beverly Hills, CA: Sage, pp. 237–58.

Schmitter, Philippe C. (1979) 'Models of Interest Intermediation and Models of Societal Change in Western Europe', in P.C. Schmitter and G. Lehmbruch (eds), *Trends towards Corporatist Intermediation*, Beverly Hills, CA, and London: Sage.

Schmitter, Philippe C. (1981) 'Interest Intermediation and Regime Governability in Contemporary Western Europe and North America', in S. Berger (ed.), *Organizing Interests in Western Europe: Pluralism, Corporatism and the Transformation of Politics*. Cambridge: Cambridge University Press.

Segrestin, Denis (1990) 'Recent Change in France', in G. Baglioni and C.J. Crouch (eds), *Industrial Relations in Europe: the Challenge of Flexibility*. London: Sage, pp. 97–126.

Shorter, Edward and Tilly, Charles (1974) *Strikes in France 1830–1968*. London: Cambridge University Press.

Shimada, Haruo (1988) 'Japanese Trade Unionism: Postwar Evolution and Future Prospects', *Labour and Society*, 13 (2): 183–201.

Spineux, Armand (1990) 'Trade Unionism in Belgium: the Difficulties of a Major Renovation', in G. Baglioni and C.J. Crouch (eds), *Industrial Relations in Europe: the Challenge of Flexibility*. London: Sage, pp. 42–70.

Squarzon, Corrado (1991) 'Sindicalizzazione e rappresentanze', in CESOS, *Le Relazioni industriali in Italia*. Rapporto 1990–1991, Rome: Edizione Lavoro.

Stephens, John D. (1990) 'Explaining Crossnational Differences in Union Strength in Bargaining and Welfare', Madrid: Twelfth World Congress of Sociology (9–13 July), mimeo.

Stevens, Mark and Wareing, A. (1990) 'Union Density and Workforce Composition, Preliminary Results from the 1989 Labour Force Survey', *Employment Gazette*, 403–13, Aug.

Stolaroff, Alan (1990) 'Labour and Redemocratization in Portugal: Changing Union–Party Relationship', Madrid: Twelfth World Congress of Sociology (9–13 July), mimeo.

Streeck, Wolfgang (1982) 'Organizational Consequences of Corporatist Cooperation in West German Labour Unions', in G. Lehmbruch and P.C. Schmitter (eds), *Patterns of Corporatist Policy-making*. London and Beverly Hills, CA: Sage, pp. 29–81.

Streeck, Wolfgang (1984) *Industrial Relations in West Germany: a Case Study of the Car Industry*. London: Heinemann.

Streeck, Wolfgang (1987) 'Industrial Relations in the Federal Republic of Germany, 1974–1985', *Bulletin of Comparative Labour Relations*, 16 (special issue), 'Unions and Industrial Relations: Recent Trends and Prospects': 151–66.

Streeck, Wolfgang (forthcoming) 'Industrial Relations in West Germany: Agenda for Change', in J. Niland and O. Clark (eds), *The Agenda of Industrial Relations*. London: Allen and Unwin.

Stroobant, Maxime (1989) 'De overheid en het collectief overleg in Belgie tijdens de sociaal-economische crisis 1970–1988', in T. Beaupain et al. *50 Jaar Arbeidsverhoudingen*, Bruges: de Keure/Belgische Vereniging voor Arbeidsverhoudingen, pp. 71–115.

Swenson, Peter (1989) *Fair Shares: Unions, Pay, and Politics in Sweden and West Germany*. Ithaca, NY: Cornell University Press.

Tarantelli, Ezio (1986) *Economia politica di lavoro*. Turin: UTET.

Terry, Michael (1986) 'How do we Know if Shop Stewards are Getting Weaker?' *British Journal of Industrial Relations*, 24 (1): 169–79.

Troy, Leo (1986) 'The Rise and Fall of American Trade Unions: The Labor Movement from FDR to RR', in S.M. Lipset (ed.), *Unions in Transition. Entering the Second Century*. San Francisco, CA: ICS Press, pp. 75–109.

Verma, Anil and Thompson, Mark (1989) 'Managerial Strategies in Industrial Relations in the 1980s: Comparing the US and Canadian Experience', Madison, WI: IRRA series, *Proceedings of the Forty-First Annual Meeting*.

Visser, Jelle (1985) 'Vakbondsgroei en vakbondsmacht in West-Europa', *Tijdschrift voor Arbeidsvraagstukken*, 1 (1): 18–38.

Visser, Jelle (1988) 'La négociation collective: une évolution sous contraintes. Quelques reflexions sur les tendances récentes en France et aux Pays-Bas', in Commissariat Général du Plan, *Négociation collective. Quels enjeux?* Report ed. by Germanin Férec and Jocelyne Loos, Paris: La documentation française, pp. 291–309.

Visser, Jelle (1989) *European Trade Unions in Figures: 1913–1985*. Deventer and Boston: Kluwer Law and Taxation.

Visser, Jelle (1990a) *In Search of Inclusive Unionism*. Deventer and Boston: Kluwer Law and Taxation (*Bulletin of Comparative Labour Relations*, no. 18).

Visser, Jelle (1990b) 'Continuity and Change in Dutch Industrial Relations', in G. Baglioni and C.J. Crouch (eds), *Industrial Relations in Europe: the Challenge of Flexibility*. London: Sage, pp. 199–242.

Visser, Jelle (1991) 'Trends in Union Membership', *Employment Outlook 1991*,

Paris: Organization of Economic Cooperation and Development, pp. 97–134.

Visser, Jelle and Ebbinghaus, Bernhard O. (1992) 'Making the Most of Diversity? European Integration and Transnational Unionism', in J. Greenwood, J. Grote and K. Rinit (eds), *European Integration and Transnational Interest Organisation*. London: Sage.

Wallerstein, Michael (1989) 'Union Organization in Advanced Industrial Democracies', *American Political Science Review*, 83 (2): 481–502.

Windmuller, John P. (1969) *Labour Relations in the Netherlands*. Ithaca, NY: Cornell University Press.

Windmuller, John P. (1975) 'The Authority of National Trade Union Confederations: a Comparative Analysis', in D.B. Lipsky (ed.), *Union Power and Public Policy*. Ithaca, NY: NYSSILR, pp. 91–107.

Windmuller, John P. (1981) 'Concentration Trends in Union Structure: An International Comparison', *Industrial and Labor Relations Review*, vol. 35, pp. 43–57.

2
Labour Movements and Political Systems: Some Variations

J. Samuel Valenzuela

With the development of proletarianization, the extension of markets, and the emergence and diffusion of socialist and syndicalist ideologies and models for worker organizations, labour movements emerged in country after country over the latter part of the nineteenth and early decades of the twentieth centuries. As they matured, they both influenced and were affected by the course of economic and social development, as well as the emergence of various forms of mass politics, democratic and non-democratic. Given the variety of national and even regional contexts which moulded their growth, labour organizations acquired many differences, which have led to an abundant comparative literature that analyses them. Much of this literature has an industrial relations focus. It examines the specific ways in which unions are organized, the considerable variety of collective bargaining procedures, the forms of state intervention in union affairs and in labour–management conflicts, and so on.[1] While the differences in such institutions are undoubtedly significant, the industrial relations perspective is too narrow to account for many variations in the characteristics of national labour movements. It is also necessary to examine the modalities such movements acquired given their insertion in national political systems; these variations depend basically on the nature of the respective political regimes and of the parties that established links with the unions during their formative processes. The characteristics of their political insertion affect the ability of labour movements to apply pressure to employers and governments in state and legislative arenas, and even affect the morphology of unions and their relations with employers.

The importance and durability of these politically related differences have usually been underestimated. Many authors have simply assumed that the political colorations of labour unions (as seen from the parties to which they are linked) matter little in the long run, since the characteristics of unions' collective actions, their militance, and even the relative radicalism of their demands and their political outlooks are determined in the last analysis by the kind of technology used at the point of production. The technology structures the work-force's level of skill, its degree of control over the productive process, its relative homogeneity or differentiation, its job security, and so on, and by creating different types of workers it generates as well very different types of unions. Hence, regardless of national political differences, artisans, miners, service employees, technicians in automated plants, and so on, have specific characteristics in common such that the political milieu in which they are inserted is clearly of secondary importance.[2] Taking a more general view, many other authors have assumed that the general course of the process of industrialization determines the characteristics of worker politics and labor relations. The early phases are marked by class conflict and radicalism, and may be led by elites having different degrees of toleration for worker organizations. However, in the long run, industrialization both moderates worker outlooks as their affluence increases and as they become used to the rhythm of industrial life, and it eventually generates the institutionalization of labour–management relations as the elites accept the necessity of worker interest representation both at the workplace and as citizens in political arenas. This perspective therefore assumes that there is a convergence between different national settings in mature industrialism.[3] Consequently, by stressing the significance of technological and economic variables in determining the political colorations of both workers and their organizations, both of these perspectives underestimate the importance of the very durable ties unions develop to various kinds of political parties as well as the impact of their insertion to different political regimes. But the long-term programmes and outlooks of labour movements, their effects on national political debates and situations, and even their internal organizational structure cannot be understood without factoring in the importance of these political differences.[4]

My purpose here is to contribute to the analysis of the politically related variations among national labour movements, exploring the differences which occur due to the specific characteristics of working-class parties, their links with the unions, and the modalities of the relations between the movements and their respective states. To this end, by focusing mainly on the historical experience of the Americas and of Western Europe (and including mainly countries with capitalist labour markets), this chapter presents five types of insertion of labour movements into national political processes. Beginning with those which may be found under democratic regimes, the types are: *the social democratic*, in

which the unions link up to form basically one national organization that in turn connects itself with a single, relatively strong
party; *the contestatory*, in which the labour movement is divided
into different ideological and partisan tendencies with a segment
linked to the Communist Party; and *the pressure group*, in which
the unions link themselves with a pre-existing party or fragments
of it. The final two types may be found under various shades of
authoritarian political regimes. These are: *the state-sponsored*, in
which both the unions and the parties are generated by political
elites from the government but attain relatively broad acceptance
among workers; and *the confrontational*, in which the leaders of
the labour movement are predominantly in opposition to the
government, but must rely principally on union organizations to
resist its policies since the regime curtails the activities of the
union-linked party or parties and the channels through which they
normally manifest their influence. The typology does not pretend
to be exhaustive, and although it is based on concrete cases, it does
not provide an in-depth discussion of any one of them. Rather, it
aims to highlight essential differences.

The variations among the types are generated by differences
along the following four dimensions: first, the manner in which
unionism achieved its organizational consolidation; secondly, the
unity or the fragmentation of the labour movement; thirdly, the
nature of the links between unions and parties; and fourthly, the
characteristics of the political regimes into which the labour
movements insert themselves. A discussion of these factors is
appropriate before presenting the typology.

Sources of Variation in the Types of Labour Movement Political Insertion

The Organizational Consolidation of Unionism
It is not possible to present here a detailed analysis of the formation of national labour movements.[5] Suffice it to say that
everywhere there were several groups of different political and
ideological orientations that rivalled in the attempt to create them,
and that the group or groups that succeeded did so because they
were able to develop their organization(s) along the following four
essential union-building dimensions: *worker allegiance*, or obtaining the trust of the work-force; *organizational linking*, or developing a national network tying the unions among each other as well
as to other organizations, such as parties and, on occasion,
churches, cooperatives, cultural associations, and so on; *plant-level
penetration*, or establishing a union presence within firms and a

regular process of collective bargaining, allowing labour leaders to become brokers between workers and management over all disputes, large and small; and *state recognition*, or obtaining the tacit or explicit authorization to build union organizations outside the plant level as well as to speak for the interests of workers in negotiations with governments and legislatures over questions of social and economic policy. The labour leadership group that succeeded in developing its organization along all four of these dimensions could be said to consolidate it, thereby virtually freezing its position as a leading sector of the labour movement, since each of these dimensions of the process of unionization becomes, once achieved, a resource which union leaders can use to stave off any challenges to their position. The analysis implies that the original consolidation of a union leadership group has the relatively lasting effect of fixing the ideological and political coloration of the labour movement as a whole. The process of union formation therefore contains one of the keys to determining the characteristics of working-class parties in each national context, since no such party can claim to represent the organized workers' interests without establishing close links to union leaderships, counting them among its members or, at least, sympathizers.

For present purposes it is only important to focus on the third dimension of the formative process. This dimension is a critical factor for unions to acquire and hold on to mass memberships (or the tacit support of many workers where labour legislation and/or the characteristics of union organizations encourage free-ridership). With the development of collective bargaining and a union presence at the plant level, the broad, usually non-militant segments of the work-force which were not participants in the earlier stages of forming union organizations were able to appreciate the protective and proactive effects of the existence of unions (Brazilian unionism as established under Vargas is a partial but peculiar exception to this). Precisely because it encouraged the massification of the unions' audience, this third dimension of the formative process was the most significant one for the consolidation of a labour leadership group, with the lasting consequences noted above. The more complete the union penetration at the plant level, the greater the facilities the unions have to call meetings at the workplace, post information, place delegates in all the sections, and so on, and the more regular, institutionalized, and comprehensive the collective bargaining, the greater will be the density of union's mass base (as membership or audience) and the importance of unionism in the national context.

The historic moment and the manner in which unions established their plant-level presence and began regular negotiations with employers therefore had great significance for the subsequent creation of the national labour movement. There were two essential ways in which the fledgling worker organizations obtained the necessary employer acceptance to institutionalize these processes: through direct negotiations with employers (including the state as such) in a context of significant worker mobilization or its threat, and through government pressure over private employers. Let us examine these in greater detail.

In order to have a decisive impact over the subsequent characteristics of the labour movement, the direct negotiation manner had to occur relatively early in its historic process of formation. By this I mean roughly before 1920, or before the global upsurge of worker mobilizations at the end of the teens, the Treaty of Versailles and its provisions addressing the social question, and the constitution and extension of the organizations of the Third International, all of which led to a greater governmental awareness of, and intervention in, labour–management issues. Given the characteristics of this form, the development of massive unionization generally had its point of origin in specific local plants and sometimes regional pockets of production. Consequently, it extended nationally in a piecemeal manner over periods of at least two decades. This process occurred where the owners did not present a strong resistance to unionization, perhaps because they chose not to do so, but principally because they were not able to do so given inadequate access to state repression, the existence of relatively tight labour markets, and expansive economic conditions. In what could be called a law of labour movement development, employer recognition of unions through direct negotiations at this early date invariably favoured the subsequent consolidation of reformist or politically moderate labour leaders. This for two reasons. It indicated that a strategy of negotiating regularly with employers was a viable route to obtaining benefits and solving other day-to-day work-related problems of the rank and file, and this buttressed the position of moderate leaders who became involved in these negotiations against those who held more extreme views. Moreover, in the absence of legislation detailing the right of union leaders to represent the collective demands of workers, the inception of a regular process of collective bargaining occurred by mutual agreement among the parties. This implied not only the employer's recognition of the representational role of the union leadership, but also the tacit recognition by the latter of the propriety of the entrepreneurial function. A radical anti-capitalist and pro-revolutionary posture was incompatible with this relationship of regular negotiations by mutual consent; such a posture could threaten its continuity by giving employers an excuse to break it off, and this threat, in turn, would simply lead – given the context of on-going negotiations – the rank and file to support a more moderate leadership.

Where employers resisted more strongly, or were able to resist more strongly, worker efforts to combine, unions achieved a plant-level presence and regular collective bargaining with legislative and state support. These settings present greater complexity than the previous ones in the manner in which the process occurred and in the kinds of labour movements it generated. Governments were more or less active in exerting pressures on employers aside from enacting a legislative framework for union and collective bargaining rights. The political colorations and coalitions of the governments that were instrumental in pressing for union rights differed considerably as well. Some included, formally or informally, all pre-existing labour leaders of the hitherto embryonic labour movement; others included only certain ideological and political segments among them; while still others fashioned what essentially became a new labour leadership group, displacing those that were active in the field previously (even if some individual labour leaders accepted the new situation and became a part of the new group). None the less, despite these different modalities, in these cases the massification of unionism occurred rapidly across broad sectors of production, thereby contrasting with the more gradual and local plant-centred massification process that took place where plant-level penetration resulted from direct negotiations between employers and workers.

The Unity or the Fragmentation of the Labour Movement

The process of development of a national labour movement can favour one or more of the principal groups which originally compete to create it. In the first case, the union movement will obviously generate one main organization from the base units to the top. When there is only one important organization, the union leaders have a monopoly of representation, which means that the rank-and-file bases generally have less possibility of pressuring the leaders, particularly if union leaderships above the plant level are selected in union congresses rather than through a broad-based vote, and if labour–management negotiations are centralized. This may lead to worker discontent spilling over into dissident although mostly ineffective movements.

In the second instance, the labour movement remains fragmented into various important organizations. When these divisions exist it is necessary to examine the spatial distribution of the fragmentation. It can either result in the creation of unions or union tendencies which extend themselves – or *may* extend themselves – to the majority of the base units, or in the formation of parallel unions which recruit workers from clearly different segments of the work-force. The effects of one or the other type of division on the dynamics of union activity are quite different. When the divisions cut widely into base organizations – which is typically the case when they are generated by ideological or political differences, or even by splits among powerful leaders for personal reasons – the various union leaders must, in spite of their occasional collaboration, compete for the support of the rank and file. This competition undermines the formation of a common front among the various organizations when confronting the employers and/or the state, since each sector will try to present itself as the most dedicated defender of the interests of the rank and file, thereby weakening – paradoxically – the union movement as a whole and diminishing its capacity to defend those very interests. Ironically, the competition between the different sectors also generates union leaderships which are very responsive to the needs and aspirations of the rank and file; hence, these divisions produce a kind of unionism which is relatively weak but very permeable to worker demands.

The second kind of fragmentation (that which occurs when the various union organizations or tendencies capture clearly different rank-and-file segments) normally results from unbridgeable ascriptive cleavages in the working class itself (along linguistic, racial, cultural, tribal, regional, and/or religious lines), for which the process of labour-movement formation has led to the creation of different organizations for each segment. In these cases, the various unions obviously do not compete with one another for the support of the workers, since each has its terrain cut out for it. However, the consequences for union action are again dramatically different according to the social standing of the various worker communities. When there is no marked difference or enmity between them, the union leaders can collaborate with relative ease in negotiations with the employer associations and/or with the state; as a result, the fragmentation does not seriously weaken the labour movement. But when there are one or more worker communities in a relatively inferior social, political, and/or economic position with respect to another or others, and/or a history of sharp conflict between them, the collaboration between the various units of the union movement becomes virtually impossible, since the unions which group the more privileged workers will normally be able to obtain advantages unattainable by, and even at the expense of, the others. The result is that the union movement as a whole is greatly weakened. Situations where there is strong racial or ethnic discrimination are the main cases in point.[6] And yet, whatever the status of the various worker communities, this type of union fragmentation normally works against the spill-over of worker discontent towards dissident organizations, given the strength of the bonds which are created by the ascriptive identities that generate the divisions.[7]

The Characteristics of Union–Party Links
Virtually everywhere national union organizations have established, either from their inception or eventually, some kind of a relationship with one or more political parties or party factions. Both organizations benefit from such links. Unions need the support of parties when pursuing some of their interests, such as when attempting to change legislation affecting them, when pressuring the state or even employer associations over specific issues, or, in general, when they need to mobilize support from sectors outside of unions for their goals and actions. Parties expect to capture the political allegiance of the mass membership affiliated to the unions, which can provide them with votes when and if there are national elections, militants, demonstrators, an organizational network, and money.

Union–party links vary in their degree of closeness. In some cases the two organizations are weakly connected. While union leaders and the rank and file may identify to a large extent with a particular party, and the latter may view them as an important part of its constituency of support, the union leaders are rarely top party leaders, the party assigns equal importance to other social segments among its supporters, and both organizations have a high degree of autonomy in adopting their policy goals. In other cases the two are closely linked. Union leaders are assumed to be party members and are often important party leaders, the party views unions as one of its main sources of support regardless of how many other constituencies may attach to it, and social and economic policies affecting unions are the object of at least some measure of consultation and discussion between the two organizations. In those settings in which union–party relationships are close, the parties can become in some cases an important unifying and directive force over unions. For this to occur, the parties must have a high degree of coherence regarding the policy issues of concern to unions, and the commitment of union leaders to the party and its overall strategy should take precedence over the particular interests of specific sectors of unions. In such situations conflicts within the union movement (at least, within those segments adhering to the same party if it does not encompass all), be they jurisdictional, political, or sectional are considerably reduced by the unifying and directive role played by the party. Unions also lose autonomy to make broad policy decisions, and although union leaders can very often convince the party to adopt the positions they espouse, the party remains an important forum for them to press their case.

These variations are largely the result of the historical origins of the parties, and of the timing of the formation of the parties and the unions.

The first factor, the historical inception of parties, refers to whether or not the party originated to articulate the interests of workers and other subordinate groups in the class cleavage of society. A close union–party tie will normally emerge where this was the case, provided that party militants or sympathizers are able to consolidate positions of leadership within the national union movement, and that its rank-and-file members and their families become an important source of party support. Most social democratic, labour, socialist, and communist parties of Europe and the Americas emerged to articulate such class interests, although many did not succeed in placing their militants at the helm of unions and/or in obtaining worker support.[8] A weak tie will result from unions establishing links with a party originally formed to articulate the interests of a variety of social segments other than (but not exclusive of) organized labour regardless of whether party sympathizers or members occupy the most important union leadership positions and of how much union households support the party. This was the case, for example, with parties formed out of the salience of social cleavages other than class, such as religious identity or a clerical/anti-clerical split. The Christian democratic parties of Chile or of Italy are cases in point.

The historical origin factor also pertains to whether the agents forming the party were in opposition to the governments of the time, or whether it was formed under governmental auspices. Assuming that union–party ties are close in both cases because the parties were formed originally to encapsulate mainly organized worker constituencies, parties formed in the opposition tend to be better able in the long run to exert a unifying and directive role over the unions. Being in the opposition forces parties to pay close attention to organization and to forging links to organized social groups since they must secure a capacity to mobilize support. It also enhances the importance of the party's ideological and programmatic discourses, since it must continually appeal for support on the basis of a certain vision of the future rather than on the ability to deliver immediate tangible benefits.[9] The result is to build bridges between party and union militants in such a way that the party strengthens its capacity to exert the above-mentioned role in the overall labour movement. By contrast, parties close to the unions but formed under government auspices – as was the case with Argentina's Peronist Party – are much weaker organizationally. They are also much more diffuse ideologically and programmatically, thereby allowing a greater dispersion of political opinions within the party that prevents it from exercising an overall leadership role in the labour movement, a feature that becomes especially evident once its founding period around the leading governmental figure is over.

The second factor has to do with the timing of the formation of unions and parties. In some exceptional situations, such as those of the United States or Colombia, the unions developed their main links to parties whose formation long anteceded them. These cases led to a weak link between the two, essentially for the above-noted reasons: the parties were originally created to channel the interests of other segments of society, and their openness to encompassing as well the representation of organized workers as these emerge is a manifestation of their great internal diversity. This weak link to a heterogeneous party leaves the national union movement bereft of the potentially unifying force that the party can exert within it, and great organizational diversity, autonomy, and jurisdictional and other conflicts can more easily develop within the various components of the national union movement. The links to the party in these cases will be most beneficial for the strongest and better financed unions that can pressure more effectively the party to adopt its positions.

In those situations where the links between the parties and the unions have been close, given a history of party formation to articulate and represent working-class interests, the timing of the formation of unions and parties still affects the latter's capacity to exert a unifying and directive role in the labour movement as a whole. Such capacity is greatest, as noted by Adolph Sturmthal, when the party emerges slightly before, or at the same time as, the most important unions that form the principal axis of the national labour organizations, as in Sweden or Germany.[10] In these cases, the party can play an active role through its workers and other militants in the formation of the unions, and it can discourage labour leaders in the stronger labour-market positions from separating themselves from the rest of the union movement by pursuing a narrow policy of accommodation with employers, sometimes to the detriment of other workers.[11] After all, given their party connections, such leaders will also be politically motivated to develop solidarity ties across the board. The result will be a union movement with comparatively fewer organizational cleavages by skill or occupation (such as those that developed so sharply in American organized labour history), thereby facilitating, in turn, the task of the party at some later point in time to exert a directive influence over the unions. By contrast, working-class parties that emerge long after the formation of large and important unions, as was the case with the British Labour Party, have much greater difficulty in becoming a unifying and leading centre for the labour movement as a whole. In these situations the labour movement is very diverse organizationally, since the successful establishment of unions before the emergence of a party linked to the labour movement necessarily means that the unions were created early on, with little employer resistance, and from the bottom up. The diversity of unionism, the already established *modus operandi* of their organizations, of their relationships with employers and among each other cannot easily be changed.[12]

These effects of the timing of party and union formation can also be observed where the parties (and to a large extent the unions as well) were created under government auspices. When, as in Perón's Argentina and in Cárdenas's Mexico, the parties and the unions were created or re-created under government auspices (the latter with leaders tied to the new party), both organizations were linked by the same founding moment and its accompanying rhetoric. Becoming a union leader normally requires adhering to the party, and identifying with its symbols and values. However, as noted above, such parties are less able to become leading forces for the labour movement as a whole in the absence of the venues of government. When the unions are created before a party that is orchestrated by the government, as was the case with the Brazilian Partido Trabalhista, the link between the two organizations is very weak and the party has even less capacity to become a leading force in the unions than is the case with the parties, such as British Labour, that also originated after the emergence of the unions but did so from the opposition.[13]

The Effects of Different Political Regimes on Party–Union Ties

Despite the previous historical determinants of the relative closeness of union–party ties, the nature of the relationship between unions and parties can vary given the characteristics of the political regime under which they operate. It is the regime that moulds, not only for labour but for all sectors of civil society, the organizational means through which political pressures must be exerted. Different types of regimes can enhance or diminish the importance of the parties for the unions and vice versa.

Although it is possible to trace the effects on the union–party relationship of different kinds of democracies and of different forms of authoritarianism, there is no space for such a detailed discussion within the confines of this chapter. Hence, although some of those differences will be alluded to, the main distinction to be highlighted here is simply that between democratic and authoritarian regimes. Democratic regimes are those in which regularly scheduled elections are the only means to determine who will constitute the national governments, in which such governments – while following the normal limitations to their power established in broadly accepted democratic constitutionalism – are not subordinate to other non-democratically generated powers such as monarchs or the military, and in which human rights, including the rights of political minorities, are fully respected. Authoritarian regimes are those that do not meet these criteria, even if some may approximate certain features of democracies, such as holding elections which are less than decisive or less than fair.

Mature democracies normally have well-established parties and party systems. This is largely a consequence of the repeated electoral contests; parties are the quintessential organizations to capture the support of the electorate, and given the electoral method for recruiting top governmental and legislative officials, the latter tend also to be affiliated in a democracy to specific parties (even if in some instances individual political leaders create their own). Although the organizations of civil society can always pressure the state directly, the presence of the parties in the governmental, legislative, and electoral arenas of democracies leads to their becoming an important means for channelling demands as well as protecting the interests of various segments of national societies, and this stimulates the development of links between parties and organized groups. The labour movement is no exception. The unions can resort to direct action to manifest their discontent through strikes, demonstrations, boycotts, and so on, but in a democratic context the party or parties linked to the unions usually become as well an important instrument for the expression of the political programme and goals of the labour movement. This is the case even when such goals include strengthening the unions, their autonomy, and their ability to negotiate directly with employers over a broader and broader agenda of issues. Corporatist interest intermediation usually develops more securely where it is accompanied by a parallel political consensus forged by well-established parties with links to the social actors.

Despite the reliance of unions on parties in democracies, the unions can rarely obtain party support for all their demands. This often leads them to put some distance between themselves and the party. When the party is in power, its reluctance to yield to many union demands is obvious; party leaders generally must implement an economic policy which does not satisfy all the aspirations of the worker constituency. When it is in the opposition, the party can certainly express itself with greater freedom in favour of union demands, but even then it cannot support them all the way. The electoral process generally leads the successful parties to acquire social bases of support which extend far beyond the purely labour-union constituency. This obliges the party leaders (and with them, on occasion, some important top-level union leaders) to disagree occasionally with certain union demands or strikes, since expressions of total agreement with them could undermine the broader support. Hence, the relation between unions and parties in a democratic regime creates a dilemma for the labour leaders. On the one hand, they hope to have a party which is supportive of their special interests, but, on the other, they require the party to be as strong as possible in order to be effective in providing that support. That strength can only be acquired in a democracy by broadening the party's electoral bases, but this necessarily means that the party cannot support exclusively the interests of the unions, and at times must even turn its back on them.[14]

To be sure, the fragmentation of the party system (which is usually buttressed by proportional representation and the existence of multiple party-generating cleavages in national societies) may limit the degree to which the party linked to the labour movement can extend its electoral bases to non-union sectors. Nevertheless, the dilemma also presents itself in the situation where there is a high degree of fragmentation of the party system, for even though this increases the viability of parties based exclusively on a union electorate, it is no less certain that in order for these to be efficacious they must enter into coalitions with parties which represent other sectors. Therefore, it can still be said, in general, that the more closely a party is identified only with unions, the greater will be its responsiveness to the union demands, but the smaller will be its capacity to protect union interests. And the greater the political capabilities of the party, the lesser the possibility that the union will be able to subordinate it to its interests.

Hence, parties that are from their inception closely identified with unions must, in order to grow electorally and/or constitute governments or governmental coalitions, either establish agreements with the union leaders which will subordinate union demands to what are understood to be the economic and political possibilities of the moment, or cultivate a relative distancing of the ties between the party and the unions. The first option has historically only been viable in a limited number of those settings where the parties had ascendancy over the unions given their role in forming them, and where the unions were relatively centralized, as will be noted later. The second alternative has been more common. Unions have therefore often been forced to exert pressures to protect the interests of workers and of their organizations against the very parties with which they are linked when these have diversified their electoral bases and acceded to governmental power.

Authoritarian regimes generate an overall context that has different effects on the relationship between unions and parties. In general, given the absence of free, regularly scheduled elections for constituting governments and legislatures, the parties (that is, all parties in the party system – not the government party of some forms of authoritarianism) do not have the fundamental means through which to express their political capabilities. Hence, it is far more difficult for them to play, if at all, the role of channels of the political pressures of the various social sectors that they partially have in democratic regimes. The organized groups of society must rely to a much greater extent on their abilities to pressure the state directly, using their own resources.

Another consequence of all authoritarian contexts is a tendency to party fragmentation, either through the formation of new political entities or in the creation of divisions in the already existing ones. The absence of free and competitive elections prevents party militants from pursuing more normal political careers apart from participating in political discussions and activities in interest groups and social movements, and this permits even very small parties that would not stand the test of voter choices to have a level of activity and status similar to the electorally much more important parties. Thus it is not uncommon for dozens of party labels to proliferate under authoritarian regimes. This, again, tends to make the leadership of significant social organizations all the more important while disabling to an even greater degree the parties from providing some form of support for them.

The sharpest contrast with democracies is provided by

authoritarian regimes that do not have any significant political arenas (such as a parliament, elections – however unfair – or local levels of government) where opposition parties and figures can act. In such especially closed regimes social mobilizations, petitions, declarations, and the like become the basic means to exert oppositional political pressures. Therefore, opposition party activists who lead groups that are able to organize such pressures acquire greater importance for the parties than they had previously. As party activities depend to a greater extent than in democracies on those of the particular interests groups, party activists will attempt to assume leadership positions in them and the parties' publicly expressed goals will tend to subordinate themselves as well to the objectives and discourses of such groups. If the authoritarian regime is, in addition, highly intolerant of demands formulated by autonomously organized social groups and of their efforts to mould public opinion, the link between opposition party activists and social organizations will be even more closely drawn. This is a consequence of the increase in personal risk involved in leading such groups, a risk that will be borne more by individuals with political commitments, and of the necessarily narrow field of possible group activities.[15] The end result is a politicization of the organizations of civil society under regimes that usually present themselves as the means to stamp out such politicization in order to realize their vision of national unity and consensus.

Other authoritarian regimes, while equally closed to party actions in the political realm may none the less provide significant room for the activities of social organizations, including unions. While opponents of the regime will still be drawn to leadership positions in such organizations, their greater viability as a means to channel social demands will stimulate a more normal functioning of their internal governance, a better communication with their social constituencies, and – as a result – a larger autonomy of the leaders from the strategies formulated by opposition parties and figures.

Still other authoritarian regimes may contain significant arenas for the actions of opposition political figures, although by definition none of them are as open as democracies. In these settings the split between those opponents who favour attempting negotiations and compromises to seek an end to the authoritarian regime and those who prefer a strategy of social mobilizations and other forms of direct action – a split that characterizes oppositions to such regimes everywhere – can develop to a much greater extent than in other cases. If the regime is highly closed and repressive of social demands and organizations, the opponents who pursue a mobilizational strategy will generally gravitate to the popular organizations, including unions. If the regime is open to union and other social demands, as is the case with populist authoritarianisms, some sectors of union and social leadership will develop accommodations with the regime while others will seek to confront it with their mobilizational efforts, thereby generating a form of this split within the social organizations themselves.

The Typology

The criteria in the preceding section can be used to analyse any specific national situation, and can be combined conceptually to create, by deduction, logically possible 'cases' which have not occurred historically. These may be useful exercises, but it is best for purposes of comparative analysis to construct types that approximate some of the principal variations that occur along these dimensions among national cases. Surely, a few cases will fit better than others into each type; but what is lost in specificity is gained in global vision.

In the previous discussion of the dimensions underlying the typology the variables were related to one another one by one; thus, the indicated effects are only to be found in that framework. In developing the various types or in analysing a concrete situation, the variables are placed in a context such that in many cases the original relationships are modified. This does not invalidate but qualify it.

The Social Democratic Type

This type approximates to the experiences of Scandinavia (except Finland), the United Kingdom, Austria, West Germany (the latter especially in the post-war period), Belgium, and the Netherlands. In the Americas the case which most closely approaches it is that of Venezuela, although the historical origins of the organized labour movement there are different. In spite of occasional references to other cases, this discussion will be based mainly on the Swedish, British, and West German experiences, since they contain the variations within the type.

Unions of the social democratic type are relatively strong, having obtained a high degree of affiliation in their respective countries.[16] They have achieved a solid plant-level presence, which enhances their national importance.[17] Generally, there is only one significant national union confederation, or certain fragmentation based on ascriptive differences, such as the linguistic ones that separate the Belgians or the religious ones that have long divided the unions and parties associated with the labour movement in the Netherlands. There is little local competition between politically and ideologically different union organizations or union tendencies; most unions are linked to a single social democratic or labour party, and this constitutes a main distinguishing feature of this type.[18]

Both the labour leaders and the allied parties have a political orientation which corresponds to a moderate socialist viewpoint with an incremental and reformist style of political action. This moderation has early roots in the historical development of the labour movement, and stems from the fact that unionism achieved an important degree of organizational consolidation at an early date (that is, before 1920, as noted above) through direct negotiations with employers.[19] For example, Turner (1962) points out that English textile unionism (including that of generally unskilled workers), began in the period prior to the 1824 abrogation of the anti-combination legislation, and in the first half of the nineteenth century there already were collective bargaining agreements. In Sweden Korpi says that 'collective bargaining on the local level was common already in the 1890s' (even though employers at the time were trying to reverse union growth); the first national agreement in an industrial sector took place in 1905, and the following year the so-called 'December compromise' led to employer acceptance of the right to unionize (Korpi, 1978: 61, 62). And although normally the German case is thought of as one in which there was considerable resistance to worker organization,[20] it does not contradict the generalization established here. Lösche says that by 1907 collective bargaining agreements covered 900,000 workers, and that by 1913 this number had risen to 2,000,000 (1973: 114).[21] In fact, the association between an early development (namely, before World War I) of regular collective bargaining and the emergence of politically moderate and reformist labour leaderships is so secure that this might well be called a law of the process of labour-movement formation, although it must be added that this is not the only route that generates reformist leaders. Given this reformist orientation the parties associated with the labour movement were also accepted early on (although obviously not preferred) by capitalists and their political allies as possible organizers of governments.

The link between unions and parties in this type is close, a result of the fact that both emerged as part of the same opposition movement, and it constitutes a unifying factor for the labour movement. This is particularly so where, as in Sweden and Norway, the party intervened in the formation of the unions, and where there has been a direct historical continuity between both organizations ever since.[22] The German case is similar, although the fusion of the union movement of Catholic origin with the social democratic one after World War II introduced – despite the relatively minor importance of the former – a certain discontinuity.[23] In Britain the unions greatly anteceded the party and virtually created it; thus, the unifying impact of the party on the unions could not take place to the same extent as in the other cases. For example, jurisdictional conflicts between unions do take place in Great Britain, whereas in Sweden they are practically unknown.

As noted in the previous section, when the labour-related parties gain electoral strength, and especially when they gain government power, it is advantageous for them either to forge agreements with the unions over incomes and labour policies that can form part of a viable package of socio-economic management, or to distance themselves from the unions. Given the size of the electoral support for the parties in the cases of this type, the frequency with which they participate in government coalitions or form governments by themselves, and the close historical associations between the parties and the unions that make any distancing between them more difficult, there are considerable pressures to reach clear party–union understandings over programmes and policies. Since the viability of such policies depends in part on their acceptance by business, the labour-linked parties become a major force pressing for agreements between labour and business associations on a wide range of socio-economic policy issues. Social democratic cases with their large, moderate parties and their strong and well-organized unions become, consequently, the principal (although by no means exclusive) grounds for the development of neo-corporatism in democracies, the analysis of which has spawned a large literature since the mid-seventies.[24] The prefix 'neo' serves to distinguish these practices from corporatism under authoritarian regimes. In democracies the parties to the agreements are organized autonomously from the state, even if they may be recognized by the state as legitimate representatives of certain interests, while in the latter they are often organized under state auspices or are subject to its oversight and intervention.[25] Moreover, under authoritarian regimes corporatism is usually of a 'sectoral' kind, as it privileges a direct relationship between favoured interest groups and the state; by contrast, while such 'sectoral' forms of corporatism can also be observed in democracies, the stress in neo-corporatism is on 'concertation', that is, the development of arenas for negotiation and compromise by a variety of partially antagonistic interests under state oversight.[26]

A central focus of attention in the literature on neo-corporatism as it pertains to labour has been the factors associated with the stability of its institutional arrangements. As noted by Regini (1984: 132), the most commonly mentioned factors are the organizational centralization and concentration of the relevant interest groups, their monopoly of representation, and the presence of the labour-linked party in the government.[27] The first of these factors prevents the lower-level leaders and even the rank and file from undermining through their job actions the agreements that are reached by the top leaderships of the associations. Centralized labour organizations, even in social democracy, are much less responsive to local level demands, and this sometimes generates the necessary discontent among workers for local-level leaders to break ranks with the main labour organization or for the surge in support for labour-leadership segments with other political and ideological attachments. The second prevents other organizations from undermining the accords. And the third stems from the pressures that have already been indicated.

Other important factors, some of them related to the previous ones, can also be drawn from the literature. First, neo-corporatist concertation is aided by the relative homogeneity of the economy, both within industrial branches and across sectors, and this condition is more easily found in smaller economies. Top-level agreements that will be satisfactory to all who are supposed to be covered by them are difficult to reach in highly heterogeneous economies; workers in its stronger components are likely to press for greater advantages, sometimes with the sympathy of employers who may prefer to deal with local-level labour representatives (especially when they are not unionized). Secondly, concertation is more likely to succeed when macroeconomic parameters are relatively stable, for this permits the various parties to the agreements a better estimate of their expected gains and costs under them. When such calculations are far off the mark, the actors will prefer to develop shorter-term strategies. Thirdly, the government and state bureacracy must want and be able to implement effectively the policies that are contained in the agreements. No rational labour leadership can, for example, agree to help fight inflation through wage restraint if the state is unable to reduce its own deficit spending. Fourthly, the agreements among the social actors must correspond to a parallel political consensus manifested in the government coalition (if it is such) and in the legislature. Otherwise political opponents of the accords may derail them. This consensus is more likely where there is an adequate transmission belt between interest associations and parties, where there is little interest group and party fragmentation, and where the parties have the necessary majorities to control the governmental and legislative process. Fifthly, concertation is aided by medium-term economic growth. This permits the social actors (especially labour) to accept limitations to taking full advantage of momentary market opportunities given the expectation that improvements will none the less ensue. Finally, the onset and stability of neo-corporatist concertation depends in part on the commitment of the labour movement to the political success of the labour-linked party, which may result as much from a positive attachment to it as well as from an attempt to prevent other parties, unsympathetic to labour, from winning elections. A similar commitment from labour may be the result of an attempt to contribute the necessary stability for a smooth transition to democracy out of an authoritarian regime, or from a perception of national economic vulnerability.

These conditions are difficult to meet. As a result, neo-corporatist concertation has not been particularly stable. Although it is not an exclusive experience of the social democratic cases, the above-noted conditions have been best met in certain cases of this type, notably in Sweden, Norway, Austria, and the Netherlands. In Great Britain the decentralization of the unions prevented the Labour Party when it was in office in the late 1970s from having a successful programme of agreements over incomes policies.[28] While neo-corporatist concertation has been more successful in Germany, the accords have also been challenged by workers in the stronger industries.[29] Even in Sweden there is evidence of wage drift as workers in the stronger industries pressure management for greater gains and to restore income differentials.[30] In fact, the tendency during the 1980s was for a greater development of plant level bargaining and 'micro-corporatism' at the firm level.

None the less, in the cases of this type, especially those with relatively centralized unions, neo-corporative institutions will continue to be a more viable option than elsewhere as a framework for the political and industrial actions of the labour movement, although their short-term use and importance may show considerable oscillation.

The Contestatory Type

This type is based on the Chilean, French, and Italian cases, most typically during the 1950s and 1960s. Other cases that approach them at various times in their history are Uruguay, Finland, Spain, and Portugal. The contestatory type occurs under democratic regimes, so the features presented here do not correspond to the authoritarian experiences in these countries. The type is characterized by a labour movement that is divided politically and ideologically, with an important segment linked to the Communist Party. This discussion will be based principally on Chile and France.[31] In both cases labour organizations underwent most of their historically formative experiences since the late nineteenth century under political regimes that, given generally free multi-party competition in regularly scheduled national elections, can be viewed as democratic.

The early efforts of worker unionization in the cases of this type were invariably resisted strongly by capitalists. This produced (as always occurs in such circumstances) embryonic groups of radicalized union leaders, one of which opted for membership in the Third International. In contrast with what happened in other contexts where the anti-union repression was also strong, in the Chilean and French cases the union leaders, both the radicalized and moderate ones, had early on a relatively broader impact in local and national politics in that they formed part of the anti-clerical (and, in France, pro-Republican as well) coalitions. Although they had little success in obliging owners to accept their unions and to develop regular collective bargaining with them (unlike in the social democratic cases), the political importance of worker organizations stimulated their development outside the plant level as cooperatives, mutual aid societies, labour exchanges, and centres for political discussion and agitation – sometimes with local or national government subsidies. There was, then, a curious disjunction between strong social repression and political openness and freedom for the early labour organizers, which created a propitious context for the development of radical worker leader-ships: they could develop the organizational capacity to disseminate their views on capitalist exploitation while the intran-sigence of employers lent credence to their arguments.[32]

Since the unusual political context that made this disjunction possible can be traced to the sharp clerical–anti-clerical division at the time in which labour organizations were in their formative stages, this explains why the contestatory cases tended to develop in Catholic countries.[33] But a contestatory type of unionism did not develop in all such countries, as illustrated by most Latin American experiences. For this type to develop fully the leaders of the embryonic labour organizations, be they radicalized or not, had to succeed in consolidating them, for which they needed to establish a plant-level presence and begin regular processes of collective bargaining with management. Unlike what occurred in social democratic cases, in all contestatory ones this took place after 1920, and only after capitalists were directly pressured by legislation and/or political events. State recognition of plant-level union rights and its initiative in establishing rules for collective bargaining were necessary before these could be obtained by the unions.

This final state-induced stage of labour movement formation was notably characterized by the absence of political repression or even discrimination against any of the pre-existent embryonic leadership groups, and by no officious attempts to create or to foster the development of competing ones. This was due to the fact that the political context at the time was one in which the parties of the left with close links to the unions were participating directly in the government or at least in the governing consensus (in Chile and France during the Popular Fronts; in Spain, partially during the Second Republic; in Italy and again in France under the immediate post-war liberation governments; and in Portugal and Spain with their recent transitions to democracy). Given the prominent political positions occupied by the parties linked to the labour movement, they played important roles in channelling the overall political and industrial actions of the labour movement. Hence, the massification of union memberships generated by the development or strengthening of a plant-level presence by labour organizations and by the inception of regular collective bargaining, as well as the consequent growth of middle-level union militants, took place at a time in which the union–party links were closely drawn. This strengthened the political and ideological identities and divisions in the expanding labour movement, to the degree that labour-union militance and even membership (where it was not obligatory, as in Chile's so-called 'industrial unions') became to a significant extent a matter of political sympathy, identity, and even choice. The result was a form of unionism which was fragmented ideologically and politically from the national to the local level.

Given these historical origins, the association between unions or segments of unions and parties in the contestatory type tend to be quite close, although many union leaders may deny it. In the case of the communist parties, the link is reinforced by the fact that they developed originally in direct relation with nuclei of organized workers, by their self-definition and identity as parties representing working-class interests (which leads them to be especially active in unions), and to the party commitment and discipline they require from their militants – including the communist union leaders. These reinforcing characteristics do not apply to the same extent, if at all, to the other parties (socialist, Christian democratic, laicist, or others) which are active in the labour movement of this group of countries. In these latter cases the union–party links, although much looser, are continually reproduced by the political divisions that are already institutionalized in the union environment, while these are, in turn, reinforced by the presence of the strong communist segment. New generations of prospective leaders are usually forced to belong to one of the organized political-ideological nucleii in order to gain the positions to which they aspire, for union militance and support networks are closely drawn around them at the local, and particularly regional and national, levels. The occasional individuals who build union-leadership careers apart from the established political-ideological nucleii in fact end up creating, sometimes unwittingly, what they usually denounce: a new organized segment that must define itself (even if using labels such as 'independent' or 'autonomous') as different from the others, which in the end only reaffirms the importance of the existing political and ideological divisions. Sometimes leaders who profess to be independent of the major segments (or those who are associated with a small group) can acquire important positions as the various political-ideological groupings need a neutral or bridge figure to lead an organization or a labour action; but this is, again, a result of the politicized environment.

The political and ideological divisions lead to a process of competition between the different tendencies for the allegiance of union militants and the rank and file. Each segment attempts to present itself as the best representative of worker interests. Unlike divisions created by ascriptive differences in the work-force, the political-ideological ones can potentially occur in all localities, although they usually do not extend at any given moment to all of them. The actual or potential competition generates union leaderships which are highly responsive and attentive to rank-and-file aspirations, and easily leads to an escalation of union demands and worker expectations. And yet unions in this type of labour movement are normally quite weak. This is partly a consequence of the very divisions that lead to the competition in the first place, and partly a result of the fact that employer resistance and repression of unions continues to be strong. Employers tend to view unions as tools of the parties of the left, especially of the Communist Party, and this serves as a convenient justification for their anti-union posture. Such attitudes have the sympathy of government authorities during periods of conservative ascendancy, which further feeds employer intransigence, and it in turn recreates a union environment in which leadership cadre self-select from among those who have ideological and political commitments. The weakness of unions is also a consequence of the fact that many rank-and-file workers view them as excessively riddled by 'politics'.

Given the combination of union weakness, the tendency towards demand escalation that stems from the competition between different segments of leadership, and the great capacity to formulate comprehensive programmes for change that comes from the ideologically charged environment, this form of unionism typically generates a large gap between what it proposes and what it obtains. It easily articulates a critical discourse regarding social and economic ills that should be corrected, but it lacks the necessary strength (except during extraordinary periods of mobilization) to pressure employers and the state effectively.

The interconnections between unions, parties, and politics ensure that labour demands and actions become quite readily matters of general political debate. The public perception of labour conflict is therefore heightened. Moreover, the influence of the left is reflected in the fact that its discourse pervades labour actions. Thus, a strike which in the United States would be no more than an attempt on the part of a limited group of workers to gain benefits, in the contestatory setting it tends to be presented as a manifestation of the class struggle by union and party circles. Partly as a reaction to this phraseology, the same events are frequently viewed as expressions of a national crisis by employers and the right.

It is not infrequent that one or more parties with union connections form part of the government while others remain in the opposition. The labour leaders linked to the government usually adopt a more moderate overall discourse, but the underlying competition in the union field makes it virtually impossible for them to develop neo-corporatist concertation with the authorities over incomes or other medium- to long-term policies. Rather, such leaders try to use their government contacts to secure specific advantages for their constituencies, often in a clientelistic rather than universalistic fashion, that will help them retain or even enhance their union bases. Meanwhile those who are linked to opposition parties try to articulate maximal worker demands and to press for them through union actions and demonstrations.[34] Rank-and-file workers may oscillate between supporting one group or the other depending on their assessments of the relative utility of government connections or of oppositional mobilization.

Despite – or perhaps because of – the divisions, there are frequent calls for unity voiced by the various segments of the labour movement. Unity of action among them, though always subject to an undercurrent of competition, can be achieved in certain periods. They require lengthy preparatory discussions and sometimes difficult accommodations to reach common denominators in union demands and objectives, as well as mechanisms for collegiate leadership. Such periods usually strengthen the labour movement, and are associated with increases in the number of unionized workers. When the parties associated to the unions are in government, top-level neo-corporatist concertation may develop, although it is not likely to prove stable. Periods of extensive unity of action increase the autonomy of the unions *vis-à-vis* the parties as union agreements over the common denominators take precedence. As a result, the contestatory type of unionism becomes more like the social democratic one of the decentralized form.

The overall political context influences the forging of labour-movement unity. It can occur when all the labour-linked parties find themselves in the opposition for a lengthy period, and a coalition between them is viewed as necessary to increase their political chances. This is what led to unity of action in France at the time of the *Programme Commun de la Gauche* in the early to mid-seventies, as socialists and communists formed an alliance to seek to end Gaullist dominance of the Fifth Republic. Unity of action may also be stimulated as one of the labour-linked parties seeks to end its overall political isolation. This was notably the case with the Italian Communist Party as it attempted to position itself in the political mainstream as a viable government coalition partner.

The crisis of Communist parties and the end of the Cold War have had a considerable impact on this type of labour movement. The decline of ideological distance among its various segments has enhanced the possibilities for greater collaboration among them, and increased union autonomy from the parties. The labour movement's agenda has changed to focus more on specific reforms than on all-encompassing programmes for change coupled with shorter-term defensiveness. And yet, it is likely that the labour movements will remain divided, partly out of bureaucratic inertia, generating a highly pluralistic labour movement whose segments, while pursuing similar goals, will continue to compete as well as collaborate as the circumstances dictate.

The Pressure-group Type

This type is based on the United States, with the situations of Britain in the last decades of the nineteenth century, and of Puerto Rico, Canada, and Colombia as ones that approximate it. The type is characterized principally by the fact that the unions developed without generating a new party; the union leaders developed, instead, links to pre-existing parties. This discussion will focus exclusively on the American case.

J. David Greenstone (1977) argued that changes on both sides of the Atlantic have virtually eliminated prior differences between American labour politics and those of European countries with a social democratic orientation. In the United States the unions strongly linked themselves to the Democratic Party, while in Europe the Social Democratic and Labour parties have moderated their political views to the degree that they cannot be distinguished from majority sentiments in the American party. This thesis has some merit, especially in the context of the sixties, and if one compares the United States primarily with Great Britain – in other words, precisely the basic comparison of Greenstone's study. At that point in the United States the Democrats had developed a consensus over expanding welfare institutions, while the leftist and neutralist currents that were to flower a decade later within British Labour still had not expressed themselves with full force.

And yet, even in the context of the sixties the Democratic Party did not have links to the unions that were as close as those between European Social Democratic and Labour parties. Just to take the British case, the unions have an institutionalized presence in Labour Party governance unlike anything in the Democratic Party; moreover, it would be inconceivable for British union leaders to ask openly for electoral support for candidates of the Conservative Party, while American union leaders can be found supporting Republican candidates. The influence of the unions in the Democratic Party depends on their always renewed effort to exchange electoral support for individual candidates for their promises of support for union causes at the legislative and governmental level; if Democratic Party candidates are not in harmony with union interests the latter may sit the election out or support the Republican candidate if he or she seems attractive enough. Moreover, while in Britain a Labour Member of Parliament will virtually by definition vote for legislation that is viewed as most favourable to union interests among the options being discussed, in the United States this by no means can be taken for granted with Democratic (or Republican) Party legislators, even after they have been elected with union support. In addition, by contrast to the British case, there is no reason why various union organizations following their perceived specific interests may not vote for different candidates. A variety of conflicts between and within unions – jurisdictional, political, and so on – are much more frequent and open in the United States than in Britain, which is itself more contentious than comparable Northern European cases. The American union heterogeneity manifests itself in an organizational structure that generates relatively strong federations but not strong confederal leadership.

In sum, to an extent unknown in Europe, the political action of American unions consists of exchanging electoral and financial support for individual candidates (of mainly the Democratic but also of the Republican parties) in the expectation that they will favour their legislative interests. And if in time American unions developed more frequently their ties to figures in the Democratic Party, this occurred primarily because the process of party differentiation generated by electoral competition led the Democrats to appeal more to popular sectors, immigrants, and non-Protestant groups (and to attract candidates who would do so), while Republicans became the party of more elite groups and nativists, and because of the experience of labour under Franklin Roosevelt's New Deal. Yet it is not in the interest of the unions to commit themselves to back the Democratic candidates loyally. This would be prejudicial to them, because it would imply losing part of their capacity to renew the exchange of promises for mutual support.[35] The candidates would simply count the union vote as secure and devote their energies to capturing the swing vote.

The fundamental question in the American case is why a new party did not develop along with the unions, as occurred in other countries. This question should not be confused (as it usually is) with the one originally formulated by Werner Sombart; namely, why did socialist parties not develop along with the unions? The abundant literature regarding American 'exceptionality' tends to conflate both questions, as if the unusual aspect of this case were the latter and not the former.[36] But many countries did not develop 'socialist' parties in connection with labour-movement formation, while only a few did not develop any major or important parties at all – socialist or otherwise. This is what should be viewed as the exceptional feature of the formation of the US labour movement.

The discussions of American exceptionality from the perspective of the absence of socialism usually contain a naïve but unstated and implicit view of the process of party formation. The implication is that parties are simply formed when a segment of the adult population discovers it has common interests opposed to those of other sectors, which then somehow gives rise to a party to defend and express those interests. In other words, the absence of socialism in the United States would be largely due to the lack of a clear conception among workers that they have common interests in opposition to those of capitalists – that is, a lack of class consciousness and its accompanying socio-economic and political solidarity. Thus, analysts have stressed the fact that American workers largely accepted the dominant liberal values of its capitalist system with its emphasis on property rights and free markets, and many hoped to forge an independent business future for themselves. They have argued that workers' sense of class solidarity was impaired by their strong ethnic and racial divisions, by the very high rates of spatial mobility, by the lack of salience of class and status divisions given the unusual egalitarianism of American society, and by the relatively high standard of living many workers enjoyed, factors that all diminished the appeal of socialist activists who tried to mobilize workers on the basis of a class identity. They have noted that white male workers did not have to organize politically to demand an extension of the franchise since they already had the vote when they emerged as a class, and therefore they did not – as in 'Europe' – undergo the politicization that such struggles produced. The United States was therefore exceptional because its workers were, in sum, different.[37]

A more nuanced conception of the process of party formation would shed greater light on this question. Very briefly, this process – as it applies to mass parties that did not emerge originally out of divisions among notables in pre-democratic parliaments – includes three elements: the first is a societal cleavage that leads sectors of the population to generate common identities and perceptions of shared interests exclusive of other sectors. This furnishes a potential mass base or constituency of support for parties and is the level of party formation that corresponds most closely to the class consciousness argument. The second ingredient is the existence of social organizations (such as churches, clubs, neighbourhood committees, cooperatives, occupational associations, or unions) that group individuals who share a common position within the social cleavage. Such organizations provide leaders, militants, and members to form the new party and to mobilize broader support for it, and often help create the perception of common identity in the relevant population. Sometimes the coincidence between the social rupture and organized groups does not readily exist, and even when it does the latter's leaders may be unwilling to attempt or discouraged from attempting to form a new party. Unions and churches (of religious minorities or dominant ones that are threatened by secularization) are usually the most party-generative of groups given their organizational continuity, and shared identities and interests. Differences and divisions among these social organizations, for whatever reasons, can be at the origin of the formation of more than one party on the basis of a single polarity in a social cleavage. And the third ingredient is composed of the constitutional, electoral, and state-administrative rules that either favoured or discouraged the formation of all as well as specific new parties.[38]

Regardless of whatever the peculiarities of American society and its working class actually were in comparison to others, and these points are always debatable, it is safe to assume from the record of occasionally bloody strikes and other labour conflicts that workers perceived the cleavage between them and the owners of the nation's firms. The discussion of the failure of a new and successful worker's party to become grafted on to that cleavage should centre, therefore, on the second and third levels of party formation. There was an available mass for a working-class party in the United States, but the union leaderships generally did not press for it, and the electoral and other state-generated rules strongly discouraged it. This chapter will not focus on the latter aspect. Suffice it to say that it was very difficult for third parties to obtain a place on the ballot for national elections given the variety of requirements set by individual states for such inclusion; the rules were rigged in favour of the – by the latter part of the nineteenth century – already well-established two-party system. Moreover, political dissidents from the established parties encountered a quite heavy fare of repression. What follows will examine the union level of the party formation process.

The single most convincing explanation for the aborted development of a new major party coupled with the emergence of the American labour movement was the great flexibility and co-optive capacity of the established two parties, which were related to their lack of national coordination and absence of specific ideological and programmatic outlooks.[39] This flexibility was accompanied by the rigidity of their virtual monopoly of access to the electoral market, providing a peculiar mix that was indeed exceptional when compared to other national experiences. The United States has a strong two-party system, but weak parties in terms of their national articulation.[40] The course of least resistance for the emerging union leaders and militants was to use the opportunities presented by the highly permeable parties to influence, first, their selection of candidates and, secondly, the outcome of the elections in ways that would enhance, or at least not prejudice, union interests. Thus, if American unions did not stimulate the formation of a new party it was, more than anything else, a product of the fact that they found greater short-term rewards in not doing so given the political opportunities and obstacles they faced.[41]

In the end, the political exchange of electoral for legislative and government (including local and state government) support that lay at the basis of the unions' associations with the parties led mainly to links with the Democrats, given, as noted above, a process of political differentiation. And yet, this exchange had a history that was complicated by the fact that, more than elsewhere, the history of American labour-union formation in the industrial sector of the economy contains not one but two distinct, albeit related, processes: one for skilled workers in mainly craft unions associated with the American Federation of Labor (AFL), and the other for the unskilled. The reasons for this are, once again, significantly tied to the political context.

The inception of regular collective bargaining and plant-level penetration for the skilled workers in craft unions occurred by direct negotiations between such workers and employers before 1920. This resulted, as noted above, in the emergence of a labour leadership whose political orientations steered clear of radical attitudes. The same process for the unskilled workers (exceptions such as the coal miners aside) began with the enactment of the New Deal's National Labor Relations Act in 1935 and extended until the beginnings of the Cold War, favouring, under legislative and other state pressures, the expansion of industrial or general forms of unionism. Some of the main leaders of the second process of union consolidation at one time belonged to the AFL, but clashed with it and eventually withdrew due to the fact that the Federation did not adequately support the difficult process of unionization of the unskilled workers; their labour-market position was not as strong as the former, and the employers (with considerable help from the state, especially the courts, the national guard, federal troops, and on occasion the police), fiercely resisted all efforts to organize them.[42]

In the early years of labour-movement formation, the skilled workers' tighter labour markets gave them everywhere a significant edge over the unskilled in forcing employers to accept their unions. They could develop a privileged bargaining relationship with management, while the latter compensated for the higher costs of skilled labour with lower wages for the non-unionized unskilled labour force. This arrangement was easily upset if the skilled workers took a leading role in the unionization of the unskilled. While some tension between the two types of workers can be found in most labour-movement histories, the usual pattern was for those with greater skills to eventually take part in forming broader worker organizations. Some analysts (for instance, Bauman, 1972: part III) have suggested that this process took place as a consequence of changes in industry at the turn of the century, that led to a deskilling of important groups of skilled workers.[43] Perhaps, but this can hardly explain why the presumed broader union-forming consequences of such changes did not show up to the same extent in the United States, which was unique regarding the depth and longevity of the conflict between the two categories of workers. That most skilled workers were white males who were native born (or long-time immigrants), and many of the unskilled included recent immigrants and some women as well as blacks of course did not help, as has been noted repeatedly, to generate solidarity between the two groups.

But there is a better explanation. The exclusive bargaining strategy of the AFL's skilled worker unions or, as Laurie calls it (1989: chap. 6), their 'prudential' form of unionism that stayed clear of the bitter conflicts staged by the broader masses of workers,[44] would not have been sustained for long if its leaders had been committed to forming a new party. Where labour-movement formation entailed as well the creation of a working-class party, the skilled worker leaderships were forced to look beyond their immediate labour markets in order to build the broadest possible support for the party. Class solidarity followed from the political-organizational imperative. The AFL did not have this imperative. It could simply rely on the above-noted political exchange to defend its interests given the openness of the established parties. And while increasing the numbers of workers it could mobilize by organizing the unskilled would perhaps have enhanced its ability to engage in the political exchange, this would have diluted the craft unions' specific political interests and threatened their already established relationship with employers, all for an uncertain gain in the political exchange. The unusually sharp organizational divisions and conflicts based on the overlapping effects of ethnicities and labour markets within American labour flourished, then, in part because of the permeability and lack of national articulation of the pre-existing parties.[45] As noted previously, party formation has a unifying impact on labour-movement formation.

The state's legislative and political pressures on employers in favour of the collective bargaining and unionization rights of unskilled workers came at a time when a Democratic administration sought a broad alliance to support its anti-depression programmes and to maximize its electoral chances. Coming on the heels of the conservative Republican administrations of the twenties, leaders of the Congress of Industrial Organizations (CIO), which had splintered off the AFL over the question of the unionization of unskilled workers, [46] jumped at the chance, and over the next decade the density of American unionism rose dramatically. This strengthened as well the association of the unions and the Democratic Party. The political exchange henceforth focused more heavily on the internal process of candidate selection and lobbying within that party. Sectors within the labour movement that favoured developing a new worker's party in the twenties and the thirties still faced the hurdles created by the electoral procedures and rules, and those that did not drew – as became plainly evident during the New Deal – the advantages of the openness of the (in this case) Democratic Party. Once again, third party formation in connection with the development of labour unions was undercut.

Moreover, there was considerable repression against the leftist segments of the labour movement. In the late teens and early twenties it strongly affected the revolutionary syndicalist Industrial Workers of the World, and later, especially with the inception of the Cold War, it fell on the communist militants who had gained a minority influence in the CIO through their activism in the unionization efforts.[47] Hence, although the American labour movement – like the contestatory ones – had to draw on state support to gain regular collective bargaining processes and to extend unionization, the overall political context – unlike those in the contestatory cases – was one which through a variety of means discriminated against the left rather than supported it. In the last analysis, the fundamental difference was that the CIO leaders did not have firm alternative party commitments. Following the style begun by the AFL, they also relied on their ability to pressure the established parties, especially the Democrats. Hence, the New Deal coalition was one of social segments and interests within the cover of the Democratic Party, whereas the Popular Front and other coalitions that pressed for the extension of unionization and collective bargaining in the contestatory cases took the form, first and foremost, of party coalitions.

Overall, American unions have probably been weakened by not having a more secure connection to the political system through a major party. As world-wide changes in the economy force a decline in the traditional areas of union strength, their capacity to use the political exchange successfully declines as well, and they cannot resort to organic party ties to compensate for their declining strength. It is also probably the case that this type of unionism generates a leadership self-selection process that favours individuals who are characterized more by attitudes and styles of functionaries than by their dedication to some larger cause.

The State-sponsored Type
This type is based primarily on Argentina during the first Peronist era (1943–55), Brazil until the mid-1970s, and Mexico. In significant aspects, this type of labour movement is also kindred to that

of communist regimes. Despite the considerable differences between them, the fundamental characteristic these cases share is the formation of a labour movement whose ability to act is significantly determined by its direct or indirect subordination to the state. This subordination is indicative of state authoritarianism in its relations with the organizations of civil society, although in the case of labour it is of a complex co-optive and populist kind that not only permits a degree of labour leadership influence over policy-makers but also provides benefits to unionized workers – especially in the formative period.

Numerous authoritarian regimes have tried to sponsor labour organizations and/or sought to impose labour leaders addicted to them only to have the former penetrated by militants that are linked to the opposition and the latter rejected by workers. Such situations are different from those of this type, in which state elites did succeed to a large measure in orchestrating a labour movement that was accepted by workers, although with variations from sector to sector and between the national cases. Such acceptance explains in part the resilience of the labour organizations in the face of changing political conditions and challenges from labour oppositions. And yet, this type of labour movement is in the long run impossible to sustain under two different – and quite opposite – political contexts: a form of democratization that fosters the development of labour's organizational autonomy by changing the laws related to unions and industrial relations as well as the behaviour of labour and state elites towards union organizations, and a turn towards a more repressive and restrictive form of authoritarianism in state–labour relations.[48] Both changes undermine the viability of the labour leaderships linked to the state; in either case they must transform their relationships with the union bases, the employers, and the state, or their opponents will gain a greater presence or even supplant them in the labour movement. During the best of times, state-sponsored cases contain significant labour oppositions to the official leaderships, but they are kept at bay as long as state elites continue to exercise their sometimes intricate mix of co-optation of labour leaders, a certain largesse in the face of worker demands, and repression.

The difference between successful and unsuccessful attempts at state sponsorship of unions has to do, once again, with the conditions that prevailed at the time unions first achieved regular collective bargaining and plant-level penetration. State-sponsored unionism only succeeded in those contexts in which, first, the leaders of the pre-existing embryonic unions had been unable to establish a plant-level presence and regular collective bargaining, thereby leaving the organizational space of the working class largely vacant; secondly, where the government stimulated the formation of unions led by individuals who professed to support it, excluding those who did not; thirdly, where the authorities were not perceived as acting simply in favour of employer interests, and had to force them to accept the worker representatives of the newly established unions and collective bargaining institutions; fourthly, where this formative process was accompanied by considerable popular mobilization, including especially a massive increase of first-time union affiliations into the state-sponsored organizations,[49] and fifthly, where the creation of these labour organizations was accompanied by a tangible flow of benefits for the working class.[50] These necessary conditions are rarely met, but they were present, though with variations in degree and form, under the governments of Perón in Argentina, Vargas in Brazil, and Cárdenas in Mexico.[51]

Union leadership careers in the cases of this type depend to a significant extent on retaining good relations with the proper government elites. The union leaderships' dependence on the government produces an ambivalent and problematical relationship between them and the rank and file. The leaders must manoeuvre between the frequently opposite pressures generated by the need to retain official support and the ability to control worker demands and actions. Both are important for union leadership success: official support, tacit or explicit, is in the last analysis decisive, but it is retained in so far as the leaders are able to prevent worker mobilizations they do not direct or cannot terminate. To this end, they must try to avoid the build-up of worker discontent that could contribute to the development of alternative opposition leadership groups among the rank and file, which means that they cannot simply accept – or be perceived as accepting – state policies that may have a visible negative impact on the rank and file's working or living conditions. For this reason, the leaderships of state-sponsored unions tend to be strong advocates of workers' rights and interests in public and semi-public state policy-making circles, and yet, despite their rhetoric sometimes to the contrary, they usually do not foster worker mobilizations against state policies lest they lose the authorities' support. In fact, with the exception of worker mobilizations in favour of the government or a certain faction within the ruling circles when these are divided, or against specific employers to whom the authorities are indifferent or want to pressure for some end, labour leaders in this type of unionism are very wary of worker actions and initiatives for fear of losing control over them. As a result, this type of unionism is very top-heavy. Union organizations are highly undemocratic in their governance, the process of collective bargaining is secluded from rank-and-file influence, rival leaderships are co-opted or repressed, union leaders at even relatively low levels are professionalized, leaders are sometimes given control over hiring, and the leaders refine the art of controlling and manipulating all union meetings and congresses.[52] This type of unionism also tends to stimulate relatively high levels of affiliation, which may seem paradoxical at first glance because the larger numbers may enhance rank-and-file mobilizational strength; but it is, on the contrary, quite consistent with this form of worker control, given the authorities' efforts to encapsulate large numbers of them in the officially sponsored organizations. And yet, in the final analysis this form of unionism's basic weakness is worker allegiance to it. It is usually under constant challenge by alternative oppositional leaderships, which sometimes take advantage of the spaces generated by the official structures to advance their leadership claims.

The cases of state sponsorship of unions led to the creation or re-creation, out of state initiatives as well, of parties linked to the labour unions (more belatedly and weakly in Brazil than in Mexico or Argentina).[53] By occupying more thoroughly the working class's organizational and political space, such parties also enhanced the ability of the authorities to generate a successful state-sponsored labour movement. An important function of these parties was to increase the co-optive capacity of the authorities over the labour leaders, since the individuals who embark on a career of labour leadership can be rewarded with sometimes lucrative party positions, seats in legislatures, governorships, or appointments in the labour ministries. And yet, placing the labour movement as one of the main constituencies of the party also enhances the ability of the labour leadership to pressure the authorities in favour of their programmes and interests. Co-optation is a two-way street. This is especially so if the authorities must periodically rely on political and/or electoral mobilization (even if these take place under conditions that are not genuinely democratic), as was the case under Perón's first government and continues to occur with each electoral period in Mexico. Naturally, if the state elites promote the diversification of the social organizations that are affiliated with the party, the relative importance of the union leaders, and therefore their capacity to use the party to pressure the government, diminishes. José Luis Reyna (1981: 23) points to this motivation as the reason for the creation of the National Confederation of Popular Organizations by the Mexican government in 1943.[54]

There are numerous differences between the unionism of the

three cases which serve as the base for this discussion, although it is not possible to develop them adequately here.[55] Briefly, Brazilian unionism developed with the least rank-and-file mobilization. Moreover, Brazilian labour legislation led to a union structure and collective bargaining institutions that limited plant-level worker organization, resulting in a notably weak form of unionism that eventually permitted the successful emergence of a labour opposition in the 'new unionism' of the mid to late seventies. By contrast, in Mexico and Argentina unions were created at a time of great social and political mobilization of workers. Union organizations effectively extend into the plant level, and in Mexico much collective bargaining takes place at that level as well. There is also a certain amount of union pluralism in Mexico that is officially accepted; in fact, it can be converted, as indicated by Erickson and Middlebrook, into one more mechanism of control over the state- and party-incorporated union sectors if they become excessive in their demands. The authorities can threaten to undermine them by favouring, sometimes tacitly or by default, the alternative union leaderships (Erickson and Middlebrook, 1982: 232).

The three main cases of this type also differ in terms of their union–party relationship. In Brazil the unions were formed during the most authoritarian period of the Vargas government (the Estado Novo), during which it was neither necessary nor desirable to have an organized political base in order to mobilize the country in support of the regime; the Partido Trabalhista Brasileiro only emerged when Vargas began to prepare for the electoral campaigns of the democratic transition he initiated at the end of World War II.[56] Thus, the union organizations and their extensive social-welfare bureacracies established their relations with the state before the creation of the party; this resulted in a much weaker union-party nexus in Brazil than in the other countries.[57] Both in Peronist Argentina and under Cárdenas in Mexico the unions were instead created in contexts during which the political mobilization of the population in support of the government and against other political and economic forces was important. The unions and the parties were created (or re-created) in order to secure (and control) that mobilization, and a strong identification between the majority of the union leaders and the party was established from the beginning. This explains in part why after the 1955 military coup in Argentina the labour leaders became (and were forced to become by the new authorities' perceptions of them) the leaders of the Peronist opposition,[58] while in Brazil the majority of the labour leaders simply continued with their specific union tasks after the

1964 military coup, leaving the Partido Trabalhista to become eventually a very minor force in Brazilian politics.

The Confrontationist Type
This type occurs under authoritarian regimes of various kinds, primarily those that can be characterized as labour-repressive. Labour movements of all the previously discussed types acquire the characteristics of this one if the overall political regime in which they are embedded changes to one of these forms of authoritarianism. In all these contexts the parties linked to the unions lose their ability to channel the political action and pressures of the labour movement, for which the unions become the primary centre for its social as well as political actions. The party militants who can do so turn their efforts to acting within the unions, generating a significant conflation of the labour-linked party or parties' interests with those of the unions. In some cases authoritarian regimes permit moderate labour-linked party leaderships to continue their political activities in what are for the unions mostly ineffective legislatures, local governments, or other such organs, in which case a split develops between the unions and the parties (as well as between the segment most closely tied to the unions and the rest within the party). Collective bargaining and other institutions through which unions could pressure the state and employers are laced with a series of restrictions, making them much less effective as vehicles to protect or enhance workers' rights and interests. In this environment, labour leaders (unless they are among the few favoured by the authorities) must rely to a greater extent than in other situations on rank-and-file support to retain their claims to leadership, for which they show an even greater sensitivity and responsiveness to the problems of the workers than in the contestatory type, although they have an even smaller capacity to do something about them. The labour-repressive authoritarian regimes (including the fascist as well as what Guillermo O'Donnell (1973, Part 1) has called the bureaucratic-authoritarian variants) that most characteristically produce this type have occurred frequently in the twentieth century, and there are therefore many examples of it, from Mussolini's Italy to Park and Chun's Korea to Pinochet's Chile.

Most authoritarian regimes would simply prefer to eliminate worker organizations altogether, but twentieth-century technology, management, and marketing provide workers with many opportunities to disrupt production, for which a totally repressive stance towards labour is counterproductive. Thus, these regimes normally allow some form of worker organization to exist, and provide mechanisms to channel their grievances. But they lace both with many limitations and controls, not only to prevent labour from exerting economic pressures but also to prevent labour organizations from becoming platforms for political oppositions to the regime. Consequently, there is a tension between permitting worker organizations to exist in order to have a semblance of normality in labour relations, and the effort to limit their effectiveness. Since this tension is in the last analysis unresolvable, authoritarian regimes undergo cycles of repression and opening towards the labour movement, repression in order to eliminate opponents and reduce labour influence, and opening so as to secure worker commitment to the process of production.

Authoritarian regime policies toward labour organizations usually follow what can be called 'corporatist' (in the sense of Schmitter's 'state corporatism' (Schmitter, 1979)) or 'market' strategies, although both forms can often be found in the same national case. The first has similarities to the state-sponsored type, but of the failed variety; that is, with very little worker acceptance or allegiance to the organizations that are established. This strategy closely monitors worker organizations and their financing, establishes compulsory membership, and sets boundaries to the sectors they cover. The leadership is designated by the authorities, or elected by workers after careful screening of candidates. Collective bargaining is generally centralized and controlled by state officials. There is little margin for autonomous action by union leaders. Many opponents of the regime will simply refuse to participate in the official structures, while trying to group workers into parallel clandestine or semi-clandestine organizations. Others will seek to turn the official channels to their advantage, while at the same time organizing an unofficial network that partly overlaps with the former. When this latter attempt is successful (as was the case, for example, with the Comisiones Obreras after 1962 in Franco's Spain), the characteristics of the workers' organizations and industrial relations eventually bear little resemblance to the original official intentions for them.

The market mechanism for union control tries to weaken unions as bargaining agents to a maximum extent. Collective bargaining is completely decentralized. Strikes are rendered as ineffective as possible by preventing the use of union funds to support them, by permitting the hiring of strike breakers and lock-outs, and by banning them outright from sectors of the economy that are considered vital. Union affiliation is voluntary, exposing its militants to being singled out by employers, and union finances depend solely on dues paid by members. While labour opponents of the regime will usually dominate the organizations, they are mostly ineffective given their restrictions. Opponents will attempt to compensate for the atomization of the unions by strengthening the union federations and confederations, and by coordinating the demands the various small unions try to formulate. And yet, during the harsh periods of authoritarian rule these activities are prime targets for state repression.

The national cases in which labour-movement formation has taken place under long-standing authoritarian regimes (sometimes interspersed with unstable periods of democratization in which labour usually makes considerable gains) present few commonalities. They include at a minimum the following: first, in all the process of formation occurred (if it has reached a minimal completion) after 1920, and often after 1945; secondly, the necessary process of state (and often employer) recognition took place under periods of regime opening, or even during processes of democratization; and thirdly, the labour leaders were closely tied to parties opposing the authoritarian regime which became important players in the politics of regime opening or democratization that permitted the development of plant-level union organizations and collective bargaining. These characteristics are well exemplified by labour-movement formation in Peru in the forties.[59] Since labour-movement formation in these settings can ultimately favour groups linked to various parties (as was the case in Peru with APRA and the Communist Party), the resulting labour organizations can become ideologically and politically fragmented to the point that they approximate the contestatory type in periods of democratic transition. If the process favours basically one political group and it is a generally moderate one, as was the case in Venezuela, a transition to democracy may lead to an approximation of the social democratic type.

Concluding Comment

By outlining five types of political insertion of the labour movements in mainly European and American capitalist contexts, this chapter has tried to demonstrate that the differences in this understudied dimension are highly significant, since they affect both the organizational forms assumed by labour movements as well as their actions. Thus, the variations in patterns of industrial relations hardly exhaust the study of the morphology of labour movements.

As is the case with the typological analysis, the conceptual abstractions that are necessary to construct the types gloss over important specificities of the cases which inform them in the first place. Moreover, it is always possible to construct more types, and even subtypes within them that will capture important additional patterns. Similarly, some cases can be found to have aspects of more than one type in different segments of the labour movement, and changing conditions – political ones, especially – can produce oscillations of specific cases from one type to another. And yet, the institutional and organizational configurations that create these various political insertions of national labour movements produce both certain rigidities as well as opportunities that, when taken together, make certain forms of change more difficult while facilitating others. As with other social organizations, labour movements are also creatures of their past circumstances.

Notes

This is a revised and translated version of a paper first written for a session chaired by Elizabeth Jelin at the World Congress of Sociology in Mexico City in 1982. It subsequently appeared unchanged in *Desarrollo Económico* (1983). I thank Robert Fishman, Jorge Domínguez, Elizabeth Jelin and Francisco Zapata for their comments on the early draft of this chapter. My gratitude as well to Alessandro Pizzorno, Marino Regini, and Peter Lange, who contributed to my understanding of labour movements. Raimundo Valenzuela assisted with the translation of the original text; his help is greatly appreciated.

1 For samples of this literature, see the many volumes of the International Labour Organization's *Labour–Management Relations Series*.

2 This argument is most prevalent in French sociology of work, and owes much to the influential work of Touraine (1955 and 1966). For an example of the influence of this conception on other works, see Durand (1971). The 'new working class' thesis was a further extension of this basic line of thinking. The classic statement is Mallet (1969).

3 The classic statements of this view are given in Kerr and Siegal (1955); Kerr et al. (1960), and from a different perspective but deriving the same conclusion regarding mature industrial society, Marcuse (1964).

4 For a study that develops these points while criticizing the now not-so-new 'new working class thesis', see Gallie (1978). For a broader view of the process of labour-movement formation from this perspective, see Berins Collier and Collier (1979 and 1991).

5 This topic is developed in Valenzuela (1981).

6 For studies of unionism in settings of racial or ethnic discrimination, see Greenberg (1980) and Frederickson (1981: chap. 5).

7 The notion that expressions of discontent lead to the formation of new collective identities in order to generate new organizations is emphasized by Pizzorno (1978: vol. 2).

8 The Argentinian Socialist Party is one of many examples of one that did not succeed on either count, although it was more important than others in the years between the teens and the 1930s. Most union leaders in the early years after the party's formation were linked primarily to the anarcho-syndicalist movement rather

than the Socialist Party. Moreover, in the early years large segments of the party's potential working-class constituencies were unable to vote given their lack of Argentine citizenship. When most workers became citizens, the party was hampered, first, by the electoral fraud of the 1930s and then by the great appeal of Peronism in the 1940s. See, among other sources, Walter (1977).

9 I thank Alessandro Pizzorno for this observation made in the context of a conversation on the characteristics of different parties.

10 Although Sturmthal does not use the 'unifying' and 'directive' terms I use here, he indicates that where the party anteceded the unions, his paradigmatic case being the German one, 'political ideas [. . .] controlled the life of the unions. [. . .] The unions appeared thus in a subordinate position to the party.' He contrasts this pattern with the British one, where the unions preceded the party (1953: 46, 48). In this case the unions have more influence over the party (1953: 39–45).

11 This point is developed by Marks (1989: chap. 6). It was also noted in the Spanish version of this chapter.

12 Marks (1989: 75) also makes this point, which, again, was included in the Spanish version of this chapter.

13 This point is developed in all its implications in Berins Collier (1982).

14 These notions, present in the original Spanish version of this chapter, have been elaborated considerably by Przeworski as the 'electoral trade-off' (1985: 104–11).

15 It is for these reasons that students of labour movements, beginning with Perlman (1928), have long noted that strong state repression of unions leads to the politicization (and radicalization) of their leaderships. This does not mean that state repression explains, as Perlman and many subsequent analysts have thought, the success of these radicalized labour leaderships in forming the national labour movements. Repression does not operate as simply as this. For an elaboration of the effects of repression on labour-movement formation, see Valenzuela (1979: Part II).

16 For example, in Sweden the unionized proportion of the labour force reaches 80 to 85 per cent; in Denmark, about 80 per cent; in Norway, about 65 per cent; in West Germany, about 40 per cent; in Great Britain, about 46 per cent. These figures are for the mid-1980s.

17 There are of course variations in the degree to which this is the case. Dutch unions, although strong at the national level, have historically been weaker at the plant level. Not surprisingly, they also have a lower level of affiliation (about 30 per cent). For an introductory summary of Dutch industrial relations, see van Zweeden (1985). This book was sponsored by the Swedish Employers Federation.

18 The Belgian labour movement created separate sections for the Flemish- and French-speaking communities of the same socialist organization, which operates under a single central direction. The Dutch labour movement has had socialist, Catholic and Protestant components. Its fragmentation was diminished by the 1976 merger of the socialist and Catholic trade-union confederations to form the Netherlands Trade Union Confederation (FNV). It is the most important workers' confederation, and it is loosely connected to the Dutch Labour Party.

19 This observation, of course, does not apply at all to Venezuela.

20 For a rather heroic vision of the development of workers' struggles in early twentieth-century Germany, see Schorske (1965). See also Nolan (1986) and Marks (1989: 55–63).

21 Even in the Ruhr area, where the employers most strongly resisted the

organization of labour, there was already a change with regard to collective bargaining by the outbreak of World War I. See Glovka Spencer (1976).

22 For useful introductory treatments of Scandinavian social democracy, see Castles (1978) and Amoroso (1980). In the Danish case the unions developed one step ahead of the Social Democratic Party. See Miller (1968: 59).

The Scandinavian cases generated welfare institutions that were unique, given the universality of access to benefits without regard for employment conditions or means. These characteristics conform to what Gøsta Esping-Andersen calls the 'social democratic' model of welfare-state institutions, and he relates their origins to the political alliances that the social democratic parties could form with peasant sectors in Scandinavia to form legislative minorities that were impossible in other countries with equally strong labour parties (Esping-Andersen, 1985: Part 1; and Esping-Andersen, 1990).

23 On the re-creation of German unionism after World War II, see Markovits (1986: 61-3).

24 For a sample of some of the best articles on the subject, see Schmitter and Lehmbruch (1979); Lehmbruch and Schmitter (1982); Goldthorpe (1984); Grant (1985); and Berger (1981).

25 This distinction is developed by Philippe Schmitter under the terms of 'societal' versus 'state' corporatism (Schmitter, 1979).

26 The distinction between 'sectoral' and 'concertive' forms of corporatism is developed by Lehmbruch (1984).

Portugal under Salazar provides a good example of corporatism under an authoritarian regime. Its actual operation did not conform to Maïnoelescu's conceptions despite the fact that they were its official ideology. Far from promoting a minimal state and the self-direction of the society and economy by organized groups, the Portuguese state intervened to an important extent in the formation of interest groups and had a heavy hand in guiding the economy. It also repressed labour organizations while it created the so-called 'National Unions' as a means of worker containment. For a detailed analysis of the relationship between interests and economic policies during the formative period of Salazar's regime, see Rosas (1986: 268-83).

27 The Spanish version of this chapter emphasized these factors as well.

28 See Regini (1984). For a detailed analysis of labour relations in a British industrial workplace, see Maitland (1983).

29 See Streeck (1984).

30 See Leion (1985: 213).

31 Works by Angell (1972) and Reynaud (1975) are especially recommended for each case.

32 For a full elaboration of the argument, see Valenzuela (1979).

33 Many analysts have tried to associate the strength of Communist parties in Latin Europe to Catholicism, by arguing that communism represents the secular form of a totalistic and authoritarian religious framework that pervades Latin culture. Even French commentators have used this argument; see Peyrefitte (1976: 338, 397). I strongly disagree.

34 Although the leftist parties (Communist and Socialist principally) tend to be in the opposition, these differences in strategy do not depend on the type of party but on whether they are in the government or in the opposition. The roles tend to be inverted rapidly when the left forms the government, as was demonstrated under Allende in Chile, dramatically so in the case of the El Teniente copper miners' strike of May and June 1973.

35 This is therefore a very different type of unionism from the contestatory type, where union leadership positions and subsequent careers as such are to a large extent predicated upon the prospective leader's loyalty to a particular party or political group.

36 For a sample of this literature, which includes articles written from different viewpoints, see Laslett and Lipset (1974). This volume contains a brief selection from Sombart (1976; first published, 1906). The 'exceptionality' derives only from a comparison to Western Europe.

37 Many of these arguments, and their detractors for one reason or another, can be found in the selections in Laslett and Lipset. Most of them were anticipated by Sombart and redeveloped by Perlman (1928). The discussions since then vary in the emphasis they assign to the different factors.

Since the publication of the original Spanish version of this chapter, only Marks (1989: 197) has defined – as far as I know – American exceptionality as the absence of a new party rather than as the absence of socialism. However, he frequently refers back to arguments that pertain to the question of why there is no socialist class consciousness among American workers. For instance, at one point he speaks of the 'absence of a revolutionary tradition' among white workers given their receipt, early on, of the 'gift' of the franchise (Marks, 1989: 221). This regularly overstated argument forgets that male workers in other countries – notably, Denmark, France, Switzerland, and Chile – also did not have to fight for the extension of the franchise as the process of building unions in the last quarter of the nineteenth century began.

A significant trend in the literature on the American working-class experience stresses that workers did indeed have class consciousness, although it was not the kind that led to socialism. See, for instance, Wilentz (1984).

38 See Lipset and Rokkan (1967) for an analysis of party formation that stresses the importance of social cleavages and of state and legal rules under the rubric of 'thresholds of representation'. They emphasize much less the role of what I have identified here as the second level of party formation.

39 This factor has been part of the repertoire of explanations for American exceptionalism since Sombart and Perlman. My point here is to give it much greater weight, and to recast its explanatory value.

The British Labour Party was, in the last analysis, a product of a lack of the same flexibility in the Liberal Party. Although many union-linked figures became Liberal MPs in the so-called Lib-Lab period, and some union segments resisted the formation of the Labour Party, a majority in the Labour movement was disappointed at the tepid reactions of the Liberals to the devastating decision rendered by the courts in the Taft Vale case. This spurred the formation of the Labour Party. The British procedural rules and constitutional system were also more favourable to the formation of third parties than those of the United States.

40 The closest case to it was the Colombian two-party system until the 1970s.

41 The same argument can be made for Catholics in the United States. The Protestant–Catholic cleavage has been a strong fault line in American society, and given the minority and originally non-elite positions of the latter, in another context, assisted by the network of parishes, the Catholic population would have been an important source of support for the formation of a new party. And yet the flexibility of the established parties, in this case again mainly of the Democrats, absorbed it as well.

42 Laurie has once again usefully stressed the strongly anti-union attitudes of

American employers (1989: 12–13, 208–9, 219). The skilled–unskilled cleavage within the American work-force also coincided with an ethnic type of split: the former tended to be native-born or older immigrants, while the latter tended to be newcomers (Laurie, 1989: 218).

For a very informative review of state actions in the labour field, including the early repressive role of the courts and the strong influence of the National Labour Relations Board in shaping the organizational structure of collective bargaining and unions, see Tomlins (1985).

43 The deskilling effects of technological change and their negative consequences on American craft unions are well documented for the iron and steel industry; see Brody (1960).

44 In referring here to the AFL's skilled worker unions I am deliberately excluding the miners and others who do not fit the skilled worker profile. They did constitute a substantial portion of the AFL's membership, though a smaller proportion of its affiliated organizations.

45 Lack of space here does not permit a fuller discussion of the relationship between the peculiarly loose organization of American parties and the working class. An important aspect of it were the political machines in cities which engaged in a form of co-optive populism, in particular with immigrant workers, that reduced the ability of third party organizers to expand their own bases of support; see Shefter (1986). The essential point was not that American workers (white and male) had the vote from early on, but who they could vote for – and, in the case of the political machines, who they were enticed to vote for.

46 The two organizations were reunited in 1955, forming the AFL-CIO.

47 For a history of the IWW, see Dubofsky (1969); and for an analysis of the communists, see Cochran (1977).

48 Brazil's imperfect democracy between 1945 and 1964 did little to change the relationship of the state towards labour, although there were some variations over the period. The state-sponsored form of unionism remained in place. The Brazilian military government after 1964 did more to undermine the system by using it exclusively as a tool for labour containment. By the mid-seventies, with the development of the so-called 'new unionism', the state-sponsored model can be said to have substantially broken down, although the leaders of the new unions took advantage of the old system in order to gain prominence in labour circles. The changes between the old and the new unions are basically two: (1) the development of leaders who favour the autonomy of labour organizations from the state, with leaderships whose careers depend primarily on rank-and-file support; and (2) an attempt to strengthen the plant-level organization of unions, engaging employers in sometimes extra-legal plant-level collective bargaining. For an analysis of the new union leaders, see Rodrigues (1990).

49 The massification of unionism in Argentina and Brazil led to the organization of large numbers of native-born and even rural workers who were not part of the European immigrant segments (or their sons and daughters) that characterized the artisanal and industrial work-force of the first decades of the twentieth century. This led analysts to think that the populist leaders of state-sponsored labour organizations could succeed only because these were 'available masses' that had no contact with the anarchist and socialist traditions of the previous generation of European migrants. For expressions of this view on Argentina, see Germani (1973), and, on Brazil, Rodrigues (1969: 98). This factor has been greatly exaggerated: the organizational variables are more important.

50 Needless to say, these characteristics do not apply to the formation of labour organizations under communist regimes.

51 There is a large literature of uneven quality on the formative period of state-sponsored unionism in these countries. The following are especially recommended as synthetic treatments: Murmis and Portantiero (1971), especially Part II; Rodrigues (1981), and Córdova (1984).

An important new book by Torre (1990) explains in careful detail why many pre-existing union leaders (principally non-communist ones) became supporters of Perón's rise to power before his election to the presidency in 1946, given his delivery of many of the benefits and recognition they had been struggling unsuccessfully to obtain during the previous decade. It also shows how Perón subsequently eliminated the most independent-minded among them, subordinating the labour movement to his cronies. And yet, Torre also argues that the strong labour base of the resulting Peronist party-movement meant that it was always open to the renewed influence of labour demands and leaders.

52 Camacho (1977) provides a nuanced analysis of the mechanisms of leadership control over unions and workers in the Mexican setting.

53 The formation of the Mexican Partido Revolucionario Institucional is the object of a thorough study in Garrido (1982). The creation of the Brazilian Partido Trabalhista Brasileiro – and other Brazilian parties – is analysed in de Souza (1990: Part II). The Argentine Justicialista Party still awaits its historian. Writings on it focus too exclusively either on the figures of Juan Domingo and Evita Perón or on the labour leaderships.

54 The labour leadership exerted greater influence and pressures over the Peronist party, which did not have other important organized constituencies, than has been the case for labour leaders in Mexico or, most certainly, in Brazil.

55 Some of the differences are discussed in Munck (1980); Erickson and Middlebrook (1982); and Berins Collier (1982).

56 See de Souza (1990: Part II) and Skidmore (1976: 39–40).

57 This point is developed by Berins Collier (1982).

Rodrigues (1981: 529) estimates that some 10,000 labour leaders had been promoted into various levels of the labour bureaucracy by the end of the Estado Novo, and points out that this number does not include the numerous employees of the unions who did not hold executive posts, nor the many professionals (lawyers, doctors, dentists, and social workers) who had permanent links with such bureaucracies.

58 On the transformation of the Peronist party from a tool of the authorities to an opposition movement, see especially Cavarozzi (1979).

59 See Cotler (1978: 265 *et passim*) and Pareja (1980).

References

Amoroso, Bruno (1980) *Rapporto dalla Scandinavia*. Rome, Bari: Editori Laterza.

Angell, Alan (1972) *Politics and the Labour Movement in Chile*. London: Oxford University Press.

Bauman, Zygmunt (1972) *Between Class and Elite*. Manchester: Manchester University Press.

Berger, Suzanne (ed.) (1981) *Organizing Interests in Western Europe*. Cambridge: Cambridge University Press.

Berins Collier, Ruth (1982) 'Popular Sector Incorporation and Political Supremacy:

Regime Evolution in Brazil and Mexico', in Sylvia Ann Hewlett and Richard S. Weinart (eds), *Brazil and Mexico: Patterns of Late Development*. Philadelphia, PA: Institute for the Study of Human Issues.

Berins Collier, Ruth and Collier, David (1979) 'Inducements versus Constraints: Disaggregating Corporatism', *American Political Science Review*, 73 (4).

Berins Collier, Ruth and Collier, David (1991) *Shaping the Political Arena: Critical Junctures, the Labor Movement and Regime Dynamics in Latin America*. Princeton, NJ: Princeton University Press.

Brody, David (1960) *Steelworkers in America: the Non-union Era*. Cambridge, MA: Harvard University Press.

Camacho, Manuel (1977) 'Control sobre el movimiento obrero en México', in Centro de Estudios Internacionales, *Lecturas de política mexicana*. Mexico, DF: El Colegio de México.

Castles, Francis (1978) *The Social Democratic Image of Society: a Study of the Achievements and Origins of Scandinavian Social Democracy in Comparative Perspective*. London: Routledge & Kegan Paul.

Cavarozzi, Marcelo (1979) *Sindicatos y Política en Argentina, 1955–1958*. Buenos Aires: Estudios CEDES, vol. 2, no. 1.

Cochran, Bert (1977) *Labor and Communism: the Conflict that Shaped American Unions*. Princeton, NJ: Princeton University Press.

Córdova, Arnaldo (1984) *La política de masas del cardenismo* (6th edn). Mexico, DF: Serie Popular Era.

Cotler, Julio (1978) *Clases, estado, y nación en el Perú*. Lima: Instituto de Estudios Peruanos.

de Souza, Maria do Carmo Campello (1990) *Estado e Partidos Políticos no Brasil (1930 a 1964)* (3rd edn). São Paulo: Editora Alfa-Omega.

Dubofsky, Melvin (1969) *We Shall be All*. Chicago, IL: Quadrangle Books.

Durand, Claude (1971) *Conscience ouvrière et action syndicale*. Paris: Mouton.

Erickson, Kenneth Paul and Middlebrook, Kevin (1982) 'The State and Organized Labor in Brazil and Mexico', in Silvia Ann Hewlett and Richard S. Weinart (eds), *Brazil and Mexico: Patterns of Late Development*. Philadelphia, PA: Institute for the Study of Human Issues.

Esping-Andersen, Gøsta (1985) *Politics against Markets: the Social Democratic Road to Power*. Princeton, NJ: Princeton University Press.

Esping-Andersen, Gøsta (1990) *The Three Worlds of Welfare Capitalism*. Princeton, NJ: Princeton University Press.

Frederickson, George M. (1981) *White Supremecy: a Comparative Study in American and South African History*. New York: Oxford University Press.

Gallie, Duncan (1978) *In Search of the New Working Class: Automation and Social Integration within the Capitalist Enterprise*. London: Cambridge University Press.

Garrido, Luis Javier (1982) *El Partido de la revolución institucionalizada. La formación del nuevo Estado en México (1928–1945)*. Mexico, DF: Siglo XXI Editores.

Germani, Gino (1973) 'El Surgimiento del peronismo: el rol de los obreros y de los migrantes internos', *Desarrollo Económico* 13 (51).

Glovka Spenser, Elaine (1976) 'Employer Responses to Unionism: Ruhr Coal Industrialists before 1914', *Journal of Social History*, 48.

Goldthorpe, John H. (ed.) (1984) *Order and Conflict in Contemporary Capitalism*. Oxford: Clarendon Press.

Grant, Winn (ed.) (1985) *The Political Economy of Corporatism*. New York: Macmillan.

Greenberg, Stanley B. (1980) *Race and State in Capitalist Development: Comparative Perspectives.* New Haven, CT: Yale University Press.

Greenstone, J. David (1977) *Labor in American Politics.* Chicago: University of Chicago Press.

Kerr, Clark, Dunlop, John T., Harbinson, Frederick and Myers, Charles (1960) *Industrialism and Industrial Man.* Cambridge, MA: Harvard University Press.

Kerr, Clark and Siegal, Abraham (1955) 'The Structuring of the Labor Force in Industrial Society: New Dimensions and New Questions', *Industrial and Labor Relations Review,* 8 (2).

Korpi, Walter (1978) *The Working Class in Welfare Capitalism: Work, Unions and Politics in Sweden.* London: Routledge & Kegan Paul.

Laslett, John H.M. and Lipset, Seymour Martin (eds) (1974) *Failure of a Dream? Essays in the History of American Socialism.* Garden City, NY: Doubleday Anchor.

Laurie, Bruce (1989) *Artisans into Workers: Labor in Nineteenth-Century America.* New York: Noonday Press.

Lehmbruch, Gerhard (1984) 'Concertation and the Structure of Corporatist Networks', in John H. Goldthorpe (ed.), *Order and Conflict in Contemporary Capitalism.* Oxford: Clarendon Press.

Lehmbruch, Gerhard and Schmitter, Philippe (eds) (1982) *Patterns of Corporatist Policy-making.* Beverly Hills, CA: Sage.

Leion, Anders (1985) 'Sweden', in B.C. Roberts (ed.), *Industrial Relations in Europe: the Imperatives of Change.* London: Croom Helm.

Lipset, Seymour Martin and Rokkan, Stein (1967) 'Cleavages, Structures, Party Systems and Voter Alignments: an Introduction', in Seymour Martin Lipset and Stein Rokkan (eds), *Party Systems and Voter Alignments: Cross-national Perspectives.* New York: The Free Press.

Lösche, Peter (1973) 'Stages in the Evolution of the German Labor Movement', in Adolph Sturmthal and James J. Scoville (eds), *The International Labor Movement in Transition: Essays on Africa, Asia, Europe and South America.* Urbana, IL: University of Illinois Press.

Maitland, Ian (1983) *The Causes of Industrial Disorder: a Comparison of a British and a German Factory.* London: Routledge & Kegan Paul.

Mallet, Serge (1969) *La nouvelle classe ouvrière.* Paris: Seuil.

Marcuse, Herbert (1964) *One Dimensional Man: Studies in the Ideology of Advanced Industrial Society.* Boston: Beacon Press.

Markovits, Andrei S. (1986) *The Politics of the West German Trade Unions: Strategies of Class and Interest Representation in Growth and Crisis.* London: Cambridge University Press.

Marks, Gary (1989) *Unions in Politics: Britain, Germany and the United States in the Nineteenth and Early Twentieth Centuries.* Princeton, NJ: Princeton University Press.

Miller, Kenneth E. (1968) *Government and Politics in Denmark.* Boston: Houghton Mifflin Co.

Munck, Rolando (1980) 'El movimiento sindical en Brasil y en Argentina: un estudio comparativo', *Coyoacán,* 3 (7–8).

Murmis, Miguel and Portantiero, Juan Carlos (1971) *Estudios sobre los orígenes del peronismo.* Buenos Aires: Siglo XXI.

Nolan, Mary (1986) 'Economic Crisis, State Policy, and Working-Class Formation in Germany, 1870–1900', in Ira Katznelson and Aristide R. Zolberg (eds),

Working-Class Formation in Germany: Nineteenth-Century Patterns in Western Europe and the United States. Princeton, NJ: Princeton University Press.

O'Donnell, Guillermo (1973) *Modernization and Bureaucratic Authoritarianism: Studies in South American Politics.* Berkley, CA: Institute of International Studies, University of California.

Pareja Pflucker, Piedad (1980) *Aprismo y sindicalismo en el Perú, 1943-1948.* Lima: Ediciones Rikchay Perú.

Perlman, Selig (1928) *A Theory of the Labor Movement.* New York: Macmillan.

Peyrefitte, Alain (1976) *Le Mal français.* Paris: Plon.

Pizzorno, Alessandro (1978) 'Political Exchange and Collective Identity in Industrial Conflict', in Colin Crouch and Alessandro Pizzorno (eds), *The Resurgence of Class Conflict in Western Europe since 1969.* New York: Holmes and Meier.

Przeworski, Adam (1985) *Capitalism and Social Democracy.* New York: Cambridge University Press.

Regini, Marino (1984) 'The Conditions for Political Exchange: How Concertation Emerged and Collapsed in Italy and Great Britain', in John H. Goldthorpe (ed.), *Order and Conflict in Contemporary Capitalism.* Oxford: Clarendon Press.

Reyna, José Luis (1981) 'El movimiento obrero en el ruizcortinismo: la redefinición del sistema económico y la consolidación política', in José Luis Reyna and Raúl Trejo Delabre (eds), *La clase obrera en la historia de México: de Adolfo Ruiz Cortines a Adolfo López Mateos (1952-1964).* Mexico: Siglo XXI Editores.

Reynaud, Jean Daniel (1975) *Les Syndicats en France.* Paris: Seuil.

Rodrigues, Leôncio Martins (1969) *La clase obrera en el Brasil.* Buenos Aires: Centro Editor de América Latina.

Rodrigues, Leôncio Martins (1981) 'Sindicalismo e classe operária (1930-1964)', in Bóris Fausto (ed.), *História Geral da Civilização Brasileira,* vol. x: *O Brasil Republicano.* São Paulo: DIFEL.

Rodrigues, Leôncio Martins (1990) *CUT: Os Militantes e a Ideologia.* São Paulo: Paz e Terra.

Rosas, Fernando (1986) *O Estado Novo nos anos trinta, 1928-1938.* Lisbon: Imprensa Universitária-Editorial Estampa.

Schmitter, Philippe (1979) 'Still the Century of Corporatism?', in Philippe C. Schmitter and G. Lehmbruch (eds), *Trends towards Corporatist Intermediation.* Beverly Hills, CA: Sage.

Schmitter, Philippe C. and Lehmbruch G. (eds) (1979) *Trends Towards Corporatist Intermediation.* Beverly Hills, CA: Sage.

Schorske, Carl E. (1965) *German Social Democracy, 1905-1917.* New York: John Wiley & Sons.

Shefter, Martin (1986) 'Trade Unions and Political Machines: the Organization and Disorganization of the American Working Class in the Late Nineteenth Century', in Ira Katznelson and Aristide R. Zolberg (eds), *Working-Class Formation: Nineteenth-Century Patterns in Western Europe and the United States.* Princeton, NJ: Princeton University Press.

Skidmore, Thomas (1976), *Politics in Brazil, 1930-1964: an Experiment in Democracy.* London: Oxford University Press.

Sombart, Werner (1976) *Why is there no Socialism in the United States?* White Plains, NY: International Arts and Sciences Press.

Streeck, Wolfgang (1984) 'Neo-corporatist Industrial Relations and the Economic Crisis in West Germany', in John H. Goldthorpe (ed.), *Order and Conflict in Contemporary Capitalism.* Oxford: Clarendon Press.

Sturmthal, Adolph (1953) *Unity and Diversity in European Labor: an Introduction to Contemporary Labor Movements.* Glencoe, IL: The Free Press.

Tomlins, Christopher L. (1985) *The State and the Unions: Labor Relations, Law and the Organized Labor Movement in America, 1880–1960.* New York: Cambridge University Press.

Torre, Juan Carlos (1990) *La vieja guardia sindical y Perón: Sobre los orígenes del peronismo.* Buenos Aires: Editorial Sudamericana, Instituto Torcuato di Tella.

Touraine, Alain (1955) *L'Evolution du travail ouvrier aux usines Renault.* Paris: Centre National de la Recherche Scientifique.

Touraine, Alain (1966) *La Conscience ouvrière.* Paris: Seuil.

Turner, H.A. (1962) *Trade Union Growth Structure and Policy: a Comparative Study of Cotton Unions in England.* Toronto: University of Toronto Press.

Valenzuela, J. Samuel (1979) 'Labour Movement Formation and Politics: Chile and France in Comparative Perspective, 1850–1950'. Ph.D. thesis, Ann Arbor, MI: University Microfilms International No. 8010420.

Valenzuela, J. Samuel (1981) 'Uno schema teórico per l'analisi della formazione del movimento operario', *Stato e Mercato,* 1 (3).

Valenzuela, J. Samuel (1983) 'Movimientos obreros y sistemas políticos: un análisis conceptual y tipológico', *Desarrollo Económico,* 23 (91).

Van Zweeden, A.F. (1985) 'The Netherlands', in B.C. Roberts (ed.), *Industrial Relations in Europe: the Imperatives of Change.* London: Croom Helm.

Walter, Richard J. (1977) *The Socialist Party of Argentina, 1890–1930.* Austin, TX: University of Texas Press.

Wilentz, Sean (1984) 'Against Exceptionalism: Class Consciousness and the American Labor Movement', *International Labor and Working Class History,* 26.

3

The Resurgence of Labour Quiescence

Michael Shalev

That labour militancy has taken a beating in recent years is hardly news. The occupational, sectoral, and social composition of the labour force has changed in ways largely detrimental to union organization and coordination. Unfavourable economic conditions, coupled in many cases with aggressive government strategies of macroeconomic management, have weakened labour's bargaining position. And there have been vigorous employer efforts to regain the initiative and impose new enterprise-orientated frameworks for labour peace. Against this backdrop, it would be safe to assume a *convergent* trend towards declining strike activity. To the extent that such declines have varied across countries, this might be accounted for by the fact that influences which everywhere have predictably negative effects on strikes (such as increasing unemployment or declining unionization) have taken a different course in different national settings.

On the other hand, earlier cross-national research suggests that labour relations are sensitive to variations in the position of labour movements in the political economy[1] – particularly as this is reflected in the political complexion of governments and the role of national labour leaders in determining and administering public policy. Social-democratic and/or neo-corporatist settings, it has been argued, are especially favourable to social peace. Assuming the continued stability of political and institutional variations, *divergent* patterns of strike activity could thus be expected to persist, even in the face of changing economic conditions.

Little light has thus far been shed on the empirical plausibility of these competing theoretical scenarios, although governments routinely publish statistical data on industrial disputes that could go a long way in this direction. Not much is known about the precise nature and scope of the contemporary resurgence of labour quiescence.[2] An earlier analysis of trends in eighteen OECD countries (Shalev, 1983) showed that, as Kalecki (1943) would have predicted, during the full-employment strike wave of the late 1960s industrial conflict became uncoupled from the rhythm of the business cycle. This remained true during a further cycle of conflict which followed in the early years of global recession after 1973. Nevertheless, by the late 1970s harsh labour-market conditions were having a clear disciplinary impact on labour militancy in most of the OECD countries. Today, when many challenging trends to past patterns of worker mobilization which were only dimly visible a decade ago have matured and become widely recognized, the time is ripe for systematic empirical investigation.

It is true that there is already a substantial case-study literature which bears on industrial conflict, including most of the contributions to the present volume (see also ILO, 1989; Baglioni and Crouch, 1990; Bamber and Lansbury, 1989). The utilization of 'hard' data on measured incidents of overt, collective conflict offers an alternative and potentially complementary approach. The limitations of official strike statistics are well known,[3] and in many ways have been aggravated by contemporary developments (most notably changes in coverage and definitions in a number of countries, and in a few cases partial suspension of the record-keeping operation).[4] Yet the equally well-rehearsed riposte is that the available information is better than nothing. We began this study with the expectation that this information could suggest answers to two sets of questions. First, in order to address the issue of convergence versus divergence, we need to know what has happened to labour militancy[5] on the plane of cross-national variation. Has the league table of *international differentials* in strike-proneness remained stable, despite declines in the *absolute level* of militancy? Can older models still predict the way that different groups of OECD nations cluster *vis-à-vis* the level and form of conflict?

A second set of questions relates to the implications of current trends in labour militancy. Does the overall drop in strike activity mean that labour has become truly pacified? As an ILO analyst has wondered out loud, 'Whether the trend to more co-operative and less conflictual industrial relations . . . comes about because of a genuine mutual desire to co-operate . . . or whether it is a reflection of a weakened or at least more defensive trade union movement, is a good question' (Gladstone, 1989: 32). A number of possibilities are worth considering in this context. First, are workers simply acting as they always have done in hard times, *'storing up' grievances* for future, more opportune moments (Rees, 1952)? If this is so, we would expect the decline in strike activity to have been pro-cyclical – that is, to have occurred in response to the sharp increases in unemployment and dramatic declines in union growth which have taken place since the mid-1970s. Along the same lines, we might also expect to see signs of reviving militancy as economic conditions improved in some countries towards the end of the 1980s. Nevertheless, responsiveness is different from amplitude. The most elementary prediction of the thesis of a transformation from conflict to cooperation must be that there has been a *radical drop in the floor level* around which industrial conflict fluctuates. Is this in fact the case?

Secondly, the abandonment of industrial action in favour of cooperation may have been *limited to certain sections* of organized labour, while others continued to sustain their militancy. This raises the question of whether there have been differential rates of decline in strike activity in different occupations, industries, and labour-market segments. We shall address this question empirically by means of a limited but suggestive analysis of changes in the contribution of a few key branches to total strike activity.

Thirdly, in the face of loss of worker cohesion and the growth of employer strategies to defuse collective worker militancy, labour may have turned to *'cut-price' forms* of industrial action, perhaps even moving dissent underground by reverting to individual or collective acts of withdrawal, or even 'sabotage' (cf. Kelly and Nicholson, 1980; Dubois, 1979). It should be possible to learn more about this by charting trends in the form, and particularly the duration, of strikes.

Comparing Countries over Time

The most elementary thing we need to know is what has been happening to work stoppages in the 1980s, from both a historical perspective (comparison with earlier periods) and a comparative one (grouping countries together). We begin with the second of these tasks. Two indicators are best suited for making cross-national comparisons using labour disputes statistics. *Relative involvement* (RI) – the number of workers involved in disputes, relative to the total number of workers in employment – is the closest approximation to the overall 'propensity to strike'. This measure avoids the pitfalls of the two most obvious alternatives. One of these, the *relative frequency* of disputes, is overly sensitive to methodological variations in the way that national statistical agencies define and count strikes. The other, *relative volume* (working days spent on strike per thousand workers) is logically the most desirable summary measure because it is mathematically the product of all three dimensions of the 'shape' of work stoppages – their frequency, size, and duration. Precisely because of its composite character, however, strike volume is difficult to interpret (many workers in brief stoppages may yield an identical volume to

Table 3.1 Industrial conflict in the OECD bloc, 1960–89[1]

	Relative involvement[2]					Duration[3]			
	1960–67	1968–73	1974–79	1960–67 to 1980–89 (% change)	1980–89	1960–67	1968–73	1974–79	1980–89
(1) Netherlands	3	6	2	16	4	3	4	2	3
Germany	2	5	5	83	4	3	2	3	1
Norway	1	1	4	140	5	12	11	7	7
Sweden	0.4	2	6	334	10	7	5	3	3
Switzerland	0.1	0.1	0.3	−14	0.1	10	7	6	3
(2) Italy	194	353	616	75	409	4	4	2	1
France	148	155	81	−178	25	1	1	3	3
Austria	117	229	277	10	129	2	2	2	2
(3) Ireland	30	50	48	10	33	14	11	16	10
Canada	23	45	59	36	33	14	18	15	15
USA[4]	17	24	15	−145	4	14	16	19	24
(4) Japan	44	48	32	−240	4	3	3	2	2
UK	41	74	57	7	44	3	6	7	6
NZ	28	74	120	131	104	3	3	3	4
Austria	21	4	1	−304	1	2	2	2	1
Finland[5]	18	26/241	178	NA	140	4	3/4	1	2
Belgium	13	21	26	−26	10	8	9	9	6
Denmark	9	17	40	110	27	3	3	2	3

Notes:
  1 Data from the ILO's *Yearbook of Labour Statistics*, various issues, supplemented by national sources. Period averages are geometric means.
  2 Workers involved in stoppages per thousand employees in employment. Data on employment from *OECD Labour Force Statistics*, various issues.
  3 Total person-days on strike per striker.
  4 Limited to stoppages involving at least 1,000 workers. Prior to the cessation in 1981 of the former comprehensive series, total relative involvement was typically some 50% higher than the figure for large strikes only.
  5 Until 1971, the series excluded stoppages lasting less than 4 hours unless attaining a volume of at least 100 person-days of work. Figures for the old and the revised series are presented for the 1968–73 subperiod.

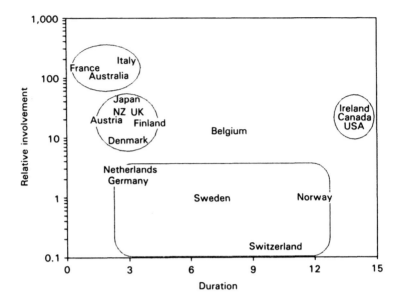

Figure 3.1 *The four strike profiles of the 'golden age'*
(1960–67)

few workers involved in protracted stoppages). Accordingly, we have chosen to eschew working with volume in favour of analysing trends in average duration (the number of days the average striker spent on strike) alongside those in RI.[6]

For the purpose of this analysis, data were collected on the contemporary evolution of strike activity in eighteen OECD countries.[7] Table 3.1 divides the last three full decades into four subperiods, in accordance with the prevailing consensus on turning points in the economic history of advanced capitalist societies during the years surveyed.

The years 1960–67
The first subperiod is representative of the interval during which most of the nations of the OECD enjoyed rapid economic growth coupled with unprecedentedly low unemployment. At this time, prior to the surging of labour militancy and wage-price inflation in the late 1960s, national patterns of strike activity in the rich democracies fell clearly and conveniently into four groups. (For a graphical presentation, see Figure 3.1.)

1 *Negligible participation in strikes* This was most conspicuously

characteristic of Switzerland and the entrenched social-democratic regimes in Scandinavia, where involvement in disputes was below one worker in every thousand. In Germany and the Netherlands RI was also very low, and stoppages typically quite short (about three days).

2 *Mass participation in brief stoppages* In France, Italy, and Australia 10–20 per cent of employed workers were involved annually in labour disputes, but on average for only a day or two (four days in Italy).

3 *Limited but protracted conflicts* In North America and Ireland strikes each year involved a limited proportion of the work-force (2–3 per cent). But they typically lasted close to three working weeks.

4 *Medium levels of strike activity* In this residual group between 1 and 4 per cent of employed workers participated in strikes, for an average of about three days. The countries concerned were Japan, Britain, and Belgium (where strike volume was more than 100 days per 1,000 workers), and New Zealand, Finland, Austria, and Denmark (with relative volume below 100).

The years 1968–73

Our second subperiod was an exceptionally turbulent one. Indeed, the years between the social explosions of the late 1960s and the first OPEC price 'shock' saw conspicuous and generalized increases in the *scope* of strike activity. Rates of increase in RI were broadly similar in most countries. And, except for Britain (where more extended conflicts joined the traditional brief dispute), national patterns of stoppage *duration* were virtually unaltered. Consequently, the division of countries between our four profiles remained almost identical. Even though Norway, France, and Japan experienced little or no overall rise in RI, from a cross-national perspective their position hardly altered. The only exceptional cases were Finland, which joined the group characterized by brief but widespread conflict, and Austria, which bucked the trend and adopted the pattern of negligible strike participation.

Since 1974

The interim period between the first and second oil shocks was a time of stagflation and rising unemployment in most countries. Despite this, there were once again few changes in the typical duration of conflicts (except in the United States, where stoppages were far fewer but even more protracted than before). In terms of striker participation, however, this was a time of transition in

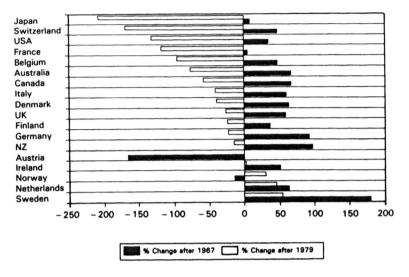

Figure 3.2   *The post-1967 surge and the post-1979 slide in participation in strikes*

many countries, offering a foretaste of trends which consolidated in the 1980s, our fourth and final subperiod. The most noteworthy of these trends characterized France, Japan, and the United States, where participation in strikes declined sharply. At the other end of the spectrum, the experience of global hard times was accompanied in Sweden, Norway, and New Zealand by substantial *increases* in participation.

As a result of these contrasting tendencies, the record for the 1980s presents a number of deviations from the international patterns which had prevailed two decades earlier. Groups 2 and 4 exchanged one member each (France and New Zealand, respectively). Strike activity in Sweden grew to the point that it became a borderline case between the negligible and medium groups (1 and 4). Most dramatic of all was Japan's movement in the opposite direction, which introduced it to the club of nations in which collective conflicts have little or no significance in labour relations.

Figure 3.2 offers additional evidence of the relative stability of cross-national differentials in earlier years, and, by contrast, the divergent trends of the more recent past. It shows that in the transition between the 'golden age' and the strike waves of the late sixties, most countries experienced roughly parallel increases in RI. The black bars indicate a modal increase of between 50 and 100 per cent between 1960–67 and 1968–73. As we mentioned earlier, only

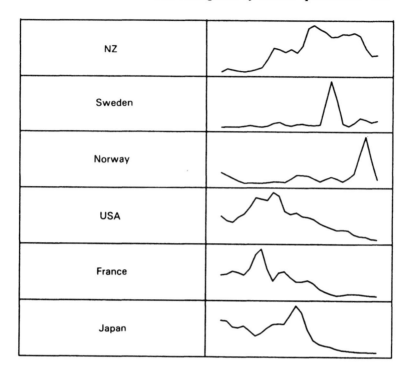

Figure 3.3 *Six cases of exceptional rise or fall in relative involvement, 1960–89*

Austria experienced a decline in stoppages in this period. In contrast, the grey bars illustrate the diversity of national responses to the political-economic climate of the 1980s. Our eighteen countries are now dispersed within a broad range set by Japan at one end (with a massive slide in striker participation) and Sweden at the other (with a substantial increase).

Despite the variability documented in Figure 3.2, it is apparent that, with few exceptions, strike activity was less extensive (or no more extensive) in the 1980s than in the immediately preceding period. From the longer perspective of Table 3.1 (thirty years), trends have been far more diverse. In nine of the thirteen countries where participation in strikes declined in the eighties, *it was still higher than it had been in 1960–67*. In comparison with that period of comparative industrial peace, the contemporary record does not then offer evidence of a general drop in the 'floor level' of industrial conflict (although this may already have changed given the continuing downward trends indicated by data for 1990).

Another important feature of the changes in RI reported in Table 3.1 is the identification of six countries that have come to deviate particularly strongly in the 1980s from the norms of the 1960s. Three of these are extreme cases of transition to labour quiescence, while the others have experienced significant increases in the scope of labour disputes.[8] Since averages sometimes conceal more than they reveal, Figure 3.3 offers a closer look at these 'deviant' cases.[9]

The three instances of rising conflict clearly divide between New Zealand, where participation in strikes twice ascended to higher plateaux and then (in the late 1980s) receded; and Norway and Sweden, where the period since 1974 has seen not only the exceptional bursts of conflict which dominate the plots, but also a more pervasive rise in strike activity. The Swedish case is particularly noteworthy. The number of workers involved in strikes grew from an annual average of only 1,000 in the 1960s to nearly 20,000 in the 1970s and 40,000 in the 1980s. And in contrast to Norway, where the *number* of conflicts remained very low, median strike frequency in Sweden since 1974 has been close to 100. The other three countries we have singled out represent in extreme form the opposite type of deviance. In each case there has been a radical fall in conflict. In France and the United States the decline had its beginnings before the onset of economic crisis, while in Japan it followed shortly afterwards. In France and Japan the most dramatic phase of the erosion of labour militancy was complete by the early 1980s, whereas in the United States the process continued to the end of the period. In 1969, 412 large strikes (1,000 or more involvements) were recorded in America; by 1989 this was down to only 51.

Can Contemporary Cross-national Variations be Explained?

We argued in the introduction that 'political economy' theories of strikes are consistent with a scenario of continuing cross-national diversity in patterns of industrial conflict. These theories did not, however, anticipate the actual trend towards *growing* diversity which this chapter has documented. Is this an indication that contemporary strike trends have crippled our capacity to explain cross-national variation in industrial conflict?

The study by Korpi and Shalev (1980) may be treated as indicative. It was argued in this study that for the period 1946–76, 'patterns of working class mobilization and political control' were closely associated with distinctive strike profiles. The purely empirical typology developed in the present chapter largely

confirms that claim. Our low-conflict Group 1 encompasses countries with stable political incorporation of either strong (Sweden
and Norway) or weak (Switzerland and the Netherlands) labour
movements (Germany was a mixed case). The cases in Group 2
were characterized by a relatively mobilized working class frozen
out of government participation. Under these circumstances,
labour conflicts were fleeting but exceptionally widespread (Italy,
France, and Australia). The nations included in Group 3 are the
antithesis of social democracy, being instances in which labour's
organizational and political weakness has been associated with
limited but intense conflict (in North America and Ireland).
Finally, Group 4 is an intermediate type in terms of both labour
mobilization/control and industrial conflict. The position of three
countries (Austria, Finland, and Japan) on our chart is inconsistent
with the findings of Korpi and Shalev, but this is mainly because
we used here data from only a limited subset (1960–67) of the
period analysed in the earlier article.

When this exercise is repeated using conflict data for the 1980s,
the results are far from satisfactory (no chart is reproduced here,
but the data can be viewed in Table 3.1). The greatest violence has
been done to the countries of Group 2, where, by Korpi and
Shalev's interpretation, political exclusion of labour parties resting
on a strong voter and trade-union base generated a politicized
pattern of demonstration strikes. Japan left this group definitively
from the late 1970s, without any fundamental changes in the
mobilization or political participation of labour. Labour disputes
also decreased substantially in France at about approximately the
same time. While in the French case it might be tempting to
attribute this sea change to the political rise of the Socialist Party,
the trend towards industrial peace preceded the Mitterrand
presidency, and the French phenomenon of 'socialism without the
workers' renders the anticipated linkage theoretically implausible in
any case (cf. Kesselman, 1983). In New Zealand, another
nominally leftward shift in government composition saw strike
activity shift in the 'wrong' direction.

A further case of unanticipated change is of course the United
States, a key member of Group 3, where a low level of labour
organization and the political marginality of the left traditionally
gave rise to distinctly confrontational disputes. Although the
element of confrontation is still clearly present (as the sharply
increased duration of stoppages attests), RI in large strikes in the
eighties was less than a quarter of its level two decades earlier. The
deteriorating organizational and political position of the American
labour movement renders this development theoretically consistent

with a labour mobilization/left politics interpretation of strikes. But in view of the strong differentiation which has developed between strike patterns in Canada, Ireland, and the United States, it must be questioned whether there is any longer a reasonable basis for considering these three countries as a discrete cluster.

Last, but by no means least, the very jewels in the crown of the social-democratic model of political economy, Norway and Sweden, both experienced large increases in RI in the 1980s. Whereas the Norwegian figure remains within the bounds of minimal strike-proneness, strike activity in Sweden has become too extensive to justify characterizing it as a country of industrial peace.

In short, every one of the half-dozen nations in which the scope of industrial conflict in the 1980s departed radically from earlier levels poses a difficult puzzle for the Korpi/Shalev strike model. With the benefit of hindsight this is not very surprising, in view of the model's failure to recognize, or anticipate, dramatic contextual changes which were already becoming visible at the time it was developed. Specifically:

1 the model paid scant attention to how the disappearance of conditions for easy economic growth would affect industrial relations practices and the scope for autonomy of public policy from the interests of business;
2 it failed to envisage an independent role for the labour organization and control strategies of employers; and
3 it was premised on overly optimistic assumptions concerning the potential for union solidarity and unity of political purpose within an increasingly heterogeneous work-force.

It may well be possible to reconstruct the Korpi/Shalev model to permit greater sensitivity to contemporary developments, but it is only reasonable to ask whether an alternative is already at hand. Five or ten years ago, the burgeoning literature on neo-corporatism appeared to offer a plausible explanation of wide national variability in the institutional and political regulation of industrial relations.[10] In particular, the emphasis in the corporatist model on the political incorporation of trade-union elites into policy-making and their acceptance of responsibility for policy implementation allowed it to deal more effectively with cases that were problematic for the 'power resources' approach. These cases comprised small countries (the Netherlands and Switzerland being the most relevant cases) and one large country (West Germany) in which organized labour was strongly inclined towards consensual incomes policies, yet without the stimulus of encompassing unions and/or a politically dominant left.

On the other side of the ledger, research into the relationship between corporatism and conflict has been handicapped by a number of conspicuous shortcomings.[11] Serious problems arise whenever analysts attempt to include non-European nations in their investigations. Japan has caused exceptional dissonance between the various authorities who have evaluated its extent of corporatism (Schmitter, n.d.; Shalev, 1990). Australia and New Zealand are comparatively high-conflict countries without corporatist traditions, which on the face of it is inconsistent with their small populations and economic vulnerability (Castles, 1985; 1987). The United States and to a somewhat lesser extent Canada are clearly the antithesis of corporatism, but Ireland – with a similar strike profile – has been seen (for example, by Lehmbruch, 1984) as no less corporatist than Germany or Switzerland. A second difficulty with the corporatist interpretation of cross-national differences in industrial conflict is that its emphasis on institutions of interest representation and processes of policy formation and implementation blurs the fact that class compromises may rest on diverse distributions of power between labour and capital, with important implications for distributional outcomes and for the long-term stability of the system.[12]

A major limitation of treating corporatism as a monolithic category was posed after 1973 by the emergence in many countries without corporatist traditions of attempts to emulate them in order to cope with conditions of economic crisis. But if the distinction between what might be called *entrenched* and *proto-corporatist systems* is taken into account, the model does a creditable job of predicting strike differentials in the seventies. Crouch (this volume) explains why the proto-corporatist nations (Finland, Britain, Ireland, and Italy) were unable to emulate the success of entrenched corporatism in defusing conflict. While organizational and political developments at the peak of the labour movement had opened the way to 'political exchange', such a strategy was severely constrained in practice by pressures from the unions' base.

In turning to more recent developments, Crouch makes an additional distinction which enables him to field a corporatist model that performs well on data for *both* the 1970s and the 1980s. He shows that over time the record of the entrenched-corporatist nations has become more internally diverse as a result of differences which only became relevant to strike activity in the changed conditions of the eighties. In 'labour-dominant' settings (Norway and Sweden), the linchpin of corporatist industrial peace – the capacity of peak associations of blue-collar workers to set the tone for labour relations throughout the economy – was severely

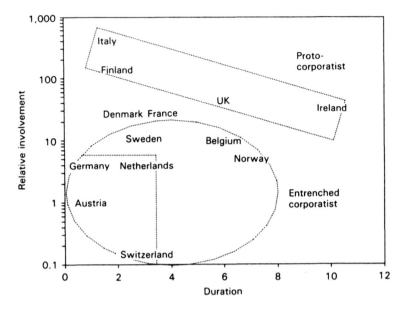

Figure 3.4   *European strike profiles in the 1980s (after Crouch)*

undermined by the growth of unions and militancy in white-collar and 'sheltered' employment. In contrast, Germany and like settings (Switzerland, Belgium, the Netherlands, and Austria) are characterized by 'weaker union movements whose articulation depended more on the strength of powerful employers' organizations and one dominant exposed sector union rather than a centralized confederation'. As we can see from Figure 3.4, this revised corporatist typology does a reasonably good job of grouping strike indicators for the thirteen European nations in our study into recognizable clusters.

The success of Crouch's revised corporatist model should not be exaggerated. Belgium and Austria ought to have changed places in the chart (although the Belgian data are unreliable, and, as Crouch points out, Austria is a mixed case with elements of both variants of entrenched corporatism). The analysis is particularly helpful in diagnosing the 'Scandinavian disease', but it offers no guidance as to why strikes have declined so precipitously in France, and would presumably have difficulty unravelling the mysteries attached to the record of a number of non-European countries (the withering away of strikes in the United States and Japan and their historically high level in New Zealand). Future efforts to develop more empirically effective frameworks for comparing patterns of industrial conflict would, however, do well to take note of the most important feature of Crouch's analysis. This is his effort to move away from a static, mechanistic typology in favour of a focus on those elements of the distribution of power and the logic of the institutions in which power is crystallized that are especially vulnerable to the effects of the type of sea changes that have occurred in recent years in the context for trade union action.

Comparing Trends across Countries

We return now to issues raised at the outset of this chapter in respect to the significance of the general trend towards declining strike activity. Do fewer strikes mean that a fundamental turning point has been reached in the evolution of labour militancy? The statistical data at our disposal permit us to carry out three types of empirical test. First, we will try to establish whether recent changes in industrial conflict can be understood as conjunctural (not necessarily structural) shifts. Secondly, we will ask whether in countries where labour militancy has apparently diminished, this is a general tendency or else has occurred with different intensity in different branches of the economy. And thirdly, we will seek evidence of whether workers are not so much refraining from entering into conflict, as limiting their engagement to more attenuated actions.

Conjunctural versus Secular Influences

Arguments that posit structural causes of labour's decline (changes in the organization of production and labour management, shifts in the composition of the working class) cast doubt on the hypothesis that the current state of labour militancy is the product of prevailing labour-market conditions. Yet there exists a venerable literature on the relationship between year-to-year strike fluctuations and the business cycle which asserts close coordination between these two. The data at our disposal show that neither expectation is fully met. There is a connection between trends in unemployment and strike frequency,[13] but the responsiveness of militancy to the threat of joblessness is not necessarily immediate or proportionate. In nearly all countries where data on the number of strikes are available and there are enough conflicts to justify the analysis,[14] we find an evident fit between *general* trends in strikes and the rate of unemployment. Once unemployment began its steady rise above the customary levels of the 'golden age', an equally steady decline in strike frequency was not far behind.

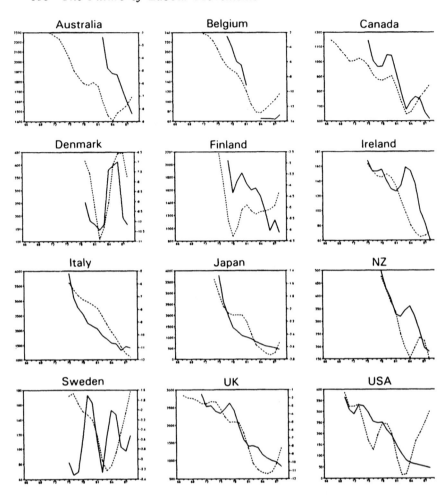

Figure 3.5   *The broadly parallel paths of strikes and unemployment, 1968–1989*

To focus attention on this relationship, Figure 3.5 juxtaposes moving averages of the number of strikes (the continuous line scaled on the left) and percentage unemployed (the dotted line scaled on the right). Unemployment was 'refracted' so that the expected inverse relationship between the two series would appear on the plots as a positive association. To simplify matters further, the computations for each series were begun just prior to the start of their transition (namely, at the onset of the secular rises in unemployment and declines in strikes). The common downward slope of the two lines is unmistakable. In a few cases (Britain,

Ireland, New Zealand) 'bubbles' of rising industrial conflict inter-
rupted the trend without any corresponding change having occurred in unemployment. But with one exception, such interruptions
were only temporary. That exception is Sweden, where the
temporal pattern of strike activity followed a cycle largely determined by the calendar of major rounds of national wage-
bargaining.

The plots also reveal significant differences in timing. In some
countries (most evidently Australia and Canada), the decline in
industrial conflict lagged behind labour-market developments,
while in other settings a high degree of simultaneity may be
observed. This indicates that the relationship between militancy
and unemployment is more that a simple conjunctural response.
That an underlying contextual change has taken place is also
suggested by what happened in cases where the trend towards
intensifying unemployment was halted or reversed (as it was in
many countries in the late 1980s). In most such cases, the easing
of unemployment did not have the effect of reversing the declining
course of labour militancy (Denmark in the period 1982–86 is,
however, a noteworthy exception).

Workers' ability to prosecute industrial action is dependent not
only on the favourability of market forces but also on their
capacity for collective action, particularly the prior extent of
labour organization. In so far as both strikes and unionization are
conditioned by the 'state of trade', both theoretical and empirical
difficulties arise in determining the role of organization *per se* in
sparking fluctuations in conflict. Nevertheless, given that unionism
is a form of institution-building as well as an expression of protest,
rates of unionization tend to be far less fluid than the movement
of strikes.[15] It might well be the case, therefore, that longer-term
shifts in the extent of worker organization (such as those that have
been noticeable in the OECD bloc over the last ten to twenty years)
have an appreciable effect on strike-proneness.

Jelle Visser's carefully constructed data on trends in union penetration of the work-force, updated in his contribution to this
volume, make it possible to test this hypothesis for a large number
of countries.[16] The graphs presented by Visser reveal that there
are only three countries in which union density has experienced
substantial declines throughout the post-1973 period. These three
are the United States, France, and Japan – the very same countries
that head the league of nations in which participation in strikes
eroded after 1974. In order to test for a broader relationship
between these two dimensions of worker mobilization, Figure 3.6
compares changes in unionization with changes in labour

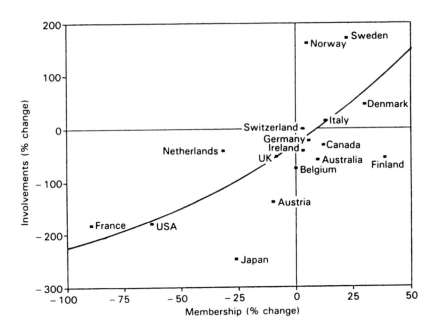

Figure 3.6   *The impact of organization on militancy*

militancy. Both comparisons pit the position in the eighties against that which prevailed prior to the advent of global economic crisis.[17] Clearly, there is a relationship – although not a tight, linear one – between the two variables. Of the six countries which experienced a decline in union density, four also exhibited the most precipitous falls in RI (more than 100 per cent). Among the remaining countries, with the exception of two outliers (Finland and Norway), there is an evident tendency for labour militancy to have been less inhibited (or even to have increased) the more that labour organization advanced.

Militancy in Declining and Expanding Sectors
The profound changes in the structure of employment in recent decades, and the difficulties they have posed for union organization and solidarity, are discussed in detail elsewhere in this book. The significance of such structural changes for industrial conflict has yet to be investigated. Specifically, to what extent does the

aggregate tendency in most countries for strikes to wane conceal differences in the militancy of labour in expanding and contracting sectors of the economy and the work-force? Unfortunately, available work stoppage data do not discriminate by gender, occupation, stability of employment, and many other widely remarked dimensions of change in the characteristics of jobs and job-holders. It is therefore impossible to estimate the extent to which the declining rate of strike activity is purely a consequence of compositional effects. Nevertheless, some of the changes taking place in the labour market can be captured, albeit crudely, by disaggregating strike trends at the branch level. In particular, there is an impression shared by many observers that industrial worker militancy has been particularly hard hit by structural changes, whereas in at least some countries, white-collar and service employees in the growing and naturally 'sheltered' public sector have become substantially more militant. How extensive are these trends in practice? To what degree have they been uniform across countries?

Methodological changes in France and the United States make it impossible to compare data for the 1980s with earlier periods. But for the remaining sixteen countries, the ILO furnishes reasonably consistent data by major branch headings for the period 1962–89. These permit simultaneous comparison across countries between changes in strike activity in two critical sectors: Manufacturing, and 'Community, Social and Personal Services' (hereafter, public services).[18] A variety of measures could be used for performing the desired comparison. We chose first to calculate, for each decade (the 1970s and the 1980s), the average proportion of total strike volume attributable to manufacturing, on the one hand, and public services, on the other. The proportion in the first period was then subtracted from that in the second, to yield the difference (in percentage points of total volume) between the two decades. The results are presented in Figure 3.7.[19]

It is clear that there has been a very widespread decline in the contribution of industrial workers to the overall strike movement; but that this decline occurred at sharply differing rates in the different countries under examination.[20] For instance, in the 1970s Britain was one of four countries in which at least two-thirds of total volume originated in manufacturing. Although in the other three cases (Germany, Denmark, and New Zealand) this situation hardly altered in the 1980s, the figure for the United Kingdom plunged to a little under one-third, generating the large drop shown at the top left of the chart. Despite such variability, the overall trend is clear: in the median country in the 1970s, half of strike volume originated in manufacturing; by the following

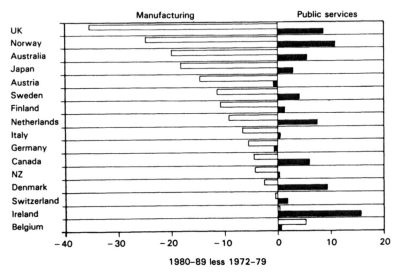

Figure 3.7   *Branch shares in total strike volume*

decade, this had fallen to a third. Moreover, even where industrial workers' *share* of volume held its own, their 'strike-proneness' almost certainly declined since *total* strike activity had been falling. By way of example, while in Ireland the proportion of total volume in manufacturing remained steady at 35 per cent through both decades, the average number of striker-days per thousand manufacturing workers fell from 400 to 250.

In contrast to manufacturing, the share of public-service strikes in total volume has been either stable or (in at least nine of the sixteen countries) experienced significant growth.[21] Nevertheless, although there is some indication of a tendency for public employees to fill the vacuum created by the fall in industrial worker militancy,[22] their increased share of strike volume generally fell well short of taking up the slack (clearly, other branches not analysed here also increased their share of the total). The rise of public-sector militancy, where it occurred, is noteworthy mainly for its novelty. In many countries (eleven out of sixteen) the public services contributed no more than 3 per cent of strike volume in the 1970s, whereas in the eighties the figure for five of these same nations had reached substantial levels (between roughly one-tenth and one-fifth of the total). Rising public-sector strike activity also tends to have taken a distinctive form. In Norway, Sweden, and the Netherlands, for instance, it has been concentrated in periodic 'bubbles' caused by major national-level confrontations, including lock-outs initiated by the state acting as employer.

Because public-sector strikes often do occur on a large scale, it would be especially interesting to chart their changing contribution to the large work stoppage. One country for which this information is available is the United Kingdom. Over the last three decades Britain has experienced fourteen massive conflicts which each accounted for one-quarter or more of total strike volume in the year of their occurrence. In the 1960s these conflicts involved metal workers (the engineering industry) and seamen, traditionally strike-prone groups. From 1970 to 1985 blue-collar workers in the public sector played the predominant role (including three national stoppages in coal mining). In contrast, all three cases in the second half of the 1980s involved public-service workers.[23] It is not unreasonable to assume that the British experience reflects a combination of trends – employment shifts, the decline of unionization and union power in traditional labour strongholds, and austerity measures in the public sector – which have been similarly profound, and have had similar effects, in other settings.

The Changing Shape of Strikes

Earlier we posed the question of whether strike activity has not only contracted in scope in the 1980s, but also undergone a change of form. A particularly significant question in this context is whether, as part of labour's overall transition to a more defensive orientation, strikes have become more attenuated. This could be the case for two quite different reasons: that workers are trying to economize on their resources; and/or that their militancy tends to evaporate in the face of determined employer resistance. On the other hand, the classic literature on strikes and the business cycle posits that conflicts become more prolonged in hard times for labour, because they pit desperate militants against employers who enjoy a bargaining advantage and have little to lose from holding out for victory. What, in practice, has been the predominant trend in the 1980s?

The principal data at our disposal have already been presented in the right-hand panel of Table 3.1. The measure of duration employed in that table divides aggregate volume by involvements, yielding the amount of time spent on strike by the average striker. Because duration tends to be more volatile than involvement, we need to be cautious about relying on the subperiod averages in Table 3.1.[24] Our conclusions therefore also take account of trends in the original year-by-year data, which it is not practical to reproduce here. These indicate that in fully half of the countries in

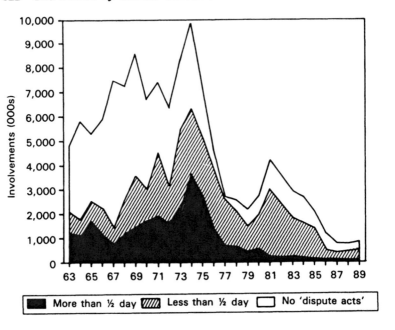

Figure 3.8 *Japan: changing forms of conflict*

this study, no clear trend is apparent in aggregate strike duration. Of the remainder, there are only two in which the length of stoppages has taken a rising course. In the United States it attained an extraordinary peak (close to forty working days) at the end of the 1980s. In the other case, France, the prolongation of conflict was only temporary. In the remaining seven countries aggregate duration has declined, although in each case the trend was in some way qualified. In Finland, the decline was only modest; in Britain and West Germany, it was countered by the occurrence of exceptionally large and prolonged disputes in a single year (1984); in Ireland and Australia the downward trend was not sustained; and in both Italy and Japan, the period of transition to shorter conflicts occurred prior to the 1980s.

Unfortunately, computing the typical duration of strikes by the mean number of work-days 'lost' per striking worker is a less than ideal procedure. One obvious limitation is that if they are large enough, occasional very long disputes may act to conceal what is happening to the duration of the bulk of strike activity. A preferable measure would therefore be the time spent on strike by the *median* striker, or some other indicator based on the distribution of involvements among different categories of stoppage duration. Not many countries furnish the necessary data, however. We managed to build a time series on the proportion of striking workers involved in 'brief' stoppages for five countries.[25] In four of the five there was no discernible trend in this proportion over the period 1970–89.[26] This in itself is a significant finding, considering that the short stoppage is a quintessential by-product of full employment and has traditionally been superseded in hard times by more drawn-out disputes.

The Japanese case is especially interesting in this context. Generally available figures for strikes in Japan (including those cited earlier in this chapter) refer only to stoppages lasting at least half a day. It is these which have taken such an extraordinary tumble since the peak reached in 1974, when one-tenth of the work-force went on strike. If, however, shorter stoppages (which also go on record) are taken into account, the picture changes quite dramatically. We can see in Figure 3.8 that when involvement in 'regular' strikes rose and then fell before and after the middle of the 1970s, so too did participation in very brief stoppages. But during the first half of the 1980s, lightning strikes apparently acted as a substitute for more extended stoppages.[27] It is only after 1985 that we witness the virtual disappearance of *both* forms of action. Similar tendencies characterized the behaviour of incidents in which no 'dispute acts' (including slowdowns) actually occurred, but the dispute itself was serious enough to be the subject of third-party mediation.[28] In sum, symbolic forms of conflict played a very extensive role in Japanese industrial relations until the period of economic crisis, reflecting the relatively low price that workers needed to pay in order to raise demands under conditions of steadily growing prosperity. In the immediate aftermath of the first oil shock these forms of action temporarily disappeared from labour's repertoire, but later they served – for a time – to take up part of the slack caused by the virtual disappearance of strikes proper.

A final dimension of the form of industrial conflict is the typical size of stoppages. Unfortunately, difficulties of measurement are particularly acute in this instance. Size is an attribute of individual outbreaks of conflict, which makes it sensitive to problems with the data on strike frequency (which are not available at all in some countries while in others their reliability has been impaired by methodological revisions). Of thirteen countries which field usable data, five experienced substantially larger stoppages in the 1980s, while in two other cases the reverse tendency prevailed. In Norway, Britain, New Zealand, and Italy the average strike was at least 50 per cent larger than in the previous decade (although in Norway the trend was delayed, and Italy experienced a decline within the 1980s). In the United States, strikes were substantially more extensive, although not in all years. In contrast, stoppages in Denmark have generally been smaller since the late 1970s. Even more notably, since the early 1960s the size of strikes in Japan has declined dramatically, from 1,000 workers to only 200.

To summarize the findings regarding the shape of strikes, it is apparent that aggregate data furnish no indication of any fundamental changes at work, either across the whole of the OECD bloc or within the more homogeneous groups of nations which share similar strike profiles. Some interesting tendencies can, however, be observed in relation to the six countries in which strikes in the 1980s have departed most dramatically from previous norms. Sweden, Norway, and New Zealand were earlier singled out as deviant instances in which strike involvements rose in recent years. In Sweden this occurred because conflicts became more numerous rather than changing shape, whereas in the other two cases growing participation was due to the larger scope of conflicts rather than more of them. The three countries which experienced exceptional reduction in RI also exhibit contrasting developments. In France and Japan, all three dimensions of strike activity – frequency, size, and duration – became more diminutive.[29] In the United States, however, conflicts became larger and considerably longer, but also far less frequent.[30]

Conclusion

This chapter has grappled with two analytical dimensions of contemporary developments in industrial conflict within the OECD bloc. One of these is the perspective of cross-national comparison, from which we queried whether the diversity of national experience has diminished or increased, and whether this diversity can be explained as satisfactorily today as it was in the past. The analysis has demonstrated that the tidy typologies of yesteryear have lost much of their mastery. The generic trend towards erosion of overt labour militancy in the course of the last decade has been subject to significantly greater national diversity than the expansive trend in industrial conflict during the period between the late 1960s and the mid-1970s. This empirical record in turn exposed important theoretical pitfalls. Comparative models built around single-factor explanations suffered especially from the fact that the same outcome (industrial peace, for example) can emerge in quite different contexts. Now that changing circumstances have brought this elementary law of comparative analysis to the forefront, it is evident that future model-building efforts will need to build in greater sensitivity to historical contingency. This is especially true for understanding the power and strategies of workers and employers, which have developed in accordance with significantly different logics under conditions of growth and conditions of crisis. Major intellectual retooling is required now that the context that Michal Kalecki so presciently defined half a century ago – the rising economic and political power of the working class – has been transformed. In particular, it is questionable whether there is still truth to the Scandinavian-inspired paradox that 'hegemonic' labour movements are the surest guarantor of labour restraint.

Both the difficulties encountered by theoretically driven general models and some of the detailed findings of our enquiry suggest that, in the near term, the best bet for comparative research will be to concentrate on 'exceptional' cases. The half-dozen countries in which industrial conflict has experienced extreme rises or falls should prove to be fruitful sites for future investigations. They are especially promising candidates for in-depth case analysis and for strategic paired comparisons (for instance, between the United States and Canada, France and Italy, Sweden and Norway, or Sweden and Austria).

The second key axis of our analysis was the time dimension. In attempting to assess the precise directions of recent strike trends, we have sought to establish the character of the current drift towards labour quiescence. Has organized labour taken a knock-out blow, or have workers accepted new cooperative strategies or opted for new forms of protest? It is apparent from the big picture (but would probably not have been had we relied on more exacting econometric techniques) that the strike movement has, as always, been responsive to declines in workers' capacities resulting from rising unemployment and falling rates of unionization. But at the same time, we have found at least presumptive evidence that structural and strategic changes are also at work. One important indication (which may well become more decisive as new data become available) is that even where labour-market conditions have revived somewhat, strikes have not. Another symptom (which again may be further reinforced as the numbers come in) is that in most cases current levels of strike-proneness are at or below the 'floor levels' defined in the period of relative industrial peace which preceded the great swings in strike activity of the last two-and-a-half decades.

Our attempts at gaining further insight by unpacking aggregate trends had mixed results. The declining contribution of blue-collar industrial workers to overall strike activity and the increasing role of public service employees indicates that structural trends can impact in contradictory directions. The evidence gathered regarding the shape of strikes was equally inconclusive. In some settings, the downward trend in labour militancy was especially pronounced for brief and localized forms of action, while in other cases these have served as a substitute for 'set-piece' conflicts.

Still, the present study has by no means exhausted the potential scope for analysis of official work stoppage statistics. More detailed disaggregation by branch, size, and duration, as well as consideration of other indicators available for some countries (strike issues and modes of settlement, for example) are obvious possibilities. There may be opportunities, where raw data can be acquired, for analysing different indicators in a multivariate framework. The goal of disaggregation can also be achieved by qualitative methods, which have an indispensable contribution to make. There is a particular need for combining macro-level perspectives with micro-studies addressing the question of whether militancy has in some sense gone underground, perhaps awaiting the return of conditions more favourable to organized protest.

The truth is that we do not know, and cannot know, what the future holds for the strike. Even educated guesses require more than just information about contemporary developments, since the analyst must also be willing to attach probabilities to plausible scenarios which take account of the wider political and economic context of labour relations. Informed attempts to do this (for example, by Crouch, 1990, and in Regini's Introduction to this book) indicate that the disappearance of industrial conflict is unlikely, and that indeed, it is entirely possible that the historical pattern of long cycles of militancy and quiescence may not yet be exhausted. The current travails of trade unionism as an encompassing social movement do not preclude the possibility of future strike waves. The question is whether on-going changes in labour markets, the organization and management of work, and political alignments will generate new opportunities and incentives for mass collective action. If the past is any guide to the future, they will.

The study of industrial conflict has been excessively sensitive to the historical waxing and waning of the phenomenon itself. The field of labour relations achieved its first major breakthrough in the English-speaking world in the early post-war period, in the aftermath of the spread of organization and militancy to blue-collar workers in the mass-production industries of the United States. With the apparent institutionalization of class conflict signalled by declining strike rates during the 1950s and early 1960s, research on strikes became transformed from a sociological to a technical enterprise and entered a period of intellectual stagnation. This period ended abruptly in the late 1960s, however, when social scientists rediscovered labour relations as an arena of social conflict and change, and labour militancy again became a focus of research and theoretical debate. The circumstances of the decade which followed engendered a further shift of focus, as the potential economic consequences of strikes (inflation, profit squeeze, and loss of international competitiveness) became painfully evident. The necessity for state intervention, and the diverse responses of labour movements, employers, and governments in different countries, sparked renewed interest in the politics of industrial relations. The neo-corporatist solution of political consensus among class and state elites became widely touted as a 'positive-sum' solution to 'zero-sum' distributional conflicts. In the 1980s, however, theory once again appeared to lag behind the real world, as labour unions and parties were forced on to the defensive. Political and economic coercion, and labour–management consensus in the enterprise, have demonstrated their efficacy as alternatives to the corporatist route to labour quiescence.

That general theories of industrial conflict have produced disappointing results is therefore due in no small measure to their exaggerated responsiveness to the twists and turns of history.[31] On the other hand, the importance of documenting this history is clear – an injunction which surely applies to periods of relative tranquillity no less than it does in the midst of strike waves. The dearth of empirical studies of industrial conflict in recent years (other than the continuing fascination of strikes to economists interested in highly abstracted bargaining models) is testament to a short-sightedness which will likely catch the scholarly community with its collective pants down the next time that there is a widespread eruption in labour markets.

Notes

1 I was a collaborator in one such study (Korpi and Shalev, 1980). For similar analyses, see also Hibbs (1978) and Cameron (1984).

2 This turn of phrase is self-consciously ironic. The contemporary resurgence of quiescence constitutes a largely unforeseen reversal of the 'resurgence of class conflict' which once preoccupied this author and several other contributors to the present volume (see Crouch and Pizzorno, 1978).

3 For details, see Franzosi (1989a); Shalev (1978); Walsh (1983); UK Department of Employment (1989).

4 The most significant development has been the suspension of record-keeping in the United States, beginning with data for 1982, for all but very large work stoppages (involving at least 1,000 workers). From 1987 published data for Canada have

incorporated a similar restriction (a threshold of 500 workers), but Labour Canada continues to keep comprehensive records, generously made available for this research. From 1981 to 1987 Belgium's Ministry of Economic Affairs published no strike statistics except for one year, 1985. Since 1986 the New Zealand of Department of Labour has published only aggregate and branch-level data, in place of the richly detailed reports made available in earlier years. Britain's Department of Employment has maintained the format of earlier annual reports, but dropped the important distinction between 'official' and 'unofficial' strikes. In a more subtle instance of how political convenience and fiscal constraints have combined to block the flow of information, the Australian Bureau of Statistics now collects non-trivial fees (cheques and credit cards are accepted) for supplying reports on industrial disputes.

5 We use the term 'labour militancy' loosely in this chapter. It is of course entirely possible that the occurrence of work stoppages reflects militancy on the part of employers rather than workers (in the extreme case, in the form of lock-outs). It is also possible, especially in the contemporary climate, that many worker-initiated disputes reflect defence of past achievements rather than the raising of 'offensive' demands.

6 Two other technical points should be noted. To avoid giving undue weight to irregular explosions of conflict, all period averages in this chapter have been calculated as geometric means. Inter-period changes have been calculated using the logarithmic method: the percentage change in X between periods t1 and t2 is 100 times the natural log of X_{t-2}/X_{t-1}.

7 The author gratefully acknowledges the cooperation of the statistical bureaux of the countries concerned, and the assistance of Professor Robert Brym of the University of Toronto, who collaborated in building the dataset. The eighteen nations studied, which were also analysed in previous works by the present author, include all OECD members except (1) tiny Iceland and Luxembourg, and (2) four 'semi-peripheral states' which have not experienced continuous democratic rule during the post-war period (Greece, Portugal, Spain, and Turkey). As stated in the text, this chapter deals only with the contemporary history of strike activity. For a longer-term perspective, see Korpi and Shalev (1980) and Shalev (1983). Table 2 of the latter article includes data from 1919 to 1982 using almost identical measures to those employed here (not precisely identical, however, because the earlier article used the non-agricultural labour force, rather than wage- and salary-earners in employment, as the denominator for calculating RI).

8 Austria and Denmark also registered change scores of at least ±100% in Table 3.1, but have not been singled out here as 'deviant'. This is because the decline in RI in Austria occurred well before the 1980s, while the recorded rise for Denmark reflects developments in the 1970s that were partially reversed during the subsequent decade.

9 Note that the purpose of Figure 3.3 is to provide a visual sense of the main trends in each country over the thirty-year period examined. For that reason the data for different countries were not plotted on a common scale. We also eliminated some of the 'noise' in the series by converting them to three-year moving averages.

10 See, for example, Goldthorpe (ed.) (1984); Panitch (1986); Marks (1988).

11 For direct tests of the impact of neo-corporatism on strikes, see Crouch (1985); and Lehner (1987); and for related contributions, Katzenstein (1985); Cameron (1984); and Schmitter (1981).

12 See Korpi (1983: chap. 2) for a critique of the corporatist model's neglect of the distribution of 'power resources'. Katzenstein's (1985) distinction between 'liberal' and 'social' corporatism illustrates the importance of the relative standing of labour and capital in the political economy. Flanagan, Soskice and Ulman (1983: chap. 5) are among those who have recognized an important specific example – the strategic role played by employer power in the quiescence of West German labour.

13 Despite serious problems of over-time reliability, strike frequency remains the preferred indicator for examining the fit between labour militancy and the business cycle. Previous research shows that rising or falling unemployment most directly affects the number of strike *decisions*. See, for example, Franzosi (1989a).

14 Time series for strike frequency are not available for Germany, Austria, and France. The absolute frequency of stoppages in Norway, the Netherlands, and Switzerland was too low for the comparison with unemployment to be meaningful.

15 For a forceful presentation of the claim that unionization is a crucial mediator of strike fluctuations, see Shorter and Tilly (1974). Bain and Elsheikh (1976) provide evidence that trends in union membership can be quantitatively accounted for by much the same economic variables as those which work satisfactorily in econometric analyses of strike trends.

16 Visser's chapter includes graphs covering sixteen of the eighteen countries analysed in this chapter. He also furnishes tabular data for Ireland, leaving New Zealand excluded.

17 In keeping with the character of unionization as a 'stock' variable and strike activity as a 'flow' variable, changes in union density were calculated from the values which pertained at the beginning and the end of the period (1970 versus the end of the 1980s), whereas changes in RI were based on the average for two subperiods (1968–73 versus 1980–89).

18 Clearly, the 'Community, Social and Personal Services' are by no means equivalent to the entire public sector, since they exclude utilities, transport, and communication, as well as nationalized industrial enterprises – leaving only public services (health, education, welfare) and public administration. Moreover, what we describe as 'public services' are actually combined by the ILO with private-sector social and personal services – although, in practice, it is doubtful that these additions are of much importance for analysing strikes.

19 The ILO data are unavailable prior to 1972. Data for one or two years are missing for a number of countries. This is not a serious problem except for Belgium, where the 1980 figures are based on only three years of data.

20 It was expedient to use strike volume (rather than involvements) in this analysis, in order to take account of potentially wide differences between the two sectors in the duration of strikes. Because the data were averaged for whole decades, there is a danger of overlooking cases in which the sectoral shifts under study occurred comparatively late. For example, in both Italy and New Zealand the bulk of the decline in manufacturing's contribution to strike volume took place in the late 1980s.

21 We have stated 'at least nine' because, in France and New Zealand, strikes by civil servants are explicitly excluded from the official statistics. It will be recalled that France could not be included in our branch analysis in any case because of lack of over-time comparability. But a report by the Ministry of Employment ('Conflits du Travail en 1989', June 1990) presents data for the public services ('Fonction publique') which indicate a pronounced rise in its share of volume in the course of the 1980s.

22 If Ireland, a clear outlier, is excluded from the calculation, the correlation between the absolute change in the shares of manufacturing and public services is − 0.31 (linear) or − 0.67 (monotonic).

23 The three stoppages were in telecommunications (1987), the postal service (1988), and local government (1989).

24 A few examples: Table 3.1 suggests that strikes in Britain did not become significantly shorter in the 1980s, but a very different picture appears if we set aside the extended conflict in coal mining in 1984–85. In Ireland, on the other hand, what appears to be a downturn in duration in the eighties is actually the result of what was only a temporary deviation during 1985–86.

25 The countries concerned are Belgium (for stoppages of less than two days), Canada (five days), Ireland (two days), Norway (eight days), and the United Kingdom (one day).

26 The exception was Belgium, where the share of involvements accounted for by strikes of less than two days' duration doubled from the late seventies, although the calculation is based on a limited sample.

27 Strictly speaking, we cannot substantiate the hypothesized substitution effect, for it is possible (but unfortunately cannot be investigated) that trends in recourse to different forms of action have not been uniform across different sectors.

28 Given that stoppages of work in large Japanese enterprises have traditionally been only one of a variety of means for staging 'rituals of rebellion' (Ben-Ari, 1990), it is reasonable to regard 'active' and 'inactive' disputes as belonging to a single underlying universe of conflictual action.

29 For France, this evaluation is based on trends in 'local' disputes, since these are the only ones for which frequency is reported (since 1975).

30 It must again be emphasized, however, that available data for the United States cover only large disputes.

31 As Franzosi (1989b) has argued in a seminal contribution, theoretical progress has also been blocked by an insistence on uni-causal models and by a failure to recognize the dialectical relationship between industrial conflict and its 'causes'.

References

Baglioni, Guido and Crouch, Colin (eds) (1990) *European Industrial Relations: the Challenge of Flexibility*. London: Sage.

Bain, George Sayers and Elsheikh, Farouk (1976) *Union Growth and the Business Cycle: an Econometric Analysis*. Oxford: Blackwell.

Bamber, Greg J. and Lansbury, Russell D. (eds) (1989) *International and Comparative Industrial Relations: a Study of Developed Market Economies*. Sydney: Unwin Hyman.

Ben-Ari, Eyal (1990) 'Ritual Strikes, Ceremonial Slowdowns: Some Thoughts on the Management of Conflict in Large Japanese Enterprises', in S.N. Eisenstadt and E. Ben-Ari (eds), *Japanese Models of Conflict Resolution*. London: Kegan Paul International, pp. 94–124.

Cameron, David R. (1984) 'Social Democracy, Corporatism, Labour Quiescence and the Representation of Economic Interest in Advanced Capitalist Society', in John H. Goldthorpe (ed.), *Order and Conflict in Contemporary Capitalism*. Oxford: Clarendon Press, pp. 143–78.

Castles, Frances G. (1985) *The Working Class and Welfare: Reflections on the Political Development of the Welfare State in Australia and New Zealand*,

1890-1980. Wellington: Allen & Unwin.

Castles, Francis G. (1987) 'The Politics of Economic Vulnerability: a Comparison of Australia and Sweden', *Acta Sociologica*, 30(3-4): 271-80.

Crouch, Colin (1985) 'Conditions for Trade Union Wage Restraint', in Leon N. Lindberg and Charles S. Maier (eds), *The Politics of Inflation and Economic Stagnation*. Washington, DC: The Brookings Institution, pp. 105-39.

Crouch, Colin (1990) 'Afterword', in Guido Baglioni and Colin Crouch (eds), *European Industrial Relations: the Challenge of Flexibility*. London: Sage, pp. 356-62.

Crouch, Colin and Alessandro Pizzorno (1978) *The Resurgence of Class Conflict in Western Europe since 1968* (2 vols). London: Macmillan.

Dubois, Pierre (1979) *Sabotage in Industry*. Harmondsworth, UK: Penguin.

Flanagan, Robert J., Soskice, David W. and Ulman, Lloyd (1983) *Unionism, Economic Stabilization, and Incomes Policies: European Experience*. Washington, DC: The Brookings Institution.

Franzosi, Roberto (1989a) 'One Hundred Years of Strike Statistics: Methodological and Theoretical Issues in Quantitative Strike Research', *Industrial and Labour Relations Review*, 42(3): 348-62.

Franzosi, Roberto (1989b) 'Strike Data in Search of a Theory: the Italian Case in the Postwar Period', *Politics and Society* 17(4): 453-87.

Gladstone, Alan (1989) 'Analysis of the Discussions', in *Current Approaches to Collective Bargaining: an ILO Symposium*. Geneva: International Labour Office, pp. 25-33.

Goldthorpe, John H. (ed.) (1984) *Order and Conflict in Contemporary Capitalism*. Oxford: Oxford University Press.

Hibbs, Douglas A., Jr. (1978) 'On the Political Economy of Long-run Trends in Strike Activity', *British Journal of Political Science*, 8(2): 153-75.

ILO (1989) *Current Approaches to Collective Bargaining: an ILO Symposium*. Geneva: International Labour Office.

Kalecki, Michal (1943) 'Political Aspects of Full Employment', *Political Quarterly*, 14(4): 322-31.

Katzenstein, Peter (1985) *Small States in World Markets: Industrial Policy in Europe*. Ithaca, NY: Cornell University Press.

Kelly, John and Nicholson, Nigel (1980) 'Strikes and other Forms of Industrial Action', *Industrial Relations Journal*, 11(5): 20-31.

Kesselman, Mark (1983) 'Socialist Possibilities and Capitalist Realities: All's Quiet on the French Leftist Front', *Research in Political Economy*, 6: 277-303.

Korpi, Walter (1983) *The Democratic Class Struggle*. London: Routledge & Kegan Paul.

Korpi, Walter and Shalev, Michael (1980) 'Strikes, Power and Politics in the Western Nations, 1900-1976', *Political Power and Social Theory*, 1: 301-34.

Lehmbruch, Gerhard (1984) 'Concertation and the Structure of Corporatist Networks', in John H. Goldthorpe (ed.), *Order and Conflict in Contemporary Capitalism*. Oxford: Oxford University Press, pp. 60-80.

Lehner, Franz (1987) 'Interest Intermediation, Institutional Structures and Public Policy', in Hans Keman, Heikki Paloheimo and Paul F. Whiteley (eds), *Coping with the Economic Crisis: Alternative Responses to Economic Recession in Advanced Industrial Societies*. London and Beverly Hills, CA: Sage, pp. 54-82.

Marks, Gary (1988) 'Neocorporatism and Incomes Policy in Western Europe and North America', *Comparative Politics*, 18(3): 253-77.

Panitch, Leo (1986) *Working-class Politics in Crisis: Essays on Labour and the State*. London: Verso.

Rees, Albert (1952) 'Industrial Conflict and Business Fluctuations', *Journal of Political Economy*, 60(5): 371–82.

Schmitter, Philippe C. (1981) 'Interest Intermediation and Regime Governability in Contemporary Western Europe and North America', in Suzanne Berger (ed.), *Organizing Interests in Western Europe*. Cambridge: Cambridge University Press, pp. 285–327.

Schmitter, Philippe (n.d.) 'A Preface and an Epilogue for Japanese Students', published in the Japanese edition of 'Trends towards Corporatist Intermediation'.

Shalev, Michael (1978) 'Lies, Damned Lies and Strike Statistics: the Measurement of Trends in Industrial Conflict', in C. Crouch and A. Pizzorno (eds), *The Resurgence of Class Conflict in Western Europe since 1968*, vol. 1. London: Macmillan, pp. 1–19, 322–34.

Shalev, Michael (1983) 'Strikes and the Crisis: Industrial Conflict and Unemployment in the Western Nations', *Economic and Industrial Democracy*, 4(4): 417–60.

Shalev, Michael (1990) 'Class Conflict, Corporatism and Comparison: the Japanese Enigma', in S.N. Eisenstadt and E. Ben-Ari (eds), *Japanese Models of Conflict Resolution*. London: Kegan Paul International, pp. 60–93.

Shorter, Edward T. and Tilly, Charles (1974) *Strikes in France 1830–1968*. Cambridge: Cambridge University Press.

UK Department of Employment (1989) 'International Comparisons of Industrial Stoppages for 1987', *Department of Employment Gazette* (June): 309–13.

Walsh, Kenneth (1983) *Strikes in Europe and the United States: Measurement and Incidence*. London: Frances Pinter.

4
The Emerging Realignment between Labour Movements and Welfare States

Gøsta Esping-Andersen

This chapter is divided into three parts. The first provides an assessment of what we know about the political impact of labour movements on welfare-state formation, an old and thoroughly researched topic, which, however, calls for some re-examination. Secondly, it examines how contemporary employment developments are intimately linked to welfare-state intervention; here, we essentially address the cybernetics of the previous relationship. Finally, the chapter moves to the more speculative terrain of how the contemporary process of de-industrialization, flexibilization, and restructuration may harbour a new nexus between industrial relations and social welfare.

Labour Movements and the Welfare State

The idea that labour would constitute the driving force behind welfare-state expansion has deep historical roots. In the nineteenth century, it found expression in the widespread fear, and occasional paranoia, among liberals and conservatives that democratic extensions would allow the working classes enough power to pervert the market with social rights. Paradoxically, the early labour movements – whether they were revolutionary or reformist – hardly ever pursued what we, today, would call a welfare state. Those who adhered strictly to the socialization strategy assumed that the welfare problem would resolve itself automatically in a post-capitalist order; those committed to immediate reforms were as much, if not more, wedded to a friendly society solution as to state responsibility.

The arrival of a fully fledged, systematically argued, and theoretically enshrined political strategy for 'social democracy' occurred during the inter-war era; its most forceful exponents, counting such figures as Eduard Heimann, Ernst Wigforss, Hjalmar Branting and the Austro-Marxists, were centred in the German, Austrian, and Scandinavian labour movements. The essence of their strategy was to employ parliamentarianism as a means to widen democracy so as to encompass social rights as well; social democracy became welfare statism in the broadest sense possible.

Thus was born the social democratic thesis, subsequently adopted as a leading hypothesis by social scientists, such as Korpi (1978, 1980, 1983), Stephens (1979), or Esping-Andersen (1990). Put simply, it argues that the level of welfare-state development is a function of strong, centralized, and unitary working-class mobilization. Its major counter-thesis springs from the functionalist tradition, which believes that class power hardly makes a difference since the larger and more pervasive forces of societal modernization, economic growth, bureaucratic maturation, and demographic transformation anyhow induce welfare statism (Flora and Heidenheimer, 1981; Pampel and Williamson, 1985, 1988; Wilensky and Lebaux, 1958; Wilensky, 1975). Indeed, the functionalist perspective as well can trace its roots back to classical political economy, in this case primarily to the work of Adolph Wagner, Max Weber, Emile Durkheim, Talcott Parsons, and Selig Perlman.

There is considerable, but absolutely no conclusive, empirical support for either position. It all depends in the end on one's choice of measurement. If welfare is measured as expenditure, the functionalists tend to be more persuasive; it is clear that expenditure on pensions correlates heavily with the size of the aged population; and it is also evident that a given level of economic development is necessary before nations can embark upon substantial redistributory adventures. The case for labour-movement power is much stronger when we focus on the *kinds* of social policies adopted. If welfare is measured in terms of indicators of social rights, equality, and full employment, the 'social democratic' thesis has greater credibility. By and large, the more encompassing the conceptualization of welfare statism, the stronger is the case for the working-class mobilization thesis. Yet there are serious qualifications to this generalization. First and foremost, purely cross-sectional studies are trapped in what Michael Shalev (1983) has called the Swedocentric fallacy: a too narrowly linear assumption that if nations which are laggards in welfare (such as the United States) had Swedish-level working-class power, they would also be blessed with Swedish-style welfare statism.

We know that such a simple linear view distorts historical reality. Virtually all studies rank Austria as a close runner-up to Swedish working-class power, but the Austrian welfare state is quite at odds with the Swedish; it lacks universalism, is hesitant to extend social services, and it spends an extraordinarily large amount on privileged civil-servant benefits. Vice versa, the Dutch welfare state is hardly inferior to the Scandinavian, despite a substantially more marginal labour movement.

If the methodological assumption of linearity is discarded, as in a recent flow of research (Castles, 1989; Esping-Andersen, 1990), we discover that welfare states cluster into distinct regime types, or, as Castles has termed it, into 'families of nations'.

A sensitivity to clustered regimes is, in my view, a prerequisite if we want to understand the role of labour movements in the construction of social welfare systems. In my own research (Esping-Andersen, 1990), three distinct clusters emerge. Defined in terms of the nature and strength of social rights, universalism, and the relative importance of private-sector welfare, it is clear that there exists a 'social democratic', largely Nordic cluster. Working-class mobilization, defined as union strength, leftist party power, or neo-corporatism (or all these) is, without doubt, the best explanation in this case (we may, however, legitimately raise the possibility that these countries were historically predisposed towards *both* social democracy and universalistic and solidaristic social rights).

The second clear regime cluster comprises the Central/Southern European nations (the EEC area), in which a combination of authoritarian-conservative, nation-building coalitions and Christian forces built regimes with strong social rights, but organized around corporatist lines and the subsidiarity principle. It is for this regime that the Wilensky argument about the impact of Catholicism holds (Wilensky, 1981). Working-class organizations – primarily trade unionism – have certainly exercised an influence on welfare expansion, but primarily via their links to, and importance within, Christian Catholic movements or, as in Holland, the pillars-system (van Kersbergen, 1991). In this cluster it seems as if the conservative heritage was so powerfully institutionalized that political efforts at 'social democratization' have largely failed: this is true for post-1960 Austria, for post-1969 Germany, for post-Mitterrand France, and even for the vaguer arrangements for historical compromise in Italy since the 1960s.

The 'conservative' regime leaves very little room for welfare in the market, such as occupational plans, but does encourage voluntary communitarian social policy initiatives, Caritas being a typical example. To a degree, the lack of employer plans is surprising. First, the idea of corporate welfare in terms of obligations of an employer towards his employees is deeply entrenched in both the Catholic and the conservative tradition. Secondly, given the conservative regime's antagonism to collective social services (especially those related to family welfare), a huge gap arises that would likely become the object of industrial bargaining. True, we find a strong work-related system of health insurance in countries like Germany, but that about exhausts the menu.

The third regime is primarily identified by its accent on residual public obligations, targeting, and on the encouragement of private-sector provision. Castles, in his most recent work, identifies two versions of this 'liberal' regime; one, in which labour movements were powerful and centrally placed (as in Australia); another, in which labour was largely excluded. Both, however, are essentially found in the Anglo-Saxon New World nations (Castles, 1985, 1989). In essence, the explanation is not far removed from the social democratic thesis: the outcome does depend on the political power of labour.

In nations where the welfare *state* is residual, the market tends to assert itself as a functional equivalent. This turns the question towards the possible direct role of trade unionism and industrial relations in promoting and organizing the usually vast system of occupational/private-sector welfare of these countries. Research on this face of the welfare system is still underdeveloped, and the evidence is rather scattered. On the positive side, indications are that trade unionism has been decisive, although not necessarily instrumental. Until the Social Security Act, for example, American trade unions (being at that time only really the AFL) distrusted government (for good reasons) and were usually blessed with a fairly convincing degree of bargaining power. Still, until 1929, trade-union welfare funds were of larger aggregate scope than were private employer plans. Private occupational plans first began to mushroom during and after World War II. The CIO embraced the bargaining approach to welfare from the late 1940s onwards (following a 1947 Supreme Court decision), and was very successful in gaining welfare extensions (especially in health care and pensions) within the primary sector of the economy.

However, on the negative side it is difficult to ascribe to trade unions in America the principal causal force behind private occupational welfare. Much of the driving force was tax policy, and much of it was employer strategy to mediate wage pressures. If anything, the principle of the 'deferred wage' is what really drove up occupational plans, the idea being that employers traded off current wage increases for future social benefits. The great advantage to employers was that they, themselves, benefited tremendously: by having at their disposal the accumulated savings, by chaining workers' loyalties to the firm, and by tax advantages. In light of the widespread termination of company or industry pension plans during the era of high unemployment of the 1970s and 1980s in the United States, the idea that they were motivated by wage pressures gains additional support. A wholly different scenario has been argued to account for the very residualist Australian social security system. Castles (1985) explains Australian residualism by reference to the power of labour – a power sufficiently strong to assure sustained and practically guaranteed full employment and, hence, a lesser need for public income maintenance. Kewley (1985) also emphasizes the successful resistance of the friendly societies to state social security in Australia.

The mix of private and public welfare provision must be taken into account if we want to understand labour-movement strategies. If we examine the issue in broad, aggregate, comparative terms, there is very little doubt that labour movements have concentrated their efforts on the public sector. But this does not imply that they are principally adverse to the private sector. A closer historical inspection will show that in many cases the labour movements first opted for a strategy based on industrial relations. This is broadly the Australian case, by and large the impulse behind French pension evolution, and describes even the Swedish LO's struggle over the ATP pensions in the 1950s.

Indeed, the relationship between labour and the private/public mix is exceedingly murky. We can identify many cases in which trade unions initially sponsored a private occupational model and subsequently shifted to a statist strategy. A plausible hypothesis is that this change was caused by power-failure; namely, the incapacity of the trade unions to obtain what they desired via direct negotiations. It would appear obvious that a trade-union decision to delegate reforms to the political level assumes a labour party in office. But, again, this may not always be the case. Take the Norwegian story of ATP pensions, in which a conservative cabinet implemented the trade-union-led reform in the 1960s.

A hallmark of private plans is their unequal distribution, benefiting primarily upper-level white-collar employees; where they extend to blue-collar workers, it is primarily within strongly unionized sectors. Originally, private plans were a prerogative of management and civil servants, only gradually disseminated to the middle layers of corporate hierarchies. It is no secret that private plans were erected for the purpose of rewarding and soliciting employee loyalties. Even in the United States, with its widely developed private welfare system, private plans remain class-distinct. The point here is that, as such, they fit more closely to a model of industrial relations which is decentralized, fragmented, and occupationally segmented. Clearly, centralized, nation-wide trade-union models like the Swedish have difficulties with the divisive and inegalitarian features of private welfare. It is telling that the occupational plans that do exist in Sweden are modelled along the lines of universalism.

Hence, a general hypothesis that emerges is that the proliferation of private welfare is more likely to occur when: (1) labour markets are segmented; (2) trade unionism and industrial relations are decentralized and heavily crafts-based; (3) where white-collar and middle-class groups have interest associations (or unions) that are sharply differentiated from general blue-collar unions; and (4) when labour markets become increasingly differentiated. This point will be addressed again below since the on-going 'post-industrialization' of the labour market is likely to crystallize a restructuration of the 'social division of welfare' and produce greater differentiation.

Summing up, the impact of labour movements on welfare policy is far from straight and direct. Where the causal mechanism is most straightforward, as in Scandinavia, the conditions were unique: a pre-existing, pre-industrial framework of social homogeneity; a pervasive sense of consensus and solidarity; a chronically weak and divided right; an unusually strong symbiosis between centralized and universalistic trade unionism and social democratic parties capable of broad popular alliances. Over the long haul, the political parties have probably been the principal actors in social policy, but often – and increasingly – basic initiatives have emerged from the unions; especially where reforms influence the labour market.

In the 'conservative' regimes, the influence of the labour movements was historically often blocked, whether through anti-socialist laws, authoritarian rule, fascism, or, occasionally, the labour movements' own decisions to oppose the state. In the post-war era, their influence has been strongly filtered through denominational trade unionism (and working-class 'Christian democratic' voting); their direct impact, as labour *per se*, has been more marginal. It should be noted, however, that true to the corporative tradition, trade unions and associations have often played a central role in setting up and administering local welfare funds.

Further, in 'liberal' regimes, the influence of labour movements has been of least consequence, being primarily confined to occupational welfare schemes through collective bargaining. In Britain, the Labour Party took much of the glory for implementing post-war welfare statism, but its design and impetus were largely liberal;

in Australia, another 'liberal' regime with strong labour influence, it is symptomatic that labour's political influence remained fairly weak, while its labour-market strength was consistently strong.

It can be argued that the entire question of labour-movement power and welfare-state development should be stood on its head. If it is the case that the regimes, or families of nations, that we can identify were, in a sense, historically prefigured during the process of nation- and state-building, industrialization, and cleavage structuration in the eighteenth and nineteenth centuries – as, for example, Rokkan (1971), Barrington Moore (1967), Flora and Alber (1981), Rimlinger (1971), and Briggs (1961) strongly suggest – the labour-movements' role cannot have been decisive in the original institutional designs, but only in their subsequent evolution. Put differently, it is very possible that the institutional characteristics that differentiate welfare-state clusters owe their origins and evolutionary logic to an epoch that antedates labour's emergence as a real political force.

If we accept this, and if we also accept the strong possibility that once a given system has been institutionalized it is more likely to dictate the terms of labour-movement evolution – rather than vice versa – we are compelled to rethink the historical role of labour movements in the development of social policy. In turn, such a rethinking would suggest the hypothesis that labour-movement power matters *little* in explaining regimes, clusters, or 'families of nations', but matters *chiefly* in explaining intra-regime variations. Thus, it is less likely that labour-movement variations can explain the differences in regime between, say, Sweden and Austria. What it can explain are differences in welfare-state accomplishment within a given regime-type; say, the unequal development of the Swedish and Norwegian welfare state, of the Canadian and American welfare state, or of the Austrian and Italian welfare state.

Turning received wisdom on its head in this way permits a major theoretical revaluation. First, it indicates that the theoretical schism between the 'modernization' and 'power mobilization' approach may find a synthesis: the question of power mobilization receives its real significance within given institutional settings, and no explanation of welfare states can be reduced to either one or the other historical force. Secondly, it accentuates the critical importance of studying the labour-movement–welfare-state problem as a cybernetic phenomenon: welfare states *may* be influenced by labour, but labour-movement evolution is, itself, affected by the institutions of the welfare state. It is to the latter that we now turn.

Welfare States in the Structuration of Labour

Most research has concentrated on the impact of labour movements on welfare policy; few have examined the issue in reverse. It is none the less clear that the welfare state cum welfare market has become a major influence in directing economic and social change. It is, indeed, hard to imagine that a welfare state which redistributes up to half of the GDP would not have a tremendous effect on social stratification and class structuration.

In this section, I shall be unable to furnish anything resembling an exhaustive overview. The aim is, rather, to highlight some of the most decisive ways in which social policies influence contemporary economic restructuration. The discussion will focus first on the formal economy; secondly, on the informal economy; and, thirdly, on the 'non-work' economy.

The Formal Economy
One of the revolutions in our time is the degree to which labour markets have become managed by welfare-state programmes. The change has been especially dramatic in the terrain of social-service production and female employment. The two intersect.

Comparatively speaking, there are great international differences in the growth of the new social-service economy (health, education, and welfare services). Scandinavia is in the undisputed and unsurprising vanguard; continental Europe is the laggard. In Sweden, it accounts for 26 per cent of total employment; 21 per cent in the United States, but only 12 per cent in Germany. These differences have, of course, many roots, but the main cause lies in the nature of welfare-state regimes, especially in their relative transfer/collective services bias. Where welfare states have been heavily weighted in favour of transfers, as is the case in Germany and the other continental European nations, the state's capacity to expand social services is fiscally limited. The bias against services is also deeply rooted in the Catholic principle of subsidiarity and the commitment to retaining the family's traditional role as the nucleus of social-care functions. When we consider the strong social Catholic influence on these countries' welfare-state designs, it is unlikely that that they would have furnished massive social-service employment growth anyhow.

In the United States, about half of the social and health services are to be found in the private economy. Certainly, private-sector social services are nourished by government tax expenditures, and their employment dividend must thus be regarded as implicitly a 'welfare-state' effect. Still, private-sector social services generate a different employment mix: a relatively large share of managers, administrators, and billing clerks. It is said, for instance, that an average American hospital employs at least thirty billing employees, and that administrative costs absorb 22 per cent of total US health expenditures.[1]

It comes as no surprise that the social services are an important source of female employment growth. In Sweden, the social services account for 85 per cent of *total* and *female* employment growth in the past two decades. With Sweden's rigorous solidarity wage policy, it is highly unlikely that female employment growth would have been so staggering had there not been the welfare state as employment generator. The lower and generally stagnant participation rates of women in countries like Germany, Italy, or Holland can best be attributed to the absence of child-care and other social services, combined with the lack of an expanding welfare-state labour market (and certainly also the lack of tax reform in the direction of complete individual taxation). In the United States, women have benefited from growth of the social services as well, although the female bias is somewhat less pronounced than in Scandinavia.

Now, if we combine these twin effects of the welfare state, we see readily the crystallization of consequences in the labour market. In Sweden, gender is sectorally divided, with women overwhelmingly concentrated in the welfare state. This has recast the framework of collective bargaining and industrial strife. Government's need to hold back wage growth has meant that tensions have mounted between public- and private-sector white-collar unions – to the point where this has become the chief axis of conflict in the labour market. Unions representing private-sector workers are increasingly unwilling to participate in solidaristic, comprehensive wage settlements, symptomized by a cascade of strikes (such as in banking) during the 1980s.

In countries like Germany, the lack of adequate progress as regards female employment is likely to generate serious tensions along the 'insider–outsider' axis (indeed, the German public sector remains heavily male-dominated). In the United States, a massive demand for female workers exists, but, unlike Sweden, its concentration in the private sector suggests that expansion in women's employment has occurred against the backdrop of significant sex-based wage differentials. It is not surprising that the debate on equal pay has come to such prominence in the United States over the past decade.

The Informal Economy

Given the absence of hard data, our discussion here can be no more than speculative. There is, however, little doubt that the informal economy is fuelled by, and maybe even dependent on, the welfare state. On one side, the informal economy represents an escape route from the high labour costs due to taxation and strong unions. On the other, it offers an entry point for welfare-state clients such as early retirees, the unemployed, and the disabled, as well as for groups excluded from the formal economy (often women and immigrants). In some cases, much of the informal economy owes its vitality to the indirect kind of wage subsidization implied by welfare-state clientelism. In Italy, it is estimated that maybe half of the early retirees and half of the workers in Cassa Integrazione (long-term unemployment) simultaneously work in the informal economy. Recipients of unemployment benefit or pensions will tend to view their work in the informal economy as a means to supplement household income. They do not need social insurance coverage and their marginal benefit may be high despite the lower pay. Clearly, this kind of 'welfare-state' labour force has a distortive impact on welfare-state finances, on wage formation, and on industrial relations generally.

It is, additionally, very likely that the informal economy is fuelled by the lack of growth in social-service jobs. Where female labour supply is in excess of demand in the official economy, it will look towards the informal economy. Del Boca (1987) argues that the Italian underground economy employs about 2.2 million women workers, very often concentrated in precarious, home-based, outwork types of production. Hence, where welfare states directly or indirectly fuel employment in the informal economy, they will tend to nourish an invisible, flexible labour force.

The Non-work Economy

There are great variations in nations' management of 'de-industrialization' and structural change. Briefly, the Scandinavian approach relied heavily on a strategy based on the welfare state of retraining and re-employing redundant workers. These countries not only averted mass unemployment and mass early retirement, but they also managed to increase overall participation in the labour force; the non-work economy actually shrank. The EEC countries, in turn, opted for the opposite strategy, seeking to reduce labour supply, especially with the aid of early retirement schemes.

The consequences can be quite dramatic. Germany's overall participation rate is a full 16 per cent less than the Swedish. A large share of this 'employment gap' is attributable to early retirement.

In the EEC group of countries, participation rates of older (male) workers has declined to less than 50 per cent. With the concomitant lack of expansion in solid employment, the result is that entry to the labour force for women and young people has been severely blocked. Thus, the incidence of long-term unemployment is particularly high.

Where this scenario obtains, we see the contours of a new insider–outsider structure, one that has close affinity to van Parijs' (1987) scenario of swelling armies of labour-force outsiders, barred from entry; a world in which jobs, as such, tend to become assets in their own right and, therefore, the object of distributional (and re-distributional) struggles.

Trade unions and industrial relations are likely to be deeply affected by such trends. First, as clearly evolved in Germany, the trade unions themselves align their strategic behaviour to the early retirement/work-reduction solution. Whether it is by means of social pacts or merely implicit deals, the unions see no other option but to participate actively in employment reduction; whether they really believe in it or not, the unions can at least hope that early retirement (or reduction of hours) redistributes the declining stock of jobs in favour of young people and women.

More broadly, where labour markets evolve into an insider system, the trade unions can hardly avoid following suit. Structurally, unions are intended to represent the employed. Where the divide between the employed and the surplus population deepens, so will the unions' imprisonment in an insider strategy solidify. They will likely be caught in the cross-fire between the employed, protesting against the mounting fiscal burden of pensions and welfare expenditures, and the outsiders, protesting against the rigidity of the labour market while at the same time demanding improved social benefits. In turn, this cross-fire may intensify by its own logic since the productivity dividend of a slimmed-down insider economy will permit the unions to negotiate what Freeman and Medoff (1984) call monopoly union wages, and because fear of future pension guarantees will motivate unions to bargain for private plans for their members.

Evolving Scenarios

There seem to be as many future scenarios as there are academics. Most of them are extrapolations from concurrent trends, but there are two or three general scenarios that adequately sum up the debate: the jobless growth model; the trend towards firm-based micro-regulation; and the new service economy model.

The Jobless Growth Model

We have already touched upon the scenario of a technology-driven growth with a low employment multiplier. In this model – largely associated with highly competitive, technologically advanced, export-led economies, such as West Germany – industry retains its international position by means of restructuration, increasing capital-intensive production technologies combined with massive lay-offs, and a strong emphasis on research. The system will shed its erstwhile 'Fordist', typically unskilled mass workers (absorbed by early retirement), and concentrate on functionally flexible, more highly qualified manpower (Kern and Schumann, 1984; Boyer, 1988). Traditionally labour-intensive production will be exported, and the macro-economy will thus be characterized by high-value-added products that can continue to support high labour costs. The jobless growth model is distinctive in its inability to stimulate compensatory employment in the services (due to high labour costs), especially if trade unionism remains fairly centralized and strong; a large informal economy is prevented from growing.

There are two principal problems regarding social policy associated with this model. One is demographic, since the combination of population ageing and work-force reduction will create huge burdens on the social security system. As the welfare-state clienteles mushroom, the system provokes a zero-sum trade-off between benefit reductions and higher taxes and contributions. Where social security benefits stagnate or decline (and where fiscal strains in the welfare state suggest an uncertain future), the chances are that private-sector welfare plans will thrive and grow – among the more privileged employee groups in particular. This is the second problem. A vicious circle may emerge as the momentum of private occupational welfare grows: the welfare state will lose its relative importance among the employed middle classes who, as a consequence, will reduce their political support for the public welfare state and, instead, use their political clout to promote favourable tax treatment of private plans.

Hence, the jobless growth model may promote an 'Americanization' of the welfare system. As employee occupational welfare spreads, the welfare state will become increasingly residualistic, catering principally to targeted social clienteles. The more vulnerable among the outsider 'surplus population', such as the unskilled early retirees, the long-term unemployed, and single parent households, are high-risk groups of the poor.

The Intra-firm Welfare State

Flexibilization is often held up as a new mode of management, work, and enterprise organization. It may go hand-in-hand with the 'German' 'post-Fordist' scenario depicted above, or with the Emilia Romagna model of small, flexible enterprises. In any case, flexibilization incurs a shift in the locus of bargaining from the central to the local and firm level, to what Regini (1991) calls micro-regulation. The tradition of uniform industry- or nation-wide agreements will fade as the emphasis shifts to local deals that are tailored to the specific demands and characteristics of the internal labour force. The outcome is almost certainly greater differentiation in the labour force, and the welfare of individual workers will be more closely tied to the performance of discrete firms.

The trend towards intra-firm welfare is emerging equally powerfully in the framework of the large transnational or multinational corporations. Firms whose operations span a diversity of nations, are developing their own internal welfare state apparatuses independently of nation-specific legislation. Thus, IBM has its own internal labour adjudication system, and the EEC Commission has granted the Airbus Industries permission to exempt itself from national social insurance, providing instead its own corporate welfare plans.

The upshot of either trajectory (and both are evolving concomitantly) is that a growing section of the labour force may be divorcing itself from dependence on the traditional, nationally confined welfare state cum industrial relations system. In the case of the multinational corporation, the drift is certainly associated with the rising internationalization of the professional/managerial class for which the conventional welfare state would appear inaccessible and irrelevant. It is also to be expected that firm-based welfare (the welfare firm?) will augment dualisms (or segmentation) in both the labour market and welfare state. If a growing proportion of the labour force bargains for its needs and interests within the firm, the conventional trade-union cum welfare-state apparatus will find its sphere reduced. Besides dualism, 'welfare firmism' will surely augment inequalities and welfare differentials. In the case of the United States, for example, it has been shown that ESOPs (employee stock ownership plans) are growing very vigorously as the new fringe benefit; however, they benefit disproportionally the new technical cadres in the high-tech vanguard industries.

In extreme cases, the entire logic of industrial relations, as we traditionally know it, may decompose as boundaries between managers, technicians, professionals, and workers become fluid, and as the labour input being transacted consists of specialized *individual* know-how. Trade unions are capable of bargaining on the price of hours – much less the price of brain-power.

The New Service Economy

There are two principal trends at play in the evolving service economy. Both pose severe problems for the future of social policy. In countries where low-level service jobs grow rapidly, such as in the American 'MacJobs' scenario, they do so precisely because of low wages. Even for a full-time worker, wages are often inadequate to guarantee against poverty.[2] In this situation, we may be facing the creation of a new service-proletariat whose size may be considerable (perhaps 8–10 per cent of the US labour force). In some countries, Scandinavia particularly, functionally equivalent unskilled service jobs grow inside the welfare state (hospital attendants and home helpers, for example), but without the associated low-pay problem. In the EEC nations, such as Germany and the Netherlands, this class cannot grow – in the private sector, due to trade-union policies and high indirect labour costs; in the public sector, due to fiscal constraints in social-service expansion.

An understanding of the new post-industrial proletariat will depend very much on its sectoral concentration, and on its life-cycle profile. If, as in Sweden, it is almost entirely concentrated in the welfare state, the social problem is less likely to involve income poverty. In any case, whether in the private or public sector, the risk is that a new service proletariat will become institutionalized and permanent. It is here that the life-cycle profile is decisive. If these jobs are largely filled with first-time entrants to the labour market (young people, older women, or immigrants) who subsequently pursue genuine careers, the welfare implications are entirely different than if it is manned by persons whose entire labour-market careers are confined therein.

In the American 'extreme' case, there is considerable evidence that the first interpretation may be true; that is, the service-sector proletariat is very much a youth/immigrant labour market. But, if it consolidates itself into a ghetto and, consequently, if the 'post-industrial' economy produces a new segmentation or dualism, the existing social policy apparatus is highly inadequate. First, service-proletarian jobs are insecure, typically temporary, usually offer no or little training or career advancement, and often virtually guarantee poverty status. In this sector, trade unions are the exception and traditional arrangements for social protection are usually marginal. And, if the probability of outward mobility is low, the average worker will be likely to face a poverty carousel: moving between low-paid jobs and various forms of social assistance, all depending on the business cycle and forces beyond individual control.

Emerging Policies

The dramatic reconstitution of our economies that has been under way for the past decade has compelled massive structural change in labour markets and industrial relations. Among the most important trends, we find the following:

1 a new burst of occupational and social differentiation, particularly centred on the new professional jobs;
2 new forms of segmentation and dualism, giving rise to, respectively, a new service proletariat or a surplus population of outsiders to the labour market;
3 micro-regulation and 'welfare firmism' at the national and international level.

In this context, new developments in social policy are under way, some of which have already been addressed. First, several factors conspire to promote a new burst in private-sector welfare. The rise of the new international managerial-professional class will promote corporate or supra-national welfare schemes; swelling of social security schemes induced by the demographic and labour supply is creating fears that future public pensions will be jeopardized. In many of the new post-industrial occupations and sectors, trade unionism is weak or absent or, perhaps, experiencing a return to the logic of craft unionism. Where this occurs, the tradition of collectively agreed wages and benefits will erode. Hence, with privatization generally, we may also expect greater individualization, or sectionalism.

Secondly, whether we see a growth of an outsider 'surplus population' or a post-industrial proletariat at the bottom end of the new class structure, the existing welfare-state apparatus is inadequate. It seems to me that the solutions to either scenario are evolving along two lines. One is a supply-side response, currently being given the main emphasis in the form of active labour-market training programmes. This approach assumes employment growth, and that the problem is mainly a mismatch of skills and vacancies. The other flows from a more pessimistic assumption about employment growth, emphasizing either reduction of working time or a guaranteed minimum citizen's income (or, perhaps, a combination of the two).

There is in the making a third model, in principle capable of synthesizing the previous two. This we could call the active life-cycle approach to social policy. In part, it is a response to existing rigidities in the relationship between the welfare state and work; in part, it is presented as a means of enhancing individual liberty and welfare. In brief, the approach would substitute existing incidence-defined social programmes (unemployment, sickness, maternity, disability, and old-age insurance) with some kind of two-tier fluid citizen's wage: a basic, minimum guarantee supplemented with a work-income-related supplement earned by way of credits. This is presented as a system in which individuals can flexibly enter and exit from the labour market across their life-cycle for a variety of reasons, such as retraining and education, family formation, vacations or sabbaticals, or temporary retirement. On one side, this kind of model holds the promise of greater mobility in the labour market; on the other, it should encourage more efficient utilization of manpower. It would, undoubtedly, be hugely expensive.

Notes

1 Information provided by Professor Vincent Navarro in private correspondence.
2 In the United States, the average hourly earnings of workers in eating and drinking establishments is only 44 per cent of average hourly manufacturing wages (Bureau of Labor Statistics, *Employment and Earnings*. Washington, DC).

References

Barrington Moore, J. (1967) *The Social Origins of Dictatorship and Democracy*. Boston: Beacon Press.

Boyer, R. (1988) *The Search for Labor Market Flexibility*. Oxford: Oxford University Press.

Briggs, A. (1961) 'The Welfare State in Historical Perspective', *European Journal of Sociology*, 1.

Castles, F. (1985) *The Working Class and Welfare*. London: Allen & Unwin.

Castles, F. (1989) 'Big Governments in Weak States', *CEPR Discussion Papers*, Canberra: Australian National University.

Del Boca, D. (1987) 'Women in a Changing Workplace', in J. Jenson, E. Hagen and C. Reddy (eds), *Feminization of the Labour Force*. Oxford: Polity Press.

Esping-Andersen, G. (1990) *The Three Worlds of Welfare Capitalism*. Oxford: Polity Press; Princeton, NJ: Princeton University Press.

Flora, P. and Alber, J. (1981) 'The Historical Core and Changing Boundaries of the Welfare State', in P. Flora and A. Heidenheimer (eds), *The Development of Welfare States in Europe and America*. London: Transaction Books.

Flora, P. and Heidenheimer, A. (1981) *The Development of Welfare States in Europe and America*. London: Transaction Books.

Freeman, R. and Medoff, J. (1984) *What do Unions Do?* New York: Basic Books.

Kern, H. and Schumann, M. (1984) *Das Ende der Arbeitsteilung?* Munich: G.H. Beck.

Kewley, T. (1985) *Social Security in Australia.* Sydney: Sydney University Press.

Korpi, W. (1978) *The Working Class in Welfare Capitalism.* London: Routledge & Kegan Paul.

Korpi, W. (1980) 'Social Policy and Distributional Conflicts in the Capitalist Democracies', *West European Politics*, 3.

Korpi, W. (1983) *The Democratic Class Struggle.* London: Routledge & Kegan Paul.

Pampel, F. and Williamson, J. (1985) 'Age Structure, Politics, and Cross-national Patterns of Public Pension Expenditures', *American Sociological Review*, 50.

Pampel, F. and Williamson, J. (1988) 'Welfare Spending in the Advanced Democracies, 1950–1980', *American Journal of Sociology*, 93.

Regini, M. (1991) *Confine Mobile.* Bologna: Il Mulino.

Rimlinger, G. (1971) *Welfare and Industrialization in Europe, America and Russia.* New York: John Wiley.

Rokkan, S. (1971) *Citizens, Elections, Parties.* Oslo: Universitetsforlaget.

Shalev, M. (1983) 'The Social Democratic Model and Beyond', *Comparative Social Research*, 6.

Stephens, J. (1979) *The Transition from Capitalism to Socialism.* London: Macmillan.

van Kersbergen, K. (1991) 'Social Capitalism'. PhD Dissertation, European University Institute, Florence.

van Parijs, P. (1987) 'A Revolution in Class Theory', *Politics and Society*, 15(4).

Wilensky, H. (1975) *The Welfare State and Equality.* Berkeley, CA: University of California Press.

Wilensky, H. (1981) 'Leftism, Catholicism, Democratic Corporatism', in P. Flora and A. Heidenheimer *The Development of Welfare States in Europe and America.* London: Transaction Books.

Wilensky, H. and Lebaux, (1958) *Industrial Society and Social Welfare.* New York: Russel Sage.

5

Trade Unions and the Disaggregation of the Working Class

Richard Hyman

In the 1970s, academic analysis of labour movements was strongly influenced by perspectives of political exchange and neo-corporatist interest intermediation. Except in certain countries where ideologically differentiated unions and confederations competed for affiliation and support, the claims of labour movements to be *representative* of labour were rarely regarded sceptically. Even where such divisions did exist, it was not usually considered problematic that the ensemble of unions were genuine and legitimate intermediators of working-class interests. There were three main reasons for most academics to take trade unions' claims at face value: neo-corporatist relations conveyed a 'public status' (Offe, 1985), underwriting unions' role as representatives (and often exclusive representatives) of their constituencies; the consequent strengthening of organizational resources helped overcome the Olsonian dilemmas of collective action; and rising union membership appeared to symbolize representational credibility. Thus analysts of trade unionism could identify a virtuous circle whereby external recognition of unions' credentials as working-class intermediators helped sustain workers' own identification with the unions, reinforcing in turn the case for recognition.

The basis for such confidence has long evaporated. According to Müller-Jentsch (1988), unions in the 1980s have faced three crises: of interest aggregation; of employee loyalty; and of representativeness. These three themes are of course interconnected. They link, moreover, to a fourth crisis, that of organizational sclerosis. 'Movements such as unionism have a life history: infancy, youth, maturity, old age, and death' (Touraine, 1986: 157). For pessimistic (or merely realistic?) analysts, trade unions have become institutionally consolidated on the basis of historically inherited constituencies and projects, and have generated procedural routines and internal systems of vested interests which are resistant to the radical changes which new circumstances require.

While it is impossible to discuss any of these issues in isolation,

the central theme of this chapter is the problem of interest aggregation and disaggregation. Many of the difficulties which beset trade
unions in the 1980s have been attributed to a growing diversification – or, indeed, conflict – of interests within each national working class. (The issue of *inter*national class relations is of growing
importance, indeed, but involves considerations too complex to be
pursued here.)

Disaggregation is not a simple concept. It denotes a variety of
processes, which are perhaps empirically but not logically
interdependent:

1 a shift from collectivism towards individualism, reflected in
declining levels of trade-union membership, and/or reduced
responsiveness to collectively determined policies and disciplines;
2 a polarization within the working class (which may largely coincide with a division between union members and non-unionists)
which many writers characterize in terms of core–periphery or
insider–outsider relations;
3 a growing particularism of collective identities and projects in
terms of employer, occupation, and/or economic sector or
industry;
4 fragmentation within the 'organized working class' expressed in
intra- and inter-union conflict, and a weakening of the authority
of national leaderships and central confederations.

The diagnosis of disaggregative tendencies is a familiar component of recent literature produced both by academic analysts and
by trade-union strategists. Trends in the (de)composition of the
working class are commonly employed *post hoc* as explanations of
the problems which (to very different degrees) affect virtually every
labour movement: declining membership, influence and/or effectiveness; a retreat from traditional 'solidaristic' programmes; a
vacuum of integrating policy and strategy. Yet what is the evidence
for the various forms of disaggregation? How closely do they
correlate with trade-union decline, fragmentation, and disorientation? What are the causal linkages, and are there counteracting
tendencies? Can trade-union movements develop any effective
response?

In the following discussion I cannot claim to offer more than
tentative (and often speculative) responses to these questions. More
complete answers based on systematic evidence would require far
more research than has yet been undertaken by the academic
community, and far more sophisticated theoretical frameworks.
What I seek to accomplish is, first, a survey of arguments which
emphasize disaggregation and its effects on trade unionism;

secondly, a summary of counter-arguments; thirdly, and briefly, an attempt to develop a synthesis from the conflicting positions.

Thesis: Disaggregation, Division and the End of Solidaristic Trade Unionism

Arguments that there has been an intensifying process of disaggregation and division may be grouped into three broad categories: the first concerning conjunctural problems of economic stagnation and recession; the second, longer-term occupational and sectoral shifts, and changes in management policy and the organization of production; the third, more diffuse cultural, institutional, ideological, and political trends.

There are various reasons why economic adversity may be seen as a source of division and disunity. In phases of economic growth it is possible to reconcile competing interests through processes of positive-sum distributional bargaining. Hence, for example, incomes policies designed to improve the relative position of the lowest paid may still permit absolute improvements in the incomes of the better off. More cynically, expansionary times may be seen as a context within which 'skilful bribery' (Streeck 1988: 314) of strategically powerful groups can occur without destroying the overall credibility of 'solidaristic' macroeconomic policies. By contrast, recession tends to transform inter-group competition within the working class into a zero-sum game, increasing the prospects of inter-group conflict. Division may spill over from collective bargaining to the broader political arena; since economic crisis and restructuring are uneven in their impact, the gainers may resist social policies designed to cushion the situation of the losers. In a 'two-thirds, one-third society' (Therborn, 1989), in which the majority prosper economically while a substantial 'underclass' suffers considerable deprivation, unions which seek to support progressive socio-economic programmes may find themselves at odds with more selfish constituents.

Recession, almost by definition, has major effects on structures of employment and unemployment. 'High unemployment changes the structure and functioning of labour markets' (Visser, 1988: 163). One consequence is often to reinforce strategies of social closure on the part of the well-organized, creating serious antagonisms of interest between core, peripheral, and unemployed workers (Kern and Schumann, 1986). For relatively secure employees who are typically most strongly unionized (and tend to dominate union policy-making) to give priority to increasing *aggregate* job opportunities 'requires more than "solidarity" . . . it requires altruism' (Offe, 1985: 89).

Labour-market segmentation has also been intensified by a trend to smaller, more dispersed workplaces; by the growth of part-time, temporary and other 'non-standard' forms of employment; and by what some term the 'flexibilization' policies of 'post-Fordist' employers, whereby a division between core and periphery is deliberately pursued (Atkinson, 1987). Some commentators would also emphasize the growing *internationalization* of labour markets as a force for division within the labour force and an obstacle to effective collective organization. The completion of the European Community's internal market is likely to reinforce such tendencies, as is the removal of barriers between East and West and the introduction of a liberal market regime in Eastern Europe.

The specific conjunctural conditions of the 1980s have inter-acted, often in complex ways, with long-term trends in industrial and occupational structures. In most advanced economies, the blue-collar industrial workers who formed the backbone of traditional labour movements are now a shrinking minority. Manual workers are now generally outnumbered by those in white-collar (or pink-collar) occupations; manufacturing jobs, by those in public and private services. (Whether the classificatory distinctions between manual and white-collar work, or manufacturing and service sectors, are scientifically illuminating can of course be debated; but that real changes have long been taking place in the structure of the economy and the labour force cannot be disputed.)

Such trends have implications, first, for the overall representativeness of trade unions. Levels of union organization are universally higher among manual than among white-collar employees, and in manufacturing as against private-sector services. The changing structure of employment thus seems biased against union membership; some would argue, because of distinctive features of the orientations and life-chances of white-collar/service sector employees. In some countries this bias was offset in the 1960s and 1970s by high and increasing levels of unionization in an expanding public sector; in the changed economic and political environment of the 1980s and 1990s, this expansion has been halted or indeed reversed. Within manufacturing itself, changes in product markets and production systems have brought a restructuring of employment: the decline of many of the old 'smokestack' industries, typically seen as a natural generator of solidaristic collectivism; the growth of new occupational groups with scarce skills and a consequential privileged situation in the labour market. In many countries, unions have faced an uphill struggle in recruiting such workers; some would argue that it is inevitable that 'new skilled workers' will 'prefer individual strategies' (Gulowsen, 1988: 168).

Conversely, many of the growing numbers of workers in private services (particularly women) perform unpleasant, insecure, and low-paid jobs. This new 'servile class' (Gorz, 1989) is expanding precisely because of inferior employment conditions, and unionization faces considerable obstacles.

To specify the problem schematically, one might identify an inverted U-curve of unionization reflecting variations in employment status and labour-market position. Those with professional qualifications or high levels of technical skill may perceive little need for trade-union support; those in the weakest labour-market position may lack the resources and cohesion for collective organization. Historically, unions in most countries have been strongest among intermediate categories of employment: traditional crafts and mass-production jobs. To the extent that patterns of work are shifting towards the extremes, unions seem fated to lose out.

Yet even if unions *do* succeed in organizing sufficient of the expanding sectors of employment to compensate for the decline in their traditional strongholds, other problems may ensue. To the extent that employees in professional, managerial, or administrative positions, or those with technologically advanced skills, possess and perceive distinctive interests, their unionization may prove a source of inter- and intra-union conflicts. Those in higher salaried positions, for example, are likely to resist egalitarian wage policies. Other, more diffuse consequences may stem from occupational and sectoral shifts in patterns of union membership. In most countries, metal workers have traditionally performed a vanguard role (Kassalow, 1987), their negotiations acting as pace-setters for the whole economy; their status within union confederations – as in the case of IG Metall – has then been pivotal. In other countries (Britain, Denmark) without a clear industrial structure to trade unionism, general unions of mainly manual workers have been predominant. But the rise of public- and service-sector, white-collar trade unions has in many cases shifted the balance of power. For example, Kommunal became the largest Swedish union in 1978; a decade later HK has overtaken SiD in Denmark; while in Britain, arrangements are well advanced for the amalgamation of three major public-sector organizations, which if consummated will create the largest union in the country. The new weight of non-traditional sectoral and occupational interests challenges old principles and priorities (Scheuer, 1986), resulting in some cases in disorientation. This may threaten the inter-union consensus which in some countries formerly provided the 'fundamental resource of the system of representation' (Regalia, 1988: 351).

The role of employers has been an important influence on trade unions in the 1980s. In general, the US experience of 'union-busting' has not been replicated in Europe; perhaps because the greater flexibility of collective-bargaining institutions, and in many cases the statutory supports for independent employee representation, present a different constellation of 'strategic choices'. Indeed, in some countries – primarily those of Southern Europe – the dominant trend has probably been the reverse of the American: the visceral anti-unionism once characteristic of the boss class giving way to a more pragmatic attitude to trade unionism and collective bargaining. However, in areas of expanding employment with few traditions of union representation and collective bargaining, employers often do still display strong resistance to unions' organizing efforts. In some countries, moreover, 'deregulation' in employment legislation has made union exclusion policies easier to accomplish.

There have, in addition, been two important trends in most countries in recent years. One has been the growing significance of the plant or company, rather than multi-employer bargaining, for the determination of employment conditions. The other has been the spread of company-level mechanisms of employee participation such as consultative committees or quality circles, typically initiated and controlled by the employer, and hence (at least implicitly) challenging the status of the union as an instrument of employee representation. The resulting 'disaggregation of industrial relations' (Crouch 1986: 10) intensifies the obstacles to solidaristic trade unionism.

Where the key arena of collective bargaining devolves to a lower level, the basis of national union authority is typically undermined (Clegg, 1976). In the 1980s, Sweden probably offered the clearest example of such a process, with a series of disintegrative moves following the initiative of the metal employers, who broke away from inter-industry coordination in 1983 in order to negotiate a separate agreement (Ahlén, 1989; Fulcher, 1987; Lash, 1985). In other countries, efforts by individual employers to achieve company-specific agreements – often linking pay structures, new technology, work reorganization, and the management of working time – have challenged the central control of both national confederations and their individual member unions.

In general, then, it is commonly concluded that the past decade has seen either increased trade-union fragmentation, or at least a relative weakening of centralized authority. A number of distinct processes have been involved. The most general experience has been that shifts in occupational structure, together with the unionization of expanding sectors, have 'tended to undermine the encompassiveness of union movements' (Visser, 1988: 167). This has been reflected, first, in the spread of professional associations, quasi-trade unions and other independent organizations, outside the framework of the central confederations (Cella and Treu, 1985); secondly, in the growth of bona fide trade unions of salaried and professional employees and public officials, affiliated to minority confederations (for example, the TCO or SACO/SR in Sweden, the CGC in France). The quantitative results have been highly significant in some countries, notably in Scandinavia: by the mid-1980s, the LO share of total union membership had fallen to 60 per cent in Sweden, 67 per cent in Norway, and 70 per cent in Denmark (Visser, 1988). In Britain, though the TUC remains one of the most comprehensive of confederations in Europe, the minority of trade unionists outside its ranks had doubled over the past decade and now stands at roughly one fifth of the total. Organizational differentiation of this kind has led Crouch (1990: 359) to pose the question: 'unions may have a long-term future, but do union *movements*?'

In the political arena there have also been major changes, only partly as a consequence of the harsher economic environment. Among the Nordic countries, a conservative regime is entrenched in Denmark, the social democrats suffered defeat in Norway (though returning to office as a minority government), while the Swedish right triumphed in 1991. Germany has undergone a *politische Wende*, the (centre) right is consolidated in power in Belgium and the Netherlands, while the 1980s was the decade of Thatcherite domination in Britain. In those countries where the political complexion of the government was more favourable to the unions than in the 1970s – France, Spain, Greece – the actual benefits were typically ambiguous. Extensions in statutory rights and protections for employees, for example, have not necessarily assisted unions in recruiting and retaining members; on the contrary, trade unions seem to have suffered from their association with the austere economic policies pursued as resolutely by governments of the left as those of the right. The *Umbruch* in Eastern Europe has transformed both state and civil society; as the dust begins to settle, the implications for industrial relations can be at best dimly discerned. Finally, we may note that those Communist parties with a traditionally hegemonic status in the working class have experienced internal conflict and instability, partly as a consequence of developments in the East, partly because of domestic electoral decline; and this has significantly influenced relationships with, and within, 'their' trade unions.

This leads to a consideration of the broader political and ideological influences on trade-union cohesion and solidarity. In the 1960s and 1970s, many trade-union movements benefited from a virtuous circle whereby governments treated them as representative bargaining partners in the determination of macroeconomic policy, and this publicly confirmed status in turn assisted unions in attracting workers' adherence to their organization and support for their policies. But the self-sustaining dynamics of political exchange came under repeated strain in the 1980s. In most countries the economic climate restricted the scope for substantive achievements. Unions had to settle increasingly for procedural and symbolic outcomes, while often being expected to perform a restraining and disciplining role. 'Pluralist political exchange' thus proved increasingly unstable (Baglioni, 1987). In much of Europe, breakdown has followed a deflationary spiral of weakened internal authority and diminished external recognition. This process is in some cases reinforced by a parallel decline in the internal authority of *employers'* organizations; to the extent that companies (particularly major, perhaps transnational firms) seek to negotiate separate agreements (or to impose employment conditions without trade-union mediation), national unions and confederations are deprived of a bargaining partner.

Manifestly, the changed political climate has also reduced external recognition of the representativeness of trade unions (though there is no simple equation between conservative governments and the abandonment of political exchange). The Thatcher regime in Britain is an extreme instance of a more general transformation: casting trade unions as scapegoats for economic decline, rejecting political exchange as a dangerous legitimation of distinctive working-class identity and interests, pursuing market discipline as an alternative and more potent mechanism for achieving moderation in the labour market. Whether or not such ideologically driven shifts in government policy have a persuasive economic rationale, their consequence nevertheless is to 'decompose the intermediary character' of trade unionism (Müller-Jentsch, 1988: 179).

If objective developments undermine collective cohesion and encourage dissaggregation, many would argue that, in addition, the *subjective* sources of sectionalism have become stronger. Whether because of the rise of a 'new individualism' (Zoll, 1988), or as part of a *sauve-qui-peut* response to economic crisis, it is widely held that employees have become less solidaristic, defining their interests either individualistically or in terms of narrow, particularistic collectivities. In the latter case, encompassing policies and projects can be threatened by forceful challenges from below. If economic crisis and the associated instability of labour markets initially reduced rank-and-file assertiveness, there are signs of revival. Where central union control has become weakened – or was never very effective – the result may be a growing disaggregation and differentiation of interest representation: individual unions become loose alliances of semi-autonomous *Betriebsegoisten*, confederations perform an even more marginal role. (Was this the fate of British trade unionism in the 1980s?) Or as in Sweden, higher-status groups held back during a long phase of 'solidaristic' macro-level concertation may use their new weight of numbers to achieve greater autonomy and hence reverse traditional confederal policies. A third variant is seen most clearly in Italy: the rise of COBAS (*comitati di base*), and more recently *rappresentanze sindacali di base*, primarily among skilled or professional groups in the public sector. In effect, this constitutes an unofficial (though increasingly institutionalized) equivalent of craft trade unionism, and seems to have achieved significant success in challenging the 'responsible' bargaining posture of the main confederal leaderships.

Other political changes have also challenged the cohesion of trade-union movements. Fiscal crisis has provoked zero-sum conflicts between public employees and tax-payers employed in private undertakings; where trade unionism is roughly evenly divided between private and public employees, the result is often confusion and instability of policy. When strikes in public services cause disruption which is used by governments as a pretext to whip up anti-union feelings, it can become particularly difficult for unions whose members are consumers of these services to maintain a solidaristic stance. In addition, new policy issues such as the environment threaten to intensify 'political' divisions within unions, and also bring antagonisms between trade unionists as employees (in the nuclear industry, for example) and as 'concerned citizens'.

In sum, the disaggregation thesis appears to match many features of the predicament (crisis?) of trade unionism in the 1980s. For a wide range of commentators, some combination of the factors outlined above can explain *ex post* the problems of trade unionism in the 1980s: membership decline, reduced effectiveness, inter- and intra-union conflict, an 'orientation vacuum' (Offe, 1985) in responding to the challenges of hard times.

Antithesis: Counterarguments and Countertendencies

For many critics, the diagnosis of a crisis of interest aggregation is oversimplified, overgeneralized, and overdeterministic. As is so often the case with both academic and popular discussion, so the counterargument runs, the plausibility of the disaggregation thesis depends heavily on a mythologized vision of the past: a golden age when workers were spontaneously collectivist, and labour organizations joined ranks behind a unifying class project.

History, of course, was never like this. As a general rule, 'labour is atomized and divided by competition' (Offe and Wiesenthal, 1985: 178); hence 'unions develop on the basis of labour market segmentation, and at the same time reinforce this segmentation' (Erd and Scherrer, 1985: 118). Anyone aware of the bitter historical conflicts between craft and general unions in Britain, for example, would perceive little novelty in the disaggregation thesis. In a paper of my own, published a dozen years ago, I argued that 'heterogeneity and uneven development have *always* been characteristic of capitalist economic relations . . . . If ideas of class identity nevertheless developed this was against the odds' (Hyman, 1978: 66). Unions as collective organizations are inevitably rooted in a heterogeneity of immediate, localized experiences and aspirations; *spontaneously* these are as likely to be in conflict as in congruence. The construction of broader solidarities has always required a deliberate and precarious *effort*, a mobilization of bias by leaders and rank-and-file activists; and success, when achieved, has usually proved temporary and partial.

There is thus considerable scope for debate about what exactly has changed, and the salience of particular transformations. Which factors are of central importance for the construction or erosion of collective solidarity, and which of at most secondary significance? Which *combinations* of changes are particularly potent? How automatic are the links between the external environment of unionism and possible outcomes in terms of disorganization and disaggregation?

It seems clear that, although many labour movements in the 1980s have been afflicted by centrifugal fragmentation and loss of representativity, there is no internationally uniform pattern. *Rappresentatività* is itself a salient public issue only in certain countries: notably, where trade-union movements are ideologically divided, and/or where an anti-union government has sought to challenge unions' public standing. The impact of occupational and sectoral shifts in employment has been very different according to national context; in some cases contributing to a sharp decline in aggregate union density, in others diminishing the relative significance (in terms of membership and influence) of the principal union confederation, in yet others resulting in far more diffuse and uncertain changes in trade-union character. The role of unions

- everywhere, indeed, composed disproportionately of relatively secure and advantaged sections of the work-force - as bearers of anti-egalitarian interests is likewise internationally variable. In part, this is because the rigidity of labour-market segmentation, and also the composition of peripheral groups, differ considerably between countries; in part because the will and ability of union policy-makers to press solidaristic strategies also display marked contrasts. Structurally, too, the impact of the crisis decade of the 1980s has been far from uniform: if organizational fragmentation has been one outcome, another has been a trend towards inter-union cooperation and even amalgamation as a means of consolidating diminished resources. Hence it is not difficult to construct a very different reading of the 1980s from that outlined above, and accordingly to draw far more optimistic conclusions for the 1990s.

Any general assertion of a trend from collectivism to individualism can be disputed as a one-sided reading of a complex and varied set of cultural processes. While trade-union activists and ideologues may have traditionally viewed collectivism as a moral value in its own right, it is perhaps realistic to assume that - apart from moments of the enthusiasm of mass mobilization - most union members have adhered to collective organization for instrumental reasons: the most effective means of realizing individual needs and aspirations. In Britain, for example, nineteenth-century craft unions functioned to an important extent as 'friendly societies', providing an extensive range of insurance benefits (covering such contingencies as death, sickness, unemployment, loss of tools, and retirement). This function became marginalized only with the development of comprehensive state welfare provision, and with fluctuations in price levels and labour-market conditions which disrupted the actuarial basis of trade-union benefit arrangements. In this sense, recent union attempts to recruit and retain members by offering a package of individual services is actually a return to an ancient tradition.

In any event, it may be misleading to view the development of collective bargaining as a predominant function of unionism as primarily an expression of collectivist and solidaristic principles. Typically, it has reflected a pragmatic recognition of individual impotence in the face of the employer: collective organization offered an insurance policy against arbitrary management, or a more effective vehicle to support individual economic goals. In this sense, to adapt Durkheim's familiar distinction, unionism has often represented a form of mechanical rather than organic solidarity. In extreme cases, indeed, rank-and-file members may have adhered passively to their union as merely one among the many other bureaucratic institutions associated with the employment relationship. If *this* mode of collectivism has been undermined by a growing anti-authoritarian and anti-productivist mood among (sections of?) the late twentieth-century working class, this is not necessarily a change to be deplored. Indeed, if the meaning of 'new individualism' is actually a greater concern with broader aspects of the quality of life than the old economistic priorities of collective bargaining, this might be seen not simply as a challenge but also as an opportunity for trade unions.

It is also possible to question the thesis that sectoral and occupational shifts in employment are an inevitable source of union weakness and decline. According to Kelly (1990: 34), 'the compositional argument is seriously flawed as an analysis of union decline [in the United Kingdom] on both empirical and theoretical grounds'. Despite the long-term movement of employment away from the traditional strongholds of organization, unions continued to expand their coverage in most countries during the 1960s and 1970s; and some national trade-union movements still grew during the hard decade of the 1980s. There is, Kelly suggests, no reason to assume that 'new' categories of worker are inherently predisposed against collective organization; if they do perceive distinctive interests, it is still in principle possible for unions to orient all their policies successfully to such new membership priorities.

Yet if such employee groups do successfully unionize, will their collective organization and action necessarily distort or dilute the efforts of (some?) labour movements to pursue solidaristic policies? If the dominance of socialist-orientated unions and confederations rooted in the 'old' working class has indeed been reduced in most countries, such trends are not universal. Despite the challenges of 'segmentation, division and centrifugality' in Germany (Markovits, 1986), for example, the DGB in the 1980s has maintained its 83 per cent of all trade unionists, in the process increasing its predominance over the DAG among *Angestellte* and retaining its narrow lead over the DBB among *Beamte*. In all countries, certainly, such traditional groups as coal miners, dockers, printers or steel workers, whose powerful trade unionism was based on close-knit occupational and often also residential communities, have diminished in numbers and influence. Yet if their unions have lost their former hegemony within their national labour movements, this may permit greater reciprocity and evenhandedness in the inter-union negotiation of policy, and may also encourage a more active initiating and coordinating role for central confederations. Greater organizational diversity need not therefore entail fragmentation.

Different issues are raised by analyses which treat the decline of trade unionism based on explicit class-political ideologies as a source of disaggregation. It is undeniable that such 'depoliticization' has been a widespread process. In Southern Europe, for example, a notable feature of recent years has been the relative (and often absolute) decline in membership of communist-orientated confederations. One can say that the CGT (probably) remains the largest confederation in France, and the CGIL in Italy, but both have fared worse than their rivals; in Spain and Portugal the CC.OO. and the CGTP have been overtaken by their socialist counterparts. (Such trends reflect not only the internal disarray within European communism, but also the actions of some governments and employers in favouring their rivals.) The weakening of the 'vanguard' role of a dominant confederation involves, at first sight, a loss of trade-union cohesion. However, this effect – reflecting as it often does the erosion of persistent ideological divisions – may be counteracted by an increase in inter-confederal solidarity (which may itself be encouraged by a more equal numerical balance between the confederations). Such cooperation, even if tentative and unstable, has for some years been evident in Italy; has existed in Spain since the *huelga general* of December 1988; and in Portugal (despite the most Stalinist Communist Party of Western Europe) was signalled by the inter-confederal agreement of March 1989. And in any event, many would dispute whether the stereotyped class rhetoric of orthodox Communist parties and their trade unions bore any real relationship to an emancipatory socialist project.

This connects with an alternative interpretation of developments in the 1980s: that what has occurred is not a crisis of trade unionism as such, but rather the crisis of a traditional style and orientation of trade unionism. In most countries, trade-union principles and practice have always displayed a tension between broad and ambitious assertions of solidarity, often linked to the goal of socialist transformation, and the mundane routines of defending the immediate employment interests of specific categories of members. Three elements of this tension are familiar to all students of industrial relations: the pressure to subordinate aspirations to transcend capitalism to the tactical imperatives of operating within it; the shaping of the agenda of collective bargaining by what can 'realistically' be demanded of employers, suppressing non-economistic aims which challenge management control; and the domination of policy formation by relatively advantaged segments of the working class. The latter tendency is particularly evident, historically, in the experience of craft unionism. In most countries, collective organization first emerged among workers whose particular skills gave them a relative advantage within the labour market. In some cases, union rules and actions were explicitly directed to sustaining and enlarging these advantages, against threatened encroachments both by employers and by other groups of workers (Rubery, 1978). While the 'doctrine of vested interests' (Webb and Webb, 1897) may have become muted over time, the practice which it articulated has remained evident: perhaps imposing on the labour movement as a whole 'the ideology of the radical artisanate [which was] frequently patronizing and intolerant of the class at large and its varying predicament [and] also ill-fitted for the particular needs of an industrial working class' (Eley, 1990: 25).

The relationship between broader and more particularistic communities of interest is complex and contradictory: 'sectional solidarities . . . may be integrative *or* divisive' (Hyman, 1975: 178), or may indeed point in both directions simultaneously. Yet if trade unionism has traditionally involved, in part at least, the mobilization of particularistic strengths in pursuit of particularistic interests, the projects and achievements of trade unionism have accordingly reflected – and perhaps reinforced – the uneven distribution of power and resources within the working class. Such factors as gender, ethnicity, education and training, structuring positions of relative advantage or disadvantage in the labour market, have in turn tended to shape collective strength: resulting both in differential degrees of unionization, and in disparities of influence *within* trade unions. Such inequalities can determine the detailed distribution of benefits (as well as costs) among workers in the process of collective bargaining; they can also shape the broader policy agenda embraced by aggregate labour movements. Hence the familiar argument of many feminists that programmes proclaimed in terms of the principles of class solidarity actually protect the aims and interests of male workers, and indeed of a particular (minority) segment of the male working class (Phillips and Taylor, 1980; Cockburn, 1981).

In many countries in recent years – particularly following the radicalism of the late 1960s – there have been efforts to reorientate trade-union policy to reflect a broader spectrum of interests. Initially, some commentators wrote optimistically of the transformatory potential of the 'new demands' of 'mass workers' (Paci, 1973; Kirchlechner, 1978); such enthusiasms, perhaps because of an oversimplified reading of trends within a 'Fordist' system of manufacturing, now seem distinctly outdated. However, the restructuring of employment *away from* manufacturing industry may be viewed as a more fundamental threat to the trade-union politics of a traditional skilled, male, manual, working-class constituency. For those who regard such trade unionism as the only authentic form, such a threat is of course viewed negatively. From a different perspective, however, the restructuring of employment creates both a need and an opportunity to reconstitute collective relations within the working class: within individual trade unions, between different organizations, and between the unionized and the non-unionized. The growing importance of the female workforce, of part-time and other 'atypical' forms of employment, of non-industrial and non-manual occupations – and the *combination* of such trends – can be seen as a powerful impetus towards a renewal of trade unionism and the development of new demands in collective bargaining, new methods of organization and action, and new forms of internal democracy. Whether such benign consequences do indeed arise depends of course on many contingencies, but cannot be discounted a priori.

What this counterargument implies, above all else, is that unions possess an area of strategic choice in responding to the changes and challenges of late twentieth-century capitalism. There are opportunities for policies which appeal to new working-class constituencies (or often, old sections whose interests have hitherto been neglected); for initiatives which address members' interests outside the workplace, and thus provide a fertile basis for transcending particularistic employment identities; and for programmes which link workers' interests as producers and consumers (as, for example, in demands for the improvement of public health care) so as to enable the construction of new types of encompassing and solidaristic alliances. On this reading, disaggregation is by no means inevitable.

Towards a Synthesis?

Much current debate on the experience of trade unionism in the 1980s and its prospects for the 1990s involves the clash of simplistic generalizations. The problems of numerical decline and lack of internal cohesion are widespread, but not universal afflictions. Individual unions, and different national movements, vary considerably in the efficacy with which they have responded to changes in the economic and political environment and in the nature of the work-force. While developments which may be categorized as instances of disaggregation are near-universal, their nature, causes, and implications differ markedly according to context. In order to understand such differences we need to develop subtle analyses of what are complex and contradictory tendencies; and in order to propose credible scenarios for the next decade we need to be able to separate cyclical (and potentially reversible) from secular trends in the environment of industrial relations. Comparative research is only beginning to suggest the basis for a more scientific approach to the questions discussed above.

In my view, it cannot plausibly be denied that most trade unions in the 1990s face harder times than during the years when economic expansion and positive-sum political exchange were common to most European nations. The risks of disaggregation are now indeed considerable. A decade ago, Ross (1981) raised the question, what is progressive about unions? Perhaps a positive and optimistic answer is even more difficult today than it was at the beginning of the 1980s. But now as then, any answer to the question must be nuanced and differentiated. Not only do the conjunctural circumstances (the depth of the recession, the extent of restructuring, the severity of unemployment and so on) vary considerably from country to country; so too do the character of established industrial relations institutions, the inherited ideologies of the labour movements, and the nature and coherence of trade-union projects and strategies. *All* these factors, I would suggest, significantly influence the scope for solidaristic outcomes from otherwise similar contexts.

Changes in the sectoral and occupational composition of employment, which have occurred universally though at varying rates and from very different origins, undoubtedly *are* important in their implications; but their impact on labour movements is mediated by an array of nationally specific factors. Perhaps the most general point which can be made is that in no country today is it possible to identify an *archetypical* proletarian: old labour-movement icons have lost their unifying force. Yet, was not the old proletarian stereotype – the muscular male hewing coal or hammering metal – always a minority within the working class? Was the hegemony of unions of such workers within national labour movements the basis of real solidarity, or rather (perhaps, also) the source of an artificial and at times narrow-minded uniformity?

The notion of a working class was always an abstraction (and also a rallying cry, in some cases perhaps a self-fulfilling prophecy), never a mere sociological description or generalization. Differentiation, division, and disunity have been omnipresent features of trade-union development. Solidarity is never a natural or fixed quality, always a goal which is at best elusive and ephemeral. Eley (1990: 26), in addressing debates on the early history of the British working class, states the issue succinctly:

> the crucial strategic problem confronting labour movements (or, for that matter, any political movement) was how to mobilize the maximum solidarity from a socially defined constituency which has no *essential unity* in the sphere of consciousness, but on the contrary a series of particularistic loyalties and preferences and a widely differing experience of everyday life, a mosaic of individual histories. The analysis of working-class politics begins with this dialectic – the contradictory and dynamic intersection of unifying and fragmenting tendencies within the class as a whole.

A mythical belief in some previous golden age of proletarian unity and unproblematic trade-union solidarity distorts our perception of current labour-movement dynamics. A more sensitive historical understanding allows us to view the question of dis-aggregation in less cataclysmic terms. Conversely, from historical experience we can learn that there are no short-cuts to the identification and (re)definition of interests in a solidaristic manner; it is always necessary to campaign and struggle for (relative) unity among workers and their organizations. Hence I am uneasy with Streeck's argument (1988: 316) that 'democracy and solidarity may have become incompatible': unity, in my view, cannot be artificially and bureaucratically imposed. Despite adverse circumstances, I suggest, scope remains for strategic initiatives by and within labour movements, allowing new means of transcending divisions and forging common interests. Yet what is certainly required is a new rationale, a new vocabulary of motives, for worker solidarity. Developing the ideals, principles, and practices required for modern forms of solidarity is a momentous, but not impossible task; it may be premature to bid farewell to the working class – or to the labour movement.

Note

My thanks for comments on versions of this chapter to Paul Edwards, Anthony Ferner, Mike Terry, Jeremy Waddington, and participants at conference discussions in Trento and Madrid.

References

Ahlén, K. (1989) 'Swedish Collective Bargaining under Pressure', *British Journal of Industrial Relations*, 27(3).
Atkinson, J. (1987) 'Flexibility or Fragmentation?', *Labour and Society*, 12(1).
Baglioni, G. (1987) 'Constants and Variants in Political Exchange', *Labour*, 1(3).

Cella, G.P. and Treu, T. (1985) 'National Trade Union Movements', in R. Blanpain, (ed.), *Comparative Labour Law and Industrial Relations*. Deventer: Kluwer.

Clegg, H.A. (1976) *Trade Unionism under Collective Bargaining*. Oxford: Blackwell.

Cockburn, C. (1981) *Brothers: Male Dominance and Technological Change*. London: Pluto Press.

Crouch, C. (1986) 'The Future Prospects for Trade Unions in Western Europe', *Political Quarterly*, 57(1).

Crouch, C. (1990) 'Afterword', in G. Baglioni and C. Crouch (eds), *European Industrial Relations*. Beverly Hills, CA: Sage.

Crouch, C. and Pizzorno, A. (eds) (1978) *The Resurgence of Class Conflict in Western Europe since 1968*. London: Macmillan.

Eley, G. (1990) 'Edward Thompson, Social History and Political Culture', in H.J. Kaye and K. McClelland (eds), *EP Thompson: Critical Perspectives*. Cambridge: Polity Press.

Erd, R. and Scherrer, C. (1985) 'Unions: Caught between Structural Competition and Temporary Solidarity', *British Journal of Industrial Relations*, 23(1).

Fulcher, J. (1987) 'Labour Movement Theory versus Corporatism', *Sociology*, 21(2).

Gorz, A. (1989) *Critique of Economic Reason*. London: Verso.

Gulowsen, J. (1988) 'Skills, Options and Unions' in R. Hyman and W. Streeck (eds), *New Technology and Industrial Relations*. Oxford: Basil Blackwell.

Hyman, R. (1975) *Industrial Relations: a Marxist Introduction*. London: Macmillan.

Hyman, R. (1978) 'Occupational Structure, Collective Organisation and Industrial Militancy', in C. Crouch and A. Pizzorno (eds), *The Resurgence of Class Conflict in Western Europe since 1968*. London: Macmillan.

Kassalow, E. (1987) 'Trade Unions and Industrial Relations: Toward the Twenty-first Century', *IRRA Proceedings, 1985*.

Kelly, J. (1990) 'British Trade Unionism 1979–89', *Work, Employment and Society*, Special Issue.

Kern, H. and Schumann, M. (1986) *Das Ende der Arbeitsteilung?* Munich: G.H. Beck.

Kirchlechner, B. (1978) 'New Demands or the Demands of New Groups?' in C. Crouch and A. Pizzorno (eds), *The Resurgence of Class Conflict in Western Europe since 1968*. London: Macmillan.

Lash, S. (1985) 'The End of Neo-corporatism? The Breakdown of Centralised Bargaining in Sweden', *British Journal of Industrial Relations*, 23(2).

Markovits, A.S. (1986) *The Politics of West German Trade Unions: Strategies of Class and Interest Representation in Growth and Crisis*. London: Cambridge University Press.

Müller-Jentsch, W. (1988) 'Industrial Relations Theory and Trade Union Strategy', *International Journal of Comparative Labour Law and Industrial Relations*, 4(3).

Offe, C. (1985) *Disorganized Capitalism*. Cambridge: Polity Press.

Offe, C. and Wiesenthal, H. (1985) 'Two Logics of Collective Action', in C. Offe, *Disorganized Capitalism*. Cambridge: Polity Press.

Paci, M. (1973) *Mercato del lavoro e classi sociali in Italia*. Bologna: Il Mulino.

Phillips, A. and Taylor, B. (1980) 'Sex and Skill', *Feminist Review*, 6.

Regalia, I. (1988) 'Democracy and Unions: Towards a Critical Appraisal', *Economic and Industrial Democracy*, 9(3).

Ross, G. (1981) 'What is Progressive About Unions?' *Theory and Society*, 10(5).

Rubery, J. (1978) 'Structured Labour Markets, Worker Organization and Low Pay', *Cambridge Journal of Economics*, 2(1).

Scheuer, S. (1986) 'Social Structure and Union Character', *Acta Sociologica*, 29(1).

Streeck, W. (1988) 'Editorial Introduction', *Economic and Industrial Democracy*, 9(3).

Therborn, G. (1989) 'The Two-Thirds, One-Third Society', in S. Hall and M. Jacques (eds), *New Times*. London: Lawrence & Wishart.

Touraine, A. (1986) 'Unionism as a Social Movement', in S.M. Lipset (ed.), *Unions in Transition*. San Francisco: Institute for Contemporary Studies.

Visser, J. (1988) 'Trade Unionism in Western Europe: Present Situation and Prospects', *Labour and Society*, 13(2).

Webb, S. and Webb, B. (1897) *Industrial Democracy*. London: Longman.

Zoll, R. (1988) 'Von der Arbeitersolidarität zur Alltagssolidarität', *Gewerkschaftliche Monatshefte*, 6.

6

The Fate of Articulated Industrial Relations Systems: a Stock-taking after the 'Neo-liberal' Decade

Colin Crouch

During the 1970s there had appeared to be a new convergence among Western European societies on a neo-corporatist pattern of industrial relations.[1] Previously the concept of a system of institutionalized collective bargaining had seemed, at least to British observers, to be the most useful way of analysing a 'mature' industrial relations system (for example, see Clegg, 1976). Most academic debate centred on a dispute between those authors who, like Clegg, regarded such a system as a substantive *summum bonum* and those who saw it as primarily a means of suppressing workers' attempts at conflict (Fox, 1974; Hyman, 1975). The idea of neo-corporatism as an extension of the conceptual range available for the delineation of system types raised some new issues. What was essentially being postulated was the possibility that trade unions and employers' organizations might share responsibility for ensuring the overall economic stability, and perhaps even social order, of the society of which they were a part.

The same old debates over whether for labour organizations this constituted a rational form of action or a betrayal of members' true interests continued unabated, and, indeed, intensified, within this framework, but some genuine novelties had been introduced. A system of collective bargaining is in a state of equilibrium when conflict issues are institutionally separated from one another and from political conflict and when there is a situation of pluralism – that is, a situation in which a mass of uncoordinated groups competes, none being able to dominate, within a political equivalent of the competitive market. But a neo-corporatist system is in equilibrium when, far from being institutionally contained within their separate sphere, industrial relations are involved in the maintenance of an overall political order. And, far from the free-market criterion of pluralist stability of a mass of competing interest groups, corporatist theory posits an oligopoly of large, non-competing organizations.

Although the concept of neo-corporatism has had its vicissitudes and misunderstandings, there is now a reasonable consensus concerning it among observers. There remains room for debate over the place of centralization as an attribute of neo-corporatist organizations. It is very common for corporatist organizations to be described as centralized, or even for levels of centralization to stand as proxies for measures of corporatism. By 'centralization' researchers usually have in mind the extent to which decisions are concentrated in the hands of leaderships at national (or possibly sectoral) level. But organizations of that kind run a considerable risk of membership revolt. For that not to be the case there must be effective devices for ensuring either (1) that the membership is passive; or (2) that any activism of the rank and file is contained within forms and goals consistent with and interdependent with the strategy of the national leadership. Kjellberg (1983), for example, points out that it is erroneous to describe Scandinavian trade unions as centralized, because there is also within them a very active shop-floor movement; but much of the time that movement has worked with rather than (as in Britain) against the grain of confederal policy.

Kjellberg does not, however, make adequately clear the need for these two (or more) levels of activism to be joined to or integrated with each other in some way if they are not to run the risk of frustrating each other's purpose. I therefore prefer to use the term 'articulated' rather than 'centralized' to describe organizations of this kind, keeping 'centralized' to describe structures where the central leadership concentrates power in itself with a *passive* membership.

Although conceptual clarity on the meaning of 'neo-corporatism' may have been achieved among academic observers during the 1980s, in the practical world many of the assumptions that favoured neo-corporatist developments were severely questioned by advocates of neo-liberal, or new right, strategies of economic management. The reasons for this will be considered in due course, and a major aim of the chapter is to examine how thorough-going was any rejection of the earlier neo-corporatist trend. First, however, we must consider how extensive that trend itself had in reality been.

Industrial Relations in the 1970s

With the exception of the two Alpine nations (Austria and Switzerland) and the Iberian nations still under dictatorial rule, all countries in Western Europe had experienced a resurgence of industrial conflict and institutional instability at some time between 1968 and 1970. Then, after 1973, the first 'oil shock' produced a wave of inflation and decline in purchasing power throughout the Western world that wreaked havoc with expectations and institutions. Virtually everywhere the response of governments to this crisis was, at least until the late 1970s, to appeal to central organizations of capital and labour to help restore stability. In turn, these organizations in the main accepted that they had some responsibility for national success and stability.[2] This was the source of an apparent neo-corporatist convergence, though in some cases these appeals were abrupt, new interventions; in others they were rooted in existing behaviour.

The Scandinavians had been engaged in relations of this kind since the late 1930s, but gradually over the years the whole process had become more intricate. During the 1970s bargaining in these countries came to be focused on the highly technical basis of models of the national economies which gave special emphasis to the relationship between domestic and 'imported' inflation levels – the Norwegian Aukrust and Swedish EFO models (Flanagan et al., 1983, chs 4 and 6; Aukrust, 1977; Edgren et al., 1973). Alongside this, unions and employer organizations were also involved with the government in the *administration* of much public policy, not just consultation. Labour-market policy (in particular, occupational training) and social policy as much as straight wage-bargaining were the meat of relations between national, cross-industry employers' organizations and national union peak organizations. But it was not just centralized action; regional, branch-level and local organizations had a place within the structure (Kjellberg, 1983). This was neo-corporatism on the basis of articulated organizations.

Similar institutions for national participation by union leaderships existed in Austria, Germany, and Switzerland, though in the latter cases in particular there was primary emphasis on the level of the economic branch and, within that framework, the individual company, rather than the nation as a whole. These systems were articulated ones but, especially on the union side, the articulation ran in a different way. Plant-level representatives (in Austria and Germany, on a statutory basis) tied to the problems and needs of individual companies but exercising in turn an important influence on unions, imparted to union policy-making a rather conservative concern for the state of individual firms. Interaction was generally limited to a narrower range of issues, though unions and employers were deeply involved in public administration (see, on Germany, Süllow, 1985), institutions which were in Austria closely linked to wage- and price-restraint mechanisms themselves (Marin, 1982). The development is seen at its most extreme in the role of business organizations in Switzerland, where many functions normally carried out by governments were performed by institutions of *Selbstverwaltung* (Kriesi, 1982).

To an extent, similar mechanisms existed in Belgium (Molitor, 1978) and the Netherlands (Akkermans and Grootings, 1978), though it is less easy here to see strongly articulated organizations, especially on the labour side. These were more clearly instances of union *centralization*, 'protection' from rank-and-file rebellion being secured by a high level of state regulation of the labour market coupled with the unusual presence of important union wings within both the social democratic and Christian political parties. Both parties were usually in coalition together in any case.

A further new phenomenon of the 1970s which has to be taken into account was, however, contrary to any neo-corporatist trend: a shift in the locus of workers' collective action towards disaggregated, localized shop-floor strength of a tenacious kind. This differed considerably from either the conservative defensiveness of traditional skilled craft workers or the transient eruptions of anger and unsettled grievance that every system had known from the early days of industrial relations. The new form of action was a product of unprecedented full employment, and it began appropriately enough in the United Kingdom, a society that had experienced both sustained full employment and a labour movement already less centralized than most.

The impact of this development was felt in most of the broadly neo-corporatist countries. In many of them the policy response was a strengthening of company-level institutions, binding worker representatives into participation at a point where they were forced to take individual companies' problems into account. The easy economic conditions of the first post-war decades were being replaced by the anxious years of high inflation; more elaborate steps had to be taken to secure the articulation of labour organizations if they were to continue to cooperate effectively. For example, in legislation of 1972 the power of German works councils was considerably extended and unions were given an explicit role in advising them; in 1976, there was some strengthening of worker directors in the largest companies. Also in 1976, the Netherlands replaced their existing weak, consultative works councils by powerful ones of the German kind (Teulings, 1985).

Finland, Britain, Ireland and Italy were countries in which the new shop-floor pressures were particularly strong, but whose institutions were clearly trying to venture down a similar road to the more clearly neo-corporatist cases. In each nation there were steps towards greatly increased national involvement by central union leaderships, probably more intensively in Finland but prominent in all these cases. The institutions did not yet have the intricate complexity of constantly growing scope for exchanges typical of the established neo-corporatist systems, but behaviour was reminiscent of the early stages of these (for example, Scandinavia in the late 1930s). Although much public debate over industrial relations during the 1970s would speak of a need for 'consensus' as a precondition for success in creating new institutions, it should be remembered that the background to the Scandinavian social settlement of the 1930s had been extraordinarily high levels of conflict, while those of Austrian post-war 'social partnership' had been pre-war civil war, fascism, and the Anschluss.

Finnish governments, faced with a high level of industrial conflict, had been trying for several years to initiate a national policy of this kind, but had been held back by divisions in the labour movement that would have made union cooperation impossible to achieve. Soon after these were healed (at any rate, at the level of formal national organizations), in 1968, the government launched its incomes-policy initiatives. While these were designed to induce cooperation and were, as the 1970s developed, accompanied by the familiar multiplication of mechanisms for tripartite cooperation, there was much recourse to statutory intervention. Union unity might have been secured at national level, but there continued to be major conflict between communist and social democratic factions at plant level, producing a massive defect in the articulation of the system. Finland was clearly trying to learn from its Nordic neighbours, but was doing so in the difficult years of the 1970s when the Danish and Swedish systems themselves were showing signs of crisis (Helander, 1984).

Britain had been engaged in a similar pattern since the early 1960s, with several initiatives for tripartite cooperation being reinforced and then hopelessly compromised by statutory intervention. In the background was the much noted decentralization of British unions – as well as a weakness of employers' associations. This major absence of any substantial articulation had been analysed as creating 'two systems' of industrial relations by a Royal Commission (Donovan Commission, 1968), but measures taken by unions to increase their linkage with the shop-floor movement seemed to do so by strengthening the influence of the latter over the former. This did not have the same implications as the union influence of German works councils, as shop-floor organizations were only rarely tied to the interests of companies. The culmination of these developments was the 'social contract' of the mid-1970s, which was eventually broken in 1979 by an upsurge of shop-floor discontent (Crouch, 1977, 1982).

Irish governments engaged in similar initiatives, achieving for much of the decade an informal, primarily bipartite (union and employer) cooperation of a more strictly corporatist kind than the statute-assisted British and Finnish cases (Hardiman, 1989).

Italy's experience was not dissimilar, opportunities for overcoming the historic alienation of the labour movement being pursued by a variety of political, union, and industrial forces (Regini, 1982). But the degree of institutional development for such integration remained weaker. As Marin has pointed out (1990), Italian unions, governments, and employers attempted to form large, once-and-for-all deals rather than the intricate patchwork of multiple relationships more typical of the Austrian and Scandinavian examples. (Indeed, the most successful of these, which was not achieved until 1983, was actually called *la trattativa*.) At the same time Italy was experiencing the development of an autonomous shop-floor movement that was much younger, but even more detached from formal national unions, than the British shop stewards. This lack of articulation meant, not only that it was difficult to secure cohesion throughout the labour movement, but also that any attempt to do so might lead to a complete dissociation between its national and shop-floor wings. Matters were not helped by the division of the national unions into three ideologically defined organizations, though in fact considerable progress towards *de facto* unity was being achieved during these years.

An important point to note is that Italy during the 1970s began to be clearly distinguishable from France, with which it is normally bracketed in accounts of industrial relations institutions. In the latter country little neo-corporatist activity took place outside moments of crisis. One such moment was, of course, the upheavals of May 1968 which, even though they soon produced a conservative political climate, also led immediately to rare tripartite talks and in subsequent years to the introduction of considerable legislation strengthening the role of unions' and workers' rights at company level (Dubois et al., 1978). This was an attempt to strengthen pluralism and collective bargaining rather than to introduce neo-corporatist arrangements.

Also in the mid-1970s, Portugal and Spain emerged from dictatorship. Unions and political parties immediately leapt out of their former clandestine existence. Initially in Spain there were

Table 6.1   *Working days lost per 1,000 dependent employees in employment, 1971–80*

Country	Days lost (rank order in parentheses)	
Austria	9.57	(2)
Belgium	228.60	(8)
Denmark	264.60	(9)
Finland	681.50	(12)
France	196.70	(7)
Germany	53.23	(5)
Ireland	665.00	(11)
Italy	1461.00	(13)
Netherlands	36.02	(3)
Norway	47.32	(4)
Sweden	162.70	(6)
Switzerland	1.92	(1)
UK	572.30	(10)

Source: ILO Yearbook

attempts to construct a collective bargaining system, though by the end of the decade there was a clear move towards a political exchange too. In Portugal, there was a more explicit corporatist attempt from the outset at national level, though with little support at the base.

Table 6.1 shows average annual industrial conflict levels for the 1970s for thirteen Western European countries. In general, cases of established neo-corporatism (Switzerland, Austria, the Netherlands, Norway, Germany, and – though with considerably higher levels than the others – Sweden) had typically low levels of industrial conflict, whereas countries that were experimenting with corporatist forms without a well-articulated labour movement had particularly high levels (Italy, Finland, Ireland, the United Kingdom).

Denmark and Belgium stand as intermediate cases of, in the former, a rapidly disintegrating articulation, and, in the latter, one in frequent need of statutory support to remedy its structural defects. Danish unions had never assumed the 'one union per industry' form common among neo-corporatist and, indeed, many other union systems. Rivalries between craft and general unions were therefore difficult to contain and began causing problems for the articulated system of wage development from the beginning of the 1960s (Rasmussen, 1985), leading to gradually increasing problems for Danish governments, employers, and unions seeking

Table 6.2　*Economic performance, 1970–74*

	1		2 (rank order in parentheses)		3	
Austria	7.30	(2)	1.82	(4)	9.12	(3)
Belgium	9.17	(8)	3.10	(10)	12.27	(10)
Denmark	9.30	(9)	2.12	(5)	11.42	(8)
Finland	12.08	(11)	2.18	(6)	14.26	(7)
France	8.90	(7)	2.94	(9)	11.84	(9)
Germany	6.14	(1)	1.54	(2)	7.68	(1)
Ireland	13.36	(13)	5.96	(13)	19.32	(13)
Italy	11.48	(10)	5.78	(12)	17.26	(12)
Netherlands	8.64	(6)	2.72	(8)	11.36	(6)
Norway	8.42	(5)	1.70	(3)	10.12	(4)
Sweden	7.98	(4)	2.26	(7)	10.24	(5)
Switzerland	7.70	(3)	(0.06	(1)	7.76	(2))
UK	13.18	(12)	3.56	(11)	16.74	(11)

Notes:
1 Annual average inflation rate.
2 Annual average unemployment rate.
3 Sum of inflation and unemployment rates.
N.B.: Swiss unemployment figures may be deceptively low because of unemployed 'guest workers' returning to their countries of origin.
Source: OECD

to follow the Scandinavian pattern of industrial relations.

France is an exception in that its conflict levels were only moderate while its level of institutional development was low.

Table 6.2 confirms a similar pattern during the early 1970s for inflation, unemployment, and the additive combination of the two, often known as the Okun or discomfort index. With the constant exception of France, we find the poorest levels of economic performance consistently recorded by the countries without settled, established routines of neo-corporatism: Ireland, Italy, and the United Kingdom, though Finland recorded a good performance on unemployment.

It is easy to see why it was the 1970s that brought neo-corporatist dynamics to the attention of academic observers, as it is then that they were fairly clearly associated with successful economic as well as industrial relations outcomes (Germany, Switzerland, Austria, Norway, Sweden, and to some extent the Netherlands, though not Denmark; one must also note that Switzerland's unemployment performance is boosted by the role of 'guest workers' who have to return to their countries of origin when there is no work for them). It is also therefore comprehensible that several countries tried to imitate these dynamics, though, as we have seen, none did so successfully.

However, one also has intimations of the strain being borne by the Scandinavian model. Manual workers' unions, especially those in the exposed sector, had since the late 1930s carried the burden of being *Ordnungsfaktoren* in these economies, a burden that they never really planned to assume. The concept of solidarity that had ostensibly guided their actions was that of the working class against its bourgeois opponents. In practice, the very centralization to which this led, together with the fact that as organizations primarily of workers in manufacturing industry in small countries they experienced keenly the need for their national economies to be internationally competitive, drove them to make their primary but implicit goal the strength of those economies. By the 1970s they were losing their hegemony, as both workers in the less heavily internationally traded tertiary sector (especially the public services) and those in white-collar employments rose in numbers. These groups were, in Scandinavia, heavily unionized, but their organizations rarely accepted any wider socio-political burden than straight representation of their members in collective bargaining. For how long could the LO unions continue to play their historical role alone?

The 1980s

In general, the inflation of the 1970s ended in recession, and in many countries the political response to the period was a political shift to the right. Domestic politics apart, international monetary agencies and powerful international investors looked to deflationary policies to remove the heat from the labour market. In many instances Keynesian demand management, the fundamental prop to workers' power since the 1940s, was abandoned. Even where forces favourable to the labour movement retained political power, they and their policies were affected by these developments; where parties of the right governed, they amplified them.

Labour had shown its potency in the decade or so following 1968, leading many conservatives to question their post-war assumptions of the wisdom of seeking to pacify unions by incorporating them. The recession of the early 1980s now led them to question whether such propitiatory policies were even necessary. Union membership levels, which had risen steadily almost everywhere in the 1970s, began to decline in all countries except those where unions retained some role in the administration of unemployment insurance schemes (Visser, 1987; Rothstein, 1988):

Belgium, Denmark, Finland, and Sweden. In these four it rose substantially. The decline was most severe in France, Italy, the United Kingdom, and, in particular, the Netherlands. However, by the end of the decade the situation had stabilized and in some countries new gains were registered.[3]

Associated with the membership decline was a sharp new decline in the proportion of the work-force in manual employment in the manufacturing sector. This either contributed to overall union weakness as the new kinds of worker were less likely to join organizations, or (should they unionize) increased the heterogeneity of the movement, intensifying the decline in the hegemony of manual workers in the exposed, export-orientated manufacturing sector already noted by the end of the 1970s (Crouch, 1990).

Further, there was in increasing need and preference among companies to tackle issues of wages and other labour questions at the company or plant level, leading to a declining importance of the sectoral and national bargains that have been so important to neo-corporatist systems. This trend was partly a response to the new, decentralized character of *labour's* action in the previous decade.

Associated with these last factors, the articulation of labour movements also declined everywhere except Belgium, Finland, the Netherlands, Spain, and Switzerland, but there are important variations. In Austria, Ireland, the United Kingdom, and throughout Scandinavia, cohesiveness declined as a result of a combined development of diminishing employment in the exposed sector, decentralizing tensions among and within unions, and a change in employer strategy. The same is broadly true of Germany, the Netherlands, and Switzerland, with one significant difference. The role of exposed-sector unions remained strong here because of the extraordinary role of one major union: in the German and Swiss cases this is the familiar metal-industry union; in the Netherlands it emerged through the formation of one new cross-branch union defined virtually explicitly as *the* exposed-sector union, following the amalgamation between the Catholic and the social democratic confederations which itself had improved the articulation of Dutch unionism in the mid-1970s (Crouch, 1990).

Overall, the situation was not favourable to neo-corporatist trends. Nowhere were these changes seen more vividly than in the United Kingdom, one of the countries that had had a difficult experience with neo-corporatist policy attempts in the 1970s. By the end of the decade research by the Confederation of British Industry (CBI) and others shows that employers' associations had given up collective bargaining in several branches, and some associations had collapsed altogether, bargaining being concentrated at company level (CBI, 1989; Purcell and Ahlstrand, 1989). The Conservative governments of the period quickly disengaged themselves from nearly all tripartite structures and contacts with trade unions. Rather than encourage a concentration and centralization of bargaining, as in the logic of neo-corporatism, they actively encouraged the fragmentation of bargaining levels within both private and public sectors. The object was to minimize the role of organizations and maximize that of the free market. The government also introduced a programme of law reform designed to weaken union power, though some of this imposed obligations on unions no more severe than those of most other Western European countries.

The British situation indeed seemed to be the 'paradigm case' of an emergent new European industrial relations system, similar to that familiar for a considerable period in the United States. However, by the end of the decade it had become clear that Britain was not so much a paradigm as an extreme example of tendencies which, while certainly found in most other countries, elsewhere appeared in far more muted form. In general, in Europe there was no abandonment of either the practice of neo-corporatist strategies where they were well entrenched or the search for them where they were absent.

It is instructive to begin the contrast with Britain by considering France, which had not only been the least neo-corporatist case in previous decades but which has also had for many years the weakest trade unionism in Western Europe. The main employers organization, the Conseil National des Patrons Français, has during the 1980s encouraged the greatest possible decentralization of pay bargaining, preferably to the individual worker; this is well in line with the 'British paradigm'. However, at the same time it has sought a number of bipartite national agreements with unions on such matters as the introduction of new technology, which agreements themselves include commitments to further negotiations with unions and *comités d'entreprise*. Similar arrangements have been made at sectoral level in several branches.

This is hardly corporatism, but rather a late encouragement of collective bargaining. It must also be noted that the substantive scope of the agreements is often very limited, that the employers have been negotiating from a position of strength, and that the main union confederation, the communist Confédération Générale du Travail, has refused to sign virtually all the deals. Nevertheless, there is evidence here of a desire by employers to have some major issues co-regulated at national or sectoral level with unions. With the important exception of pay bargaining, France has not been an example of a radical attack on the organized economy.

The other countries that had, like Britain, experienced relatively unsuccessful neo-corporatist attempts during the 1970s, continued with them for much of the new decade. In the early 1980s the Italians attempted, with temporary success, major national deals on wage restraint. At the end of the decade there were major attempts by both employers and the unions at sector-level agreements incorporating widespread bipartite agreement and lower-level participation. Most of this work was, however, frustrated by the radical disarticulation of the Italian labour movement and the growth of rank-and-file activist groups (*comitati di base*, COBAS) autonomous of the unions.

Spanish and, to a lesser extent, Portuguese and Greek governments tried throughout the decade to encourage national systems of *concertación social*, almost as much in order to stabilize their young democracies as to control inflation. Again, these suffered from the low levels of articulation of the labour movement. Nevertheless the strategy persisted.

Ostensibly more successful in their continued pursuit of neo-corporatist policies have been the governments of Ireland and Finland. Although the former followed a moderate version of British policy for much of the decade, a change of government in 1987 led to the re-admission of the Irish Congress of Trade Unions as a valued interlocutor by government, and a new tripartite programme for economic recovery. The unions receive an enhanced public role in exchange for undertakings about the control of wages and industrial conflict. Although some unions have opposed this, the experiment has to date been generally judged successful, and constitutes an unusual departure from British policy in a 'Scandinavian' direction by Irish institutions.

Scandinavian imitations have understandably been easier for the Finns who, despite continuing problems of articulation in the labour movement and the return of the Conservatives to the governing coalition, have continued to construct an elaborate network of neo-corporatist institutions.

Meanwhile, ironically, many employers in the heartland countries of the Scandinavian model were beginning to seek new 'British' approaches and – albeit with considerable ambivalence – to reject neo-corporatism. In Denmark these tendencies were considerably reinforced by the policies of the main governing parties for much of the decade. Scandinavian employers have confronted, not only powerful labour movements at a time when those in other countries have been weakening, but a neo-corporatist structure that has been becoming ineffective. As already noted, the articulation of Scandinavian labour organizations has been in serious decline. Central employers' confederations, together with powerfully placed individual unions, have therefore advocated a radical decentralization of bargaining to sectoral or company level, leaving union confederations and social democratic parties to defend and try to shore up the centralized system.

However, when Scandinavian employers' organizations speak of decentralization, they mean a controlled and deliberate decision by themselves to have bargaining take place at a decentralized level, a decision which in some years they choose to reverse. This is very different from the institutional collapse that has affected British associations as employers have simply chosen to opt out of branch-level arrangements. An interesting illustration of this ambivalence occurred in 1988 when, the Swedish central employers' body, Svenska Arbetsgivarföreningen (SAF), having declared that it wanted decentralized bargaining, the bakery employers proceeded to reach an agreement with their union. They did not, however, consult SAF about its terms first, which therefore fined it 1 million kronor.

Swedish, Norwegian, and Danish institutions are clearly unable to function in the way they once did. The central union confederations are responding by trying to shore up a structure based on the dominance of manual workers' unions in the export-orientated sector when this no longer reflects the structure of either employment or union membership. The employers, on the other hand are, albeit inconsistently, seeking further to undermine the existing structure without having clear ideas as to how they will manage decentralized structures alongside powerful individual unions. This crisis came to a head in Sweden when, following the election of a new-right government in late 1991, the SAF began to withdraw from *all* tripartite arrangements, leaving considerable uncertainty over the future of Swedish institutions.

The remaining countries of Western Europe are those that had developed structures which, while strongly neo-corporatist, have incorporated trade-union systems less powerful than in Scandinavia and have been more 'employer-driven': Germany, Switzerland, Belgium, the Netherlands, and (though with a more 'Scandinavian' level of union power) Austria.

As noted, labour's articulation has been under less pressure in most of these countries. While there have been movements to greater decentralization and company-level bargaining, these have been within the framework of continuing strong associational policies by employers. German employers, for example, continue to work through their powerful associations not only for labour issues but also for many other questions and have shown few tendencies to follow the US and UK economies into a more individualistic form of capitalism. The reunification of the country has seen the importance of the German model confirmed, as associations moved to incorporate their East German counterparts.

The form of labour's articulation in the 'German' countries already incorporated a considerable subordination to the needs of individual companies and was therefore more amenable to adaptation to the conditions of the 1980s without major disturbance. It is notable that in 1989 the Christian-Liberal government of the Federal Republic introduced legislation *strengthening* the role of works councils in the introduction of new technology.

Belgium and the Netherlands depart somewhat from this pattern in that labour is more centralized than articulated, its local structures long having been weakly developed. This has often meant, and continues to mean, that national economic concertation requires a heavier input of government regulation than is implied by the neo-corporatist model; but it has also meant, as in the other three countries, that there is no fundamental challenge to the existing rights of labour's organizations – even in the Netherlands, where labour's loss of members was particularly severe. In any case, by the end of the decade labour's political representation in government had been strengthened in both countries.

The conflict data in Table 6.3 for the latter 1980s give a far more confused picture than in the 1970s. (We are now able to include data on Spain and Portugal, but lose Belgium from the series as the Belgian government stopped publishing strike statistics.) The established neo-corporatist cases are now associated with low conflict only in Austria, the Netherlands, Germany, and Switzerland. The distinction between these cases and the Scandinavian countries demonstrates the importance of the point made above: a division between forms of neo-corporatism dependent on powerful, articulated, and centralized union movements (as in Scandinavia), and those built on weaker union movements whose articulation depended more on the strength of powerful employers' organizations and one dominant exposed-sector union rather than a centralized confederation (Germany, Switzerland, and now the Netherlands). This was not really anticipated by any theories of industrial relations organization.

Only Austria remains a clearly low-conflict example of a 'labour-dominant' neo-corporatism, and it will be noted that the inclusive nature of the Austrian union confederation, the Österreichische

Table 6.3 *Working days lost per 1,000 dependent employees in employment, 1986–90*

Country	Days lost (rank order in parentheses)	
Austria	1.42	(2)
Denmark	41.24	(5)
Finland	401.47	(12)
France*	65.06	(6)
Germany	4.58	(3)
Ireland	282.01	(11)
Italy	2499.70	(14)
Netherlands	12.75	(4)
Norway	149.94	(10)
Portugal	79.78	(7)
Spain	618.11	(13)
Sweden	132.47	(8)
Switzerland	0.36	(1)
UK	141.31	(9)

* Following changes in the method of calculation, it is now difficult to compare French strike statistics with those of other countries.
Source: ILO Yearbook

Gewerkschaftsbund, does not involve the Scandinavian division between manual and non-manual workers.

If reducing conflict was one of the aims of the continuing experiments with neo-corporatism by the Finns, Italians, and Irish, and the new ventures of that kind by the Spanish, they achieved little. On the other hand, the rejection of such strategies by the British seemed to bring only a modest return in relative strike performance. France becomes even more exceptional than in the 1970s, and Portugal emerges as a relatively low-conflict case.

The evidence on inflation and unemployment is more complex (Table 6.4). The lowest inflation levels were scored by four 'employer-dominated' corporatist cases (Belgium, Germany, the Netherlands, Switzerland) plus Austria. The clearly labour-dominated neo-corporatisms (the Nordic countries) had very indifferent records, being indistinguishable as a group from those either attempting neo-corporatism on a weak basis or (primarily the United Kingdom) rejecting it entirely. On the other hand, if one takes account of the special factors in the low unemployment level of Switzerland, the countries with the best records on unemployment were the 'social-democratic' neo-corporatist ones, including Austria and now Finland but not the 'decayed' case of Denmark.

Table 6.4   *Economic performance, 1986–90*

	1		2		3	
			(rank order in parentheses)			
Austria	2.19	(4)	4.08	(4)	6.27	(2)
Belgium	2.13	(3)	9.58	(11)	11.71	(8)
Denmark	3.92	(8)	8.64	(8)	12.56	(9)
Finland	4.83	(9)	4.32	(5)	9.15	(5)
France	3.09	(6)	9.84	(12)	12.93	(10)
Germany	1.36	(2)	5.90	(6)	7.26	(3)
Ireland	3.29	(7)	16.04	(14)	19.33	(14)
Italy	5.75	(11)	10.64	(13)	16.39	(12)
Netherlands	0.75	(1)	8.90	(10)	9.65	(6)
Norway	6.27	(13)	3.48	(3)	9.75	(7)
Portugal	11.34	(15)	(6.46	(7)	17.80	(13))
Spain	6.46	(14)	18.60	(15)	26.06	(15)
Sweden	6.25	(12)	1.82	(2)	8.07	(4)
Switzerland	2.52	(5)	(0.67	(1)	3.19	(1))
UK	5.96	(10)	8.80	(9)	14.76	(11)

Notes:
1 Annual average inflation rate.
2 Annual average unemployment rate.
3 Sum of inflation and unemployment rates.
N.B.: Portuguese and Swiss unemployment figures may be deceptively low
because of, in the former case, unemployed workers returning to family land in
the countryside and, in the latter, unemployed 'guest workers' returning to their
countries of origin.
Source: OECD

   Given the different relative preferences of employers and
workers for good records on inflation and unemployment, these
interesting outcomes are comprehensible. It would appear that the
leading partner in a neo-corporatist system was able to steer the
economy in its preferred direction in a manner not possible in
pluralist cases. However, in doing so they were all, in their
different ways, clearly straining the high-trust legacy of their
corporatist past, when shared goals between capital and labour had
been easier to find and achieve. Employers' widespread preferences
for moving away from national organizations to plant-level
bargaining suggest declining confidence by them in the existing
arrangements; and, as we have noted, the decline of manual work
and employment in the exposed sector suggests major problems on
the labour side for the neo-corporatist model.
   Nevertheless, when we consider the combined inflation and
unemployment measure of the Okun index during the late 1980s,

the third column in Table 6.4, both kinds of neo-corporatist economy – the employer-dominated and those with particularly strong labour – turn in the best performances: Switzerland (admittedly with its unusual unemployment situation), Austria, Germany, Sweden, Finland (which of the neo-corporatist 'imitators' of the 1970s stood the best chance of adopting Scandinavian institutions), the Netherlands, Norway and Belgium, followed by the decayed case of Denmark. The bottom six places in the ranking are occupied by those countries that cannot be described as neo-corporatist.

In retrospect, we can now see that the conflict between neo-liberal policies and neo-corporatism that seemed to be the central policy debate of the 1980s was in fact only part of the story. First, any idea of a general disillusion with neo-corporatism among employers is an oversimplification. A further important trend was the remarkable bifurcation around two different forms of 'success' (over unemployment where there was labour-dominated corporatism, over inflation where corporatism was dominated by employers and strong exposed-sector unions). The paradigm neo-liberal case of the United Kingdom shared neither of these forms of success, and was indeed not clearly a major paradigm at all.

It is probably an error to seek major trends in the rapid fluctuations of contemporary advanced economies. Policy and practice shifted as the recession of the early 1980s gave way to new labour shortages in the latter part of the decade, and the 1990s will see new adjustments. The eastern part of Germany and some other Eastern European countries will be absorbed into an enlarged European division of labour. The development of a single European economy within the European Community will change the pattern of intra-Community competition, robbing government, business, and organized labour of many accustomed policy instruments and thus encouraging experimentation with new ones.

Although, outside the United Kingdom, there is, as of the early 1990s, still something of a shared Western European preference for at least elements of neo-corporatism, it would be unwise to predict any strong convergence. In any event, new developments cannot take the form of a return to patterns of the 1970s: the organization of the labour movement is hardly appropriate outside Germany, Switzerland, and possibly the Netherlands; and employers will not wish quickly to dismantle their new company-level structures. There may, however, be further experiments of the kind launched in Finland and, outside Europe, in Australia, whereby national coordination tries to span the differences between public and private, manual and non-manual.

Beyond that, it is important to remember that there has never really been a 'Western European' pattern of industrial relations. The systems of the two major continental powers, France and Germany, differ about as much as two advanced industrial democracies could do. However, if France has – surviving dictatorships apart – been the main non-corporatist outlier for most of the post-war period, that position was, by the end of the 1980s, occupied by Britain.

Notes

Earlier versions of this chapter were presented at meetings of the working group 'Labour Movements in the State and Industrial Arenas' of the International Sociological Association, at Trento in December 1989, and at the World Sociological Congress at Madrid in July 1990.

1 I assume here a basic knowledge of the debate over neo-corporatism. Those to whom it is unfamiliar should consult Schmitter and Lehmbruch (eds) (1979), Lehmbruch and Schmitter (eds) (1982), Crouch (1983), and Martin (1983).

2 A major source for much of what follows is Crouch and Pizzorno (1978).

3 A major source for much of what follows is Baglioni and Crouch (1990), supplemented by various national sources.

References

Akkermans, T. and Grootings, P. (1978) 'From Corporatism to Polarisation: Elements of the Development of Dutch Industrial Relations', in C.J. Crouch and A. Pizzorno (eds), *The Resurgence of Class Conflict in Western Europe since 1968*, vol. 1., *National Studies*. London: Macmillan.

Aukrust, O. (1977) 'Inflation in the World Economy: a Norwegian Model', in L.B. Krause and W.S. Salent (eds), *Worldwide Inflation: Theory and Recent Experience*. Washington, DC: Brookings Institution.

Baglioni, G. and Crouch, C.J. (eds) (1990) *European Industrial Relations: the Challenge of Flexibility*. London: Sage.

CBI (1989) *The Structure and Process of Pay Determination in the Private Sector, 1979–86*. London: CBI.

Clegg, H.A. (1976) *Trade Unionism under Collective Bargaining*. Oxford: Blackwell.

Crouch, C.J. (1977) *Class Conflict and the Industrial Relations Crisis*. London: Heinemann.

Crouch C.J. (1982) *The Politics of Industrial Relations* (2nd edn). London: Fontana.

Crouch C.J. (1983) 'Pluralism and the New Corporatism: a Rejoinder', *Political Studies*, 31: 452–60.

Crouch C.J. (1990) 'Trade Unions in the Exposed Sector: Their Influence on Neo-corporatist Behaviour', in R. Brunetta and C. Dell'Aringa (eds), *Labour Relations and Economic Performance*. Basingstoke: Macmillan and International Economic Association.

Crouch C.J. and Pizzorno, A. (eds) (1978) *The Resurgence of Class Conflict in*

Western Europe since 1968, vol. 1, *National Studies*. London: Macmillan.

Donovan Commission (1968) *Report* of the Royal Commission on Trade Unions and Employers' Associations. London: HMSO.

Dubois, P., Durand, C. and Erbès-Seguin, S. (1978) 'The Contradictions of French Trade Unionism', in C.J. Crouch and A. Pizzorno (eds), *The Resurgence of Class Conflict in Western Europe since 1968*, vol. 1, *National Studies*. London: Macmillan.

Edgren, G., Faxén, K-O. and Odhner, C-E. (1973) *Wage Formation and the Economy*. London: Allen & Unwin.

Flanagan, R.J., Soskice, D.W. and Ulman, L. (1983) *Unionism, Economic Stabilization and Incomes Policies*. Washington, DC: Brookings Institution.

Fox, A. (1974) *Beyond Contract: Work, Power and Trust Relations*. London: Faber.

Hardiman, N. (1989) *The Search for Consensus: Centralised Collective Bargaining: Trade Unions, Employers and Government in the Republic of Ireland*. Oxford: Oxford University Press.

Helander, V. (1984) 'Corporatism or Quasi-corporatism: the Development of Prices Policy Mechanisms in Finland 1968–1978', in H. Paloheimo (ed.), *Politics in the Era of Corporatism and Planning*. Tampere: Finnish Political Science Association.

Hyman, R. (1975) *Industrial Relations: a Marxist Introduction*. London: Macmillan.

Kjellberg, A. (1983) *Fackliga organisering i tolv länder*. Lund: Arkiv fürlag.

Kriesi, H. (1982) 'The Structure of the Swiss Political System', in G. Lehmbruch and P.C. Schmitter (eds), *Patterns of Corporatist Policy-making*. London: Sage.

Lehmbruch G. and Schmitter, P.C. (eds) (1982) *Patterns of Corporatist Policy-making*. London: Sage.

Marin, B. (1982) *Die paritätische Kommission*. Vienna: Internationale Publikationen.

Marin, B. (1990) 'Generalized Political Exchange: Preliminary Considerations', in B. Marin (ed.), *Generalized Political Exchange*. Frankfurt am Main: Campus.

Martin, R. (1983) 'Corporatism and the New Pluralism', *Political Studies*, 31: 86–102.

Molitor, M. (1978) 'Social Conflicts in Belgium', in C.J. Crouch and A. Pizzorno (eds), *The Resurgence of Class Conflict in Western Europe since 1968*, vol. 1, *National Studies*. London: Macmillan.

Purcell, J. and Ahlstrand, B. (1989) 'Corporate Strategy and the Management of Employee Relations in the Multi-divisional Company', *British Journal of Industrial Relations*, 27(3).

Rasmussen, E.J. (1985) 'Twenty-five Years of Labour Government and Incomes Policy', Unpublished doctoral thesis, European University Institute, Florence.

Regini, M. (1982) 'Changing Relationships between Labour and the State in Italy: Towards a Neo-corporatist System?', in G. Lehmbruch and P.C. Schmitter (eds), *Patterns of Corporatist Policy-making*. London: Sage.

Rothstein, B. (1988) 'Trade unions and social security programmes', Stockholm, mimeo.

Schmitter, P.C. and Lehmbruch, G. (eds) (1979) *Trends towards Corporatist Intermediation*. London: Sage. ·

Süllow, B. (1985) *Die Selbstverwaltung in der Sozialversicherung als korporatistische Einrichtung*. Frankfurt am Main: Lang.

Teulings, A. (1985) 'The New Dutch Works Councils', University of Amsterdam, mimeo.

Visser, J. (1987) 'In Search of Inclusive Unionism', Unpublished doctoral thesis, University of Amsterdam.

7
Europe's Internal Market, Business Associability and the Labour Movement

Luca Lanzalaco and Philippe C. Schmitter

The Logic (or Logics) of Collective Action for Capitalists and Workers

According to the 'orthodox perspective', capitalists are individualists in behaviour and ideology and only engage in collective action when compelled to do so by others (Schmitter and Brand, 1979). Belatedly and reluctantly, they respond to the prior activity of trade unions formed by their workers. The more militant, class conscious, and solidaristic the workers' collective action, the greater the reliance of capitalists upon business interest associations (BIAs) and the more encompassing their organizational format. Hence, their characteristics, strategies, and probable role in the interest politics of any given country are conceived as dependent variables, and those of unions are treated as their independent determinants.

Seen from this perspective, the project to complete Europe's internal market by 31 December 1992 – by itself – should make little or no difference in business associability, unless the multiple directives and regulations pouring out of the Commission and slowly being implemented by national administrations were to have the prior effect of weakening or strengthening the role of trade unions. As several other chapters in this volume testify convincingly, there are many reasons to suspect that worker militancy, solidarity, and collective action will decline in Europe – regardless of whether or not the Twelve manage to meet their self-imposed deadline. Hence, the orthodox expectation would be that the role of BIAs, especially of peak associations representing the comprehensive interests of capitalists as a class or of major sectors of the economy, should decline in the Europe of the future.

Before accepting this as a working hypothesis, perhaps we should re-examine the historical pattern of business associability a bit more closely to discover if the orthodox perspective is as well justified as it seems. An analysis of that record would show that relatively few BIAs were formed simply as a reaction to the challenge of trade unions or other forms of worker organization. In most countries (from France to Great Britain, from the Netherlands to Germany), the first wave of specialized business associability and the first efforts of establishing federations or confederations were aimed at regulating competition among firms within or across sectors and/or at exerting pressure upon the state for protection, improvements in infrastructure, standardization, and so on. Only later did the problem of coping collectively with industrial conflict and the labour movement emerge and employers' organizations form (Lanzalaco, 1990b: chap. 10).

Furthermore, strictly from an abstract theoretical perspective, it is difficult to understand *why* and *how* relatively powerless actors (workers) – even when acting collectively – should be able to determine the behaviour of more powerful ones (capitalists). In generic terms, power is precisely the capacity to control intentionally the conduct of others. Not surprisingly, the usual assumption in most fields of research is that it is the powerful, not the powerless, who are the initiating and guiding forces behind social and political transformations. Only in special contexts is it meaningful to speak of 'the power of the weak'. Lipset and Rokkan (1967), for example, routinely assumed that the alliance patterns involved in the building of party systems in Western Europe depended on the configuration of dominant interests that emerged from varying lines of cleavage. Similarly, industrial relations specialists have argued that the strategic and organizational choices of management tend to determine the behaviour of workers both in the collective bargaining arena and at the firm level (for example, Ingham, 1974; Clegg, 1976; Kochan, McKersie and Cappelli, 1984; Streeck, 1987). From a broader perspective, several seminal theorists of industrial conflict have sought to explain the similarities and differences between national labour movements by relating them to the type and timing of capitalist development that prevailed in specific countries (for example, Commons, 1932; Perlman, 1928; Shalev, 1980).

Not only do these general perspectives suggest that business associability might play an active and not just a passive role, but the specific approach which dominated the study of regional integration, neo-functionalism, also assigned major importance to the activities of organized interests. It assumed that the integration process would be driven forward by ambitious Eurocrats and cautious interest representatives. With the new policy responsibilities in Brussels, national associations were expected to regroup at the supranational 'European' level. These new peak and sectoral federations would provide the necessary political support and technical information for 'spill-overs' into new areas and enlarged *compétences* for the Commission authorities. Political parties and mass publics were expected to remain preoccupied with national issues and identities and indifferent to this gradual, almost surreptitious accumulation of power. Eventually, they would be convinced to shift their attention and affection to the European Community – once they had experienced the consequences of its enlightened and efficient policies. Now, the actual course of the integration process did not strictly follow this scenario, especially during the 1970s when it degenerated into inter-governmental haggling, but the neo-functionalist assumption that the Treaty of Rome would provide incentives for enhanced associability, especially, as we shall see, for business interests, and eventually lead to task expansion, was fundamentally correct.

One way to cut through this morass of conflicting perspectives is to focus generically on the logic (or logics) of associability by labour and capital. Why do persons in specific social categories – classes, sectors, or professions – engage in associative action? What determines the organizational format and political role of these specialized intermediaries? To what extent do interacting or, better, conflicting group interests respond to the same motives and incentives and, therefore, tend to mirror each other's structures and behaviours? How are these patterns affected across time by changes in technology, ideology, diffusion? If we had compelling answers to these questions, we could be fairly confident of predicting the impact upon existing BIAs of even such an uncertain process as the completion of Europe's internal market.

Alas, the systematic study of associability is in its theoretical infancy – despite the attention focused on it so long ago by Alexis de Tocqueville in his magisterial study of *Democracy in America*. The assumption by pluralists that 'like-minded persons would just naturally group together in defense of their common interests' (Truman, 1951) has been effectively dispelled by rational choice theorists who demonstrated that 'free-riding' on the efforts of others was an omnipresent temptation (Olson, 1965). Both of these approaches implicitly argued for an equivalence of motive *and* need for collective action across social categories, the latter discriminating only according to the size and dispersion of the group to be organized. Claus Offe and Helmut Wiesenthal (1980) were the first to suggest that there might be systematic differences in the logic of associability between capital and labour. Following a Marxist tradition, they argued that employers acted initially by organizing 'dead labour' into the production process at the level of individual enterprises. Workers reacted collectively by forming trade unions; to which capitalists subsequently responded as a class by creating employer associations. They concluded that employers and workers must follow two different logics of collective action: the latter can only act effectively through their respective unions; while the former continue to have sufficient resources to act individually at the initial, firm level of organization, where they can expect to dominate workers through the employment relation and, hence, have much less need to rely on collective action.

This provocative thesis has been much discussed. Many of its pitfalls have been identified (especially in Streeck, 1988), but one has been largely neglected. Offe and Wiesenthal refer exclusively to 'capital', not 'capitalists'. In other words, they fall into what could be called *'the reifying fallacy'*, namely, to treat as purely physical objects (that is, quantities of capital or repositories of 'dead labour') persons who are subjects capable of engaging in action endowed with meaning, intention, and strategic calculation (namely, individual, living, breathing, egotistical capitalists). Business interest associations do not combine abstract *things* with objective needs, but *social actors* with subjective preferences. They do not defend the long-term reproductive – let alone expansive – imperatives of capitalism; they defend the relatively short-term interests of their capitalist members. In this central regard, they do not differ from trade unions. This does not obviate the possibility that BIAs may be less essential and play a different role with regard to the interests of their members, but it does suggest that the logic of associability surrounding them may not be all that different.[1]

Our approach rejects both the 'orthodox' and the 'heterodox' perspective. In line with corporatist theory, we do not assume the substantive content of interests as given but as a problem to be resolved through an on-going political process (Schmitter, 1981; Berger, 1981). We presume no structural or substantive difference a priori between worker and capitalist logics of associability, since to do so would be to assume not only that interests are determined by socio-economic structure, but also that members of conflicting classes, sectors, and professions engaged in different modes of interest calculation. We do, however, recognize that many conditions can influence differentially whether groups will be successful in organizing for collective action and, even more, whether they will be successful in obtaining what they want. Both capitalists and workers can associate to increase their power resources (by combining those already controlled by individuals and by generating new resources through collective mobilization and discipline). Moreover, once they have been formed, the conduct of these associations can become relatively autonomous from the preferences and demands of their members, introducing yet another element of dynamism and unintended consequence into the process. Both business associations and trade unions can be influenced 'from within' by organizational imperatives and 'from above' by state intervention, although the latter is often deliberately skewed to favour one class over the other (Schmitter, 1977).

The implications of our approach should, by now, be clear: (1) no logical asymmetry distorts the associative efforts of classes, sectors, or professions; (2) the outcome of these efforts will be affected not just by the reciprocal antagonisms of interest groups, but also by their own internal processes and by the interventions of affected outsiders, especially public authorities; (3) at the European level, the response will be compounded by the heterogeneity of patterns that have emerged historically in its member states and by the differential resources that the European Community can expend to encourage the collective action of capitalists and workers.

This affirmation of logical symmetry contrasts with some flagrant empirical differences in the structure and behaviour of business associations and trade unions. For example, the Organization of Business Interests project demonstrated unambiguously that BIAs greatly outnumbered trade unions in all countries and in every sector in its sample.[2] The history of worker collective action is punctuated with monumental public demonstrations, uprisings, and strikes; that of capitalists is much more prosaic and secretive. Wolfgang Streeck in a article in 1988 has shown that these can be explained by differences in conditions and resources, not by differences in their respective logics of associability. Most obvious of these differences is the simple fact that capitalists as owners or managers of individual enterprises command greater resources than do workers as individual producers. This alone, plus the dependence of the state upon the general condition of the economy for its revenues, ensures that capitalists will play an important political role – irrespective of whether or not they act intentionally and collectively to influence public policies. Hence, Offe and Wiesenthal are substantively correct when they assert that, under normal conditions, employers are not as dependent upon associative action as workers and that BIAs play a less significant role in both defining and protecting interests than do trade unions (1980).[3] Contrary to Offe and Wiesenthal, who arrive at the conclusion that associability among consenting capitalists is not only less necessary than among mobilizing workers but is also

Table 7.1   *The differences between representing class interests and producer interests to capitalists*

	Class interests	Producer interests
Market on which these interests emerge	Labour market	Product market
Cleavage around which these interests emerge	Class	Sector
Distinction that these interests produce	Inter-group (categorical)	Intra-group
Tendencies that these interests bring about	Cohesive	Divisive
Type of association representing these interests	Employers' association	Trade association
Main interlocutor	Trade unions	State agencies
Main legitimacy principle of action	General interests of capitalists as buyers of labour	Specific interests of capitalists as sellers of products
Main organizational principle	Integration	Differentiation
Preferred parameter for organization	Territory	Sector
Historical impetus	Class conflict	Sectoral clashes

easier to accomplish, we would argue that it is more difficult for the former to create and sustain effective intermediary organizations. The main reason for this – one that was initially undervalued by recent scholars of business associability – is that BIAs must develop a dualistic set of activities. On the one hand, they must represent capitalists in their role as *employers* in the labour market *vis-à-vis* trade unions; on the other, they must represent their members as *competitive producers* in specific product markets *vis-à-vis* capitalists in other sectors and/or *vis-à-vis* potential regulators, protectors, and sponsors in state agencies (Streeck, 1988). In both of these areas, collective action is aimed at defending and advancing the perceived interests of owners and managers. In the former, it usually emerges only when association members are jeopardized by the actions of organized labour; in the latter, it is triggered by the 'traps' set by competition between capitalists themselves (Bowman, 1982).[4] These two tasks of representation are difficult to satisfy simultaneously within the same association. They impose quite different *organization* and *legitimation* imperatives, which are summarized in ideal-typical form in Table 7.1.

So distinctive are these two sets of requirements that it has

Table 7.2   *Functional specialization between trade and employers' peak associations in some countries*

Country	Employer ass.	Functions performed Trade ass.	Both functions
Germany	BDA	BDI	
Switzerland	ZVSAO	VORORT	
Ireland	FUE	CII	
Denmark	DA	IR	
Finland	STK	TKL	
Norway	NAF	NI	
Sweden	SAF	SI	
Portugal		AIP	CIP
France			CNPF
Belgium			FEB/VBO
Italy			CII
UK			CBI
Spain			CEOE
Netherlands			VNO/NCW
Luxembourg			FIL
Austria			BWK/VOEI
Greece			SEV
Turkey			TISK

frequently led historically to *functional specialization* and *structural differentiation* in business associability. For example, in Germany, Switzerland, Denmark, Sweden, Norway, Finland, and Ireland two distinct peak organizations were formed: one specialized in dealing with trade unions and social issues (employer associations); the other one with interactions with state agencies and other capitalist groups (trade associations). And also in those numerous national peak associations that nominally perform both functions, such as the British CBI, the French CNPF, the Italian Confindustria, we find a more or less sharp distinction between the structures (member associations or, more frequently, offices, representative and advisory bodies) operating in the social field and those operating in the economic one. Furthermore, these peak associations often play a little or no role in direct bargaining with organized labour (see Table 7.2).

It is important to observe that, while this tension between the social and the economic also applies *in principle* to trade unions, they have typically chosen *in practice* not to represent the interests of their members as producers, only their interests as workers. This has left the field of defending specific sectors from competition with other sectors and predation by the state exclusively to trade associations of business.

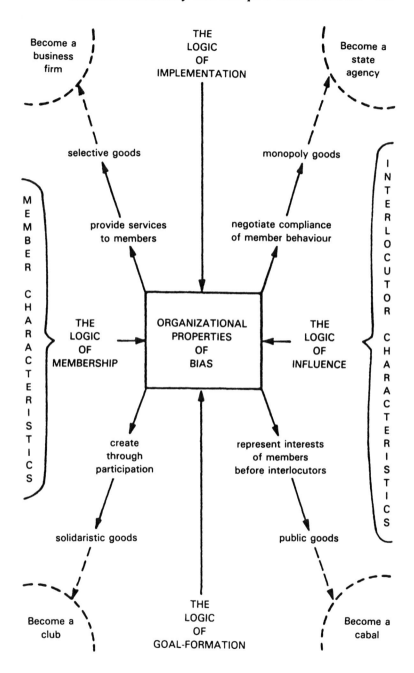

Figure 7.1 *A diagram of the four logics of associability*

As we now turn to the analysis of the prospective impact of the 1992 Project on organized interests, we will focus primarily on the strategic choices facing capitalists. Specifically, we will be concerned with whether they are likely to respond collectively to its challenges and uncertainties in terms of their position in the labour market (hence, by emphasizing their interests as a class and using employer associations) or in terms of their product market position (by accentuating their interests as managers, competitors and recipients of state favours and relying on trade associations). A second issue is whether this choice will strengthen associability at the *national* or the *supra-national* level – with even the possibility that *sub-national* (regional) groups may be given a boost by means of the distribution of so-called 'structural funds'. Throughout, it will be our assumption that the organizational response of labour will be predetermined by that of business associations – contrary to the orthodox perspective.

Europe's Internal Market and the Competing Logics of Business Associability

Our approach to understanding what sort of associational response will emerge rests on three assertions. First, it questions the liberal notion that only the characteristics and preferences of potential members will determine the structure of emerging interest organizations (Schmitter, 1977). Secondly, it pays equal attention to all the *interlocutors* of a given business interest category and does not treat organized labour as a privileged actor. This may even mean suspending the assumption of voluntarism and recognizing the power of state agencies to compel capitalists to adopt (or adapt) a specific organizational format. Thirdly, it takes into consideration not only the socio-political constraints to organized action, but also the technical imperatives emerging from the organizing process itself.

According to Schmitter and Streeck (1981), the organization of BIAs may be conceptualized as a compromise among four competing 'logics' of associability. The *logic of membership* leads to associative structures that reflect the fragmented and specialized preferences of members; the *logic of influence* tends to produce more unitary and encompassing structures in response to the demands of its principal interlocutors, state agencies and trade unions; finally, the *logic of goal formation* and the *logic of implementation* determine the association's response to the political problem of efficaciously aggregating member preferences into a more-or-less coherent organizational programme, and to the administrative problem of scale in delivering efficiently a particular mix of public, selective, monopolistic, and solidaristic goods and services (Child, Loveridge and Warner, 1973). If and when the Single European Act leads to an internal market among the twelve countries, it will affect all these logics in that the potential membership of associations will increase in number and heterogeneity, the nature and characteristics of their public and private interlocutors will change, the scale on which associational goods and services must be distributed will expand, and the rules for making collective decisions will have to take into account the multiplicity of levels of aggregation of member preferences.

In terms of the *logic of membership*, the creation of the European Internal Market should lead to the restructuring of capital, labour, and product markets on a subnational, national, and supranational scale. This will affect differentially firms of varying size, sector, and location – depending on the extent to which EC norms are harmonized or are based on 'mutual recognition', and on the extent to which local and national exemptions are tolerated. What we can confidentially forecast are increasing differentiation, fragmentation, and internal conflict among capitalist interests – leading to greater problems in the *management of diversity* within their associations. In general terms, the sectors and regions most penalized will be those at present most sheltered from competition by distinctive national 'regimes', while those that have a long experience of international competition will be better equipped to respond to the challenge of 1992 (Jacobi, 1989). Advantages will accrue mainly to those sectors (and to the countries and regions where they are sited) that are characterized by large firm size, strong demand growth, a high R&D component and increasing returns to scale in production and/or distribution. Not coincidentally, these were the firms that actively promoted the passage of the Single European Act through their special unit of collective action, the European Business Roundtable (Katseli, 1989). However, it is not yet clear whether their project of deregulation and mutual recognition will prevail over the demands of competing sectors and firms for re-regulation and policy harmonization by the EC. Nor can those firms which have performed well in the past in the semi-regulated climate of European business necessarily be expected to do as well in the future, if the eventual internal market is fully exposed to extra-European competitors. Threatened in this way, they may well prefer opting for new forms of 'sheltering', and this could provide a potent incentive for more corporatist forms of business associability. In any case, these alternatives will be subject to future political choices as the Twelve meet (or do not meet) the obligation to agree upon (and, eventually, to implement) the 279 EC directives implied by the 1992 Project. In other words, we can forecast increasing divisiveness across sectors and, perhaps, within sectors – but not their direction or intensity.

As far as the *logic of influence* is concerned, the future is even more uncertain since it is not clear what the end-state of the integration process will be. The Single European Act is notoriously silent on the issue of Community institutions. It increases modestly the role of the Parliament, shifts some (but not all) issues to weighted majority voting in the Council of Ministers, expands greatly the policy initiation role of the Commission, and hints at an expansion of its responsibility for direct administration of Community decisions, but the eventual configuration of its policy-making institutions remains to be seen (Schmitter, 1990).

We can, however, make a number of assumptions: (1) the institutions of the Community will be multilayered and, possibly, overlapping in their *compétences*; (2) the predominant decision-making style, whatever the formal rules, will be consociational, not majoritarian, and few measures will be pushed through against the intense resistance of a member state, especially a large member state; (3) the capacity of the Commission, Council, Parliament, or any other EC institution to mobilize mass pressures against the concentrated resistance of specialized interests will be limited; (4) the efforts of the Commission to expand their authority to administer EC policies directly will be limited and only sporadically accorded by member states, many of which will continue to use 'selective implementation' as a means of avoiding collective obligations they cannot otherwise prevent; (5) the Commission will seek to forge 'discretionary alliances' not only with specific sectors as in the past (such as agriculture, coal and steel, and artificial fibres, but also with particular subnational regions).

All this does not yet 'prefigure' the sort of polity that is likely to emerge in the aftermath of 1992. Several key questions remain:

First, will the substance of authoritative policy-making at the Community level follow *functional* or *territorial* lines of aggregation and, if territorial as in a federalist system, will the constituent units be existing national states of their subnational units?

Secondly, will the 'format' of post-1992 Europe be *concentric* with all its institutions rotating around and being coordinated by the Eurocracy in Brussels, or will it adopt an *eccentric* pattern with a multitude of relatively independent, policy-specialized authorities dispersed across the European continent – each with different levels of member obligation and, even, with different sets of members?

Thirdly, which countries will eventually join the *acquis communautaire*, and will the prospective increase in number of member states, as well as their variety, change the basic rules of the game?

Fourthly, will the *identities* and *allegiances* of individual citizens eventually 'migrate' from their present national and subnational sites to that of Europe as a whole, and will its overarching authorities manage to mobilize them in defence of the continent's 'general interests'?

Needless to say, these are quite different institutional outcomes. Movement in any of these directions would set up significantly different incentives within the logic of influence and its subsequent impact on the organization of business interests at the European level.[5] Similar choices during the process of state-building in the nineteenth century had a major influence on the formation and role of national peak associations of business (Lanzalaco, 1990b: chap. 10).

As far as the *logic of goal formation* and the *logic of effective implementation* are concerned, it is virtually assured that the enlargement of the market will raise new problems of scale, different from those embedded in nationally protected markets. This will require associative structures able both to provide goods and services on the level of the Community and to aggregate preferences and demands across and within national borders. The supra- and the sub-national scales are probably more efficient and effective that the national ones in coping with these exigencies, but they would require increasing autonomy of regional and supranational BIAs at the expense of national peak associations – something that surely will be resisted. It may well be that the 'economies of scale' in the distribution of collective goods will clash with the 'politics of scale' in terms of established identities and organizational interests. There is no guarantee that the imperatives of a more rational division of labour between different associative levels will necessarily overcome the inertial forces of existing national BIAs.

Summing up, some forces are pushing towards the decline of national peak associations; others are strengthening them. The extension of Community tasks and authority should promote a marked shift to the European level as the deadline approaches, but it is far from clear whether this will benefit supra-national peak associations or sectorally and territorially differentiated associations. From whatever 'logical' perspective one adopts, it is simply not possible a priori to determine the likely impact of the 1992 Package on the organizational properties of BIAs. The only certainty is that the magnitude of unfolding and impending changes is sufficient to change the political strategy of capitalists – whether or not it affects the collective behaviour of workers and employees. Somewhere in the contested terrain between the likelihood of a radical de-regulation of markets within the Community, the threat of competition from producers outside the Community, the varying capacity of each member government to protect and exempt its clients, and the pervasive inertia of existing lines of interest intermediation, the decisions (and non-decisions) will be made. What is at stake is not just a matter of organizational tinkering and social engineering, but a *strategic choice*[6] of dramatic and far-reaching importance. It will determine, in the long run, the collective identity of capitalists as a class, the integrity of their norms and institutions, and the conditions of their social reproduction. If we assume that the organizational properties of business associations are not just the passive outcome of fixed member preferences, but can actively mould the nature, boundaries, and interests of the categories they represent (Sartori, 1969; Schmitter, 1983), then, what could be at stake is nothing less than the possible emergence of a Euro-bourgeoisie, along with its potential Executive Committee, the EC. The alternative – should the project of an integrated market not succeed or fail to produce a significant restructuring of class or sectoral interests – is likely to be the resurgence of national bourgeoisies, each with its distinctive system of interest politics and industrial relations.

Since the margins of manoeuvre are wide and the discretion of actors correspondingly great, all we can do is to sketch out the range of possible courses of action and to analyse their strategic implications. We propose four plausible future scenarios.

First, *relative decline of business associability at all levels, coupled with the emergence of other forms of governance at the sectoral level.* In this scenario, capitalists (especially those in sectors favoured by the newly integrated market) would react to the increasing specialization and fragmentation of interests caused by a radical de-regulation of national markets and the failure to harmonize these arrangements with a set of European re-regulations. These new lines of cleavage and opportunity would 'spill over' existing BIAs, national or European, that are much too bounded by a traditional definitions of interest and much too binding on their members (Streeck, 1988). In this Thatcherian scenario, other forms of governance would come to dominate at the sectoral level: *hierarchies* (trusts, conglomerates, mergers, vertically integrated firms); *markets* (with or without informal collusive arrangements); *clans* (family connections, industrial districts, local communities); *alliances* (joint ventures, strategic combinations, cooperative research and marketing arrangements; Schmitter, 1989). Firms would be confident of the ability to pursue their objectives in the economic arena, free from the constraints imposed by state agencies or their associations. When necessary, individual capitalists or firms would resort to direct lobbying in Brussels or Strasbourg.

Secondly, *increased territorial and sectoral differentiation of business associability at both the supra- and sub-national levels.* Faced with the challenge of the integrated market, capitalists – especially those in previously sheltered, less competitive sectors – may be compelled to produce an adaptive response through associative channels, but not necessarily thorough existing ones. In order to cope with the likely fragmentation of interests along regional and product lines, they might diminish their support for national, intersectoral, peak associations and rely increasingly on associations specialized by territory and sector. These national organizations, in turn, might create supranational networks linking specific producers to Community institutions in defence of sectoral subsidies, exemptions, and re-regulations when faced with 'unfair competition' from extra-European producers. One could even imagine alliances between subnational associations representing regions in different countries with similar product mixes or infra-structural problems. Depending on the size, number, and diversity of firms involved, as well as the intervention of public agencies, it may prove impossible to satisfy their interests by resorting to the more privatistic solutions of markets, communities, alliances, or corporate hierarchies.

Thirdly, *greater reliance on national peak associations.* So far, we have assumed that capitalists react to changing contexts by following the line of least resistance. Faced with a shift in scale and a fragmentation of interests, they would either abandon their reliance on associative action altogether or adapt bits and pieces of it to the new opportunity structure. But what if capitalists were 'proactive' and responded by strengthening existing national peak associations such as the CBI, BDI and BDA, CNPF, Con-findustria, CEOE, and so forth? The 1992 Package means greater market volatility and strong pressures on firms to enhance their flexibility in order to compete effectively. The de-regulation of national regimes undermines not only well-entrenched business practices, but also arrangements that have long governed the training and employment of workers. All this could be perceived as a threat to the historical identity of business as a 'national' class and to the distinctive sources of 'national' productivity.

Capitalists – perhaps in alliance with a national labour movement that also sees its coherence and rights being menaced – could react by demanding protection from 'social dumping' and respect the 'mutual recognition' of each member's peculiar socio-economic institutions. To do this, they would have to increase the resources and governing capacity of their respective peak associations.

Fourthly, *emergence of supranational business associability, culminating in an enhanced role for European peak associations.* In this case, the response would be both proactive and reactive in nature. In order to cope collectively with the increasing dispersion and specialization of business interests and the imperative of restructuring markets on a wider scale, capitalists could strengthen existing, but weakly functioning, sectoral and intersectoral organizations at the level of Europe as a whole. The 'unity of the capitalist class' – already a precarious matter at the level of most national states – would be asserted by coordinating centrally the responses of functionally or territorially specialized units of representation. Such national and subnational associations would persist, but – contrary to the second and third scenarios – they would lose their autonomy to overarching organizations at the level of the Community as a whole.

The Likely Strategic Choice and its Organizational Consequences

The successful accomplishment of the 1992 objectives would involve an institutional restructuring of both labour and product markets. Therefore, it would be bound to affect, even if to differing degrees and in different ways, the interests of capitalists both as authoritative employers of workers and competitive producers of goods and services. As the process of completing the internal market unfolds, they will have to choose whether to base their associative response on the former or the latter. And this, as we have seen above in Tables 7.1 and 7.2, is likely to make a difference, since the two orientations have significantly different organizational requirements. Moreover, given the size and complexity of the EC, it would seem highly unlikely that European capitalists could effectively include both within the same organizational structure. Already at the national level, those associations that formally claim to be covering both sets of interests, in fact are incapable of dealing with them simultaneously. Needless to say, this orientation towards employer versus producer interests has major implications for which of the four scenarios is most likely to occur.

If we assume (1) that the effects of restructuring the labour market at the European level are likely to be very favourable for employers and disadvantageous for workers (Streeck, 1990a, 1990b); (2) that labour is already less organized and less resourced at the EC level than business interests (Sargent, 1985; de Vroom, 1987; Grant, 1990); (3) that no collective bargaining is at present conducted at the EC level and that the chances are slim that a 'Social Dimension' will be added to the 1992 Package (Streeck, 1990a); and (4) that capitalists will be likely to organize to defend or promote those interests of theirs that are most challenged and jeopardized; then, we are easily led to the conclusion that *capitalists in the context of the Community will have much stronger incentives to privilege their sectoral interests as producers and to down-play (even to disregard altogether) their class interests as employers.* In terms of the variables in Table 7.1, they will be prone to adopt divisive conceptions of interest along sectoral or product lines and to support the more differentiated forms of representation characteristic of trade associations – eschewing the more cohesive and encompassing format of employers' associations.

This hypothesis, however, does not provide us with a clear expectation about which of the four scenarios is most likely to emerge. Concretely, it fails to specify which *principle of differentiation* (the sectoral or the territorial) and which *level of aggregation* (the subnational, the national, or the supranational) will predominate.

The first and second scenarios are the most congruent with a producer mode of defining business interests. Both involve a passive and adaptive response. Both would lead to a diversity of strategies along lines of sectoral or territorial differentiation and would produce a fragmentation of units of collective action – even if the former would operate outside associative channels, while the latter would make extensive use of them.

The first scenario would imply the most radical change from the *status quo*, at least in continental Europe. It forecasts the decline of all collective forms of interest representation, and their replacement by either non-political forms of collective action – for example, buy-outs and mergers into single hierarchical structures, strategic alliances among firms or informal, collusive arrangements between competitors – or by political forms of individual action – such as the development of the government-relations function by firms at the EC level, the hiring of specialized lobbyists and lawyers in Brussels. The adoption of this strategy is contingent, first and foremost, upon the de-regulatory impact of 1992 upon national policies and, secondly, upon the emergence of some autonomous capability at the new centre to reward and punish individual enterprises – with subsidies, credits, standards, protections, and so on.

To a certain extent, the first scenario has already become a reality. Numerous commentators have observed the extraordinary rush to Brussels by law firms and free-lance lobbyists. One particularly knowledgeable student of business politics has noted 'the extent to which large multinational firms increasingly find it necessary to have permanent government affairs representatives in Brussels' (Grant, 1990: 4). One of the major impacts of the Single European Act has been the unprecedented wave of cross-national mergers, acquisitions, and buy-outs (Schmitter and Streeck, 1990: 3). This is a strategic response that is available only to big business and is likely to meet with rising resistance from the ranks of small and medium-sized enterprises – where and when they are not simply bought out. Moreover, the scramble by large firms to acquire particularistic advantage for themselves from the completed market will leave underprotected and, often, unrepresented the interests of the capitalist class as a whole. It is one thing to stress *ad nauseam* the need for decentralized flexibility in 'the global market place'; it is quite another to ignore the sorts of 'public goods' – worker training, stable currency, infrastructure provision, protection from predators, policing of contracts, enforcement of standards, and so forth – that only a state (or state-like) coercive body can provide. One could assume that 'big business' in Europe will eventually acquire the hegemony it has long enjoyed in the United States, but this seems highly unlikely within the timeframe of the Single European Act. To protect itself politically, big business will need allies among small and medium-sized firms.[7] In the meantime, the EC will be vulnerable to the accusation that its initials really stand for 'Executive Committee of the Dominant Class' (Schmitter and Streeck, 1990). In order to protect themselves against such defamation, Eurocrats may well seek to popularize their activities by appealing to workers and employees by means of such measures as adding a 'Social Dimension' to the 1992 Package. Our assessment is that, whatever merits the first Scenario might have from the perspective of economic efficiency, it will be both socially and politically vulnerable in the Europe of the 1990s.

The Second scenario would seem the most plausible, if only because it is most compatible with the *status quo ante*. European capitalists have already expressed a preference for specialized trade associations at the Community level (de Vroom, 1987; Grant, 1990). After an initial period in which EC officials actively promoted the formation of broadly encompassing peak associations for business and provided them with special recognition, privileged access, and some subsidization (Schmitter and Streeck, 1990), since the mid-1960s,

> neither the Commission not any other EEC body appears to have encouraged simplification of the organization of European representatives of capital [since] there has been no encouragement of mergers between the organisations which represent similar interests, nor support for greater hierarchical ordering of European representatives of capital. (Sargent, 1985: 233)[8]

Moreover, these sectoral associations have operated in Brussels quite independently of the Union of Industrial and Employers Confederations of Europe (UNICE), whose membership is composed exclusively of some thirty-two intersectoral, national peak associations from the twelve EC members and ten other European countries. As its current secretary-general prudently put it, 'UNICE does not usually intervene on "vertical" matters, i.e. those which are "sector-specific" . . . [unless] no relevant sectoral organization exists or when the issue is of exceptional importance' (Tyszkiewicz, 1990: 3).

The process of European interest differentiation and association formation has, so far, been much more pronounced along sectoral than territorial lines.[9] While there is considerable evidence that regionally based intersectoral associations are being reinforced within such national peak associations as the French CNPF, the British CBI, the Italian Confindustria and the Dutch NCW and VNO (Schmitter and Lanzalaco, 1989), there is not yet much sign of a shift in focus towards Brussels by these subnational business representatives. What has been occurring on a substantial and accelerating scale is the establishment there of 'quasi-embassies' by subnational governments: virtually all of the German *Länder*, Catalonia, Emilia-Romagna, Lombardy, Rhône-Alpes, and so forth. Whether this will eventually provide a cover for the permanent representation of local business interests remains to be seen. Their delegations to Brussels already seem to be richly stocked with such spokespersons.

The ultimate viability of the second scenario depends very much on the policy mix that will emerge from the directives and spill-overs of the 1992 Process. If de-regulation does not substantially undermine the functional approach that has characterized European integration since its inception, and if the regional funds that were part of its political quid pro quo continue to expand, then we have every reason to expect a strengthening of both supranationally structured sectoral associations and subnationally specified peak associations. The former are already well entrenched in Brussels, although they still have to compete with direct interventions from specialized national organizations and individual firms. The latter are merely a glimmer on the Community's horizon, but their significance could increase considerably – especially with a boost from the Commission anxious to escape the limitations of dealing exclusively with national-level governments and associations (Greenwood, Grote and Ronit, 1990).

Nor can the third scenario, based on a proactive strengthening of national peak associations, be ruled out. The 1992 commitments may well meet increasing resistance. The most difficult issues – taxation, welfare policy, and monetary union – have yet to be resolved, and these are issues of deep-rooted national concern. They are also issues which are exempt from the weighted majority voting procedure. In the past, national peak associations have played a significant role in shaping the response of business to measures before the EC (Kirchner, 1986; Sargent, 1985; Grant, 1990). Once they realized the import of the Single European Act, they have greatly stepped up their attention to Community affairs (Grant, 1990) and begun to restructure their internal committee and governance systems accordingly.[10] In addition to their long-standing membership in UNICE (which, in any case, is not very binding upon them), each of these associations has its own bureau in Brussels and, as long as the Council of Ministers has the definitive say in the adoption of directives, each has its privileged line of defence through the national government representatives who sit on the Council. We have already seen signs that some national peak associations are adapting to the new opportunity structure by restructuring their internal processes so as to provide more of a role for subnational representation in their activities.

Whether national peak associations will be able to contain both sectoral specialization and territorial differentiation within their ranks and continue to occupy the sort of strategic position astride Community legislation that they did in conjunction with national governments during the 1970s is problematic – but not impossible. They are also suffering from strong pressure within their own national contexts to devolve their roles as 'bargaining agents', 'dispute handlers', and 'service providers' to smaller units of representation or even to individual firms (Sisson, 1990). However, in favour of this outcome is the likelihood that the strategy of capitalists will be based, not on the *actual impact* of the 1992 Package, but on the *uncertain expectations* that have been aroused by its provisions. When actors perceive such uncertainty, they are likely to cling to old and well-consolidated institutions (Crouch,

1986). And existing national peak associations readily offer such a familiar and reassuring framework for collective action. Moreover, during the ensuing negotiations, they will remain important instruments for exerting pressure upon member governments and the Council of Ministers on behalf of exemptions and exclusions. Should they succeed in protecting the basis of national productivity from 'social dumping' and 'regime competition', these associations could well acquire an enhanced role and salience in the supranational politics of the Community.

The fourth scenario would entail the transmigration of business-interest representation from the national to the supranational plane. If one regards the contemporary integration of Europe as a repetition of the previous patterns of national economic and political integration in the same area, this must appear to be a virtually inevitable outcome. As local markets were replaced by national ones, so local business associations were displaced by national ones. Why should the same not happen at the European level in response to the completion of 'its' market?

One simple reason is that national economies and national associations are far more entrenched and resilient than were the less formal local arrangements they displaced. Another is that the European Community is still far from becoming a supranational state – even with the added *compétences* stemming from the 1992 Package. Not only must the EC share its decision-making with member states, but it is also almost completely dependent upon them for the direct implementation of its policies. Another way of putting the point is that comprehensive, concentrated, and hier-archically coordinated national peak associations have only emerged historically under two conditions: (1) strong and relatively autonomous state intervention in economic matters, especially in general policy arenas that affect several sectors simultaneously; and (2) a relative balance of class forces in which organized labour has the capacity to deter independent action by capital and to influence the agenda of public choice. Behind both of these lies a single political phenomenon: the emergence of social democracy in the electoral and, eventually, the governing arena.

In the context of the EC, neither of these conditions presently obtains, but they could eventually. Existing European peak associations were artificially created 'from above', shortly after the founding of the Community and before the creation of sectoral associations (de Vroom, 1987). Subsequently, they were displaced by the more specialized interlocutors in policy deliberations within the Commission and by national peak associations at the level of the Council of Ministers. Currently, there are efforts under way to strengthen their role and expand their resources (Grant, 1990). In the case of UNICE, this involves the development of closer relations with selected large firms and an increase in their contributions to its budget (Tyszkiewicz, 1990). Nevertheless, without a serious challenge from organized labour at the Community level which could compel capitalists to shift from a producer to an employer conception of their interests, it is hard to imagine that could be successful in convincing them to give up their 'traditional' reliance on national and sectoral associations. The only chance of that lies, not with the autonomous efforts of the European Trade Union Confederation (ETUC), but with the (at present unlikely) prospect that Europe could be engulfed by a wave of social democratic electoral triumphs at the national level; for example, the SPD in Germany and Labour in the United Kingdom. This, along with their continued role in France, Spain, and Italy, and the eventual accession of countries that have long been dominated by such parties – Austria, Norway, Sweden, even Finland – would radically change the composition of the Euro-parliament (where the socialists already form the largest voting bloc) and shift the priorities of the Commission. Issues such as a 'Social Dimension' and a 'European Company Law' with important provisions for worker representation would be revived and could sharpen the lines of class cleavage, forcing capitalists to respond collectively by strengthening their peak associations at the European level.

Of the four possible scenarios, it is easiest to estimate which is the least probable. That would be the fourth scenario because it is contingent on the most significant deviations from current practice in terms both of the politics of member countries and of the Community. The first scenario is not only more likely, but there is already considerable evidence of experimentation in that direction. It would be the clear preference of those large industrial and service firms that are capable of operating in the completed internal market and that have sufficient resources to intervene directly in the politics of Community institutions. This strategy is risky, however, for two reasons: (1) it would reinforce existing cleavages between capitalists based on differences in size of firm and market orientation; and (2), it would leave the class as a whole without much capability for collective action – if and when the European workers' movement re-acquires its sense of solidarity and militancy.

This leaves us with the second and third scenarios. The latter is predicated on a failure of the 1992 Project. Either there would be a manifest inability of the Twelve to meet the commitments contained in the Single European Act (and, needless to say, an even greater inability to negotiate its spill-over into monetary union or the Social Dimension), or the 279 directives would be formally issued, but their actual implementation would be so deficient and divergent that national-level regulatory regimes would remain intact and still effective in protecting national producers. Business interests would respond by regrouping in their national peak associations and defending themselves against 'unfair competition' and 'social dumping' – often in cahoots with trade-union confederations. So far, this has not happened. Admittedly, the most difficult measures have yet to be tackled, and resistance to further extensions of the Commission's role has been rising, but the momentum is considerable – as would be the disappointment of popular expectations if the whole notion of 'open frontiers' were to fade from sight.

The second scenario is, if only by elimination, the most likely outcome. It is the closest to the institutional pattern which set in during the 1960s and 1970s, and offers the most flexible response both to the immediate demands for differentiation according to policy area and to the eventual demands of organized labour. By grouping simultaneously at the supranational sectoral and the subnational territorial levels, business interests can ensure that they will be present in the forging of specific functional directives and in the distributing of regional funds. This provides few incentives for a comprehensive organizational response by labour (which it is, in any case, not capable of producing) and it reduces the visibility of the connection of capitalism to the Integrated Market.

The Implications for the Labour Movement

The completion of Europe's internal market will lead inevitably to harsher conditions of competition. It will pose a differential challenge to the prosperity of firms in specific sectors, sizes, regions, and countries. It seems likely to involve a substantial de-regulation of labour markets and unlikely to include a significant commitment to the Social Dimension (Streeck, 1990a). How will this affect existing trade unions and their confederations? More specifically, will the 1992 Project provide organized labour with an opportunity for aggregating and articulating its interests at the supranational level? Or, conversely, will it obstruct this process and encourage further divisions within the labour movement along sectoral or territorial lines?

Our first and overriding assumption should be already apparent: *capitalists may have the option of choosing between several reactive and proactive strategies; the response of workers can only be reactive.* It will depend primarily on what capitalists collectively decide to do and only secondarily on the preferences of Eurocrats or Euro-voters, not to mention Euro-workers.

Our second (and obvious) assumption is that, *while capitalists will be better equipped collectively to respond to the challenges of 1992, they will not necessarily be more affected by them.* Workers will suffer and benefit even more intensively, given their vulnerability in particular labour markets. The general level of employment, the conditions of working life, the extent of regulation of labour markets, the provision of welfare benefits, the provision of vocational training, the rights and obligations of trade unions, the composition of demand for skills, as well as the prosperity of specific sectors and firms, could all be determined by Community processes in the future – much in the way that most of what affects the interests of European agriculturists is already dependent upon decisions made at that level. Depending on how the 1992 Process advances, trade unions may have to deal with these issues at the EC level, even if they will have very little influence over whether or not such matters will be taken up by Community institutions.

Nor, as the other chapters in this volume testify, is the moment propitious. Not only have many, if not most, of the national labour movements lost members, financial strength, and their policy role in corporatist arrangements, but there has also been a marked tendency towards a decentralization of bargaining processes within national industrial relations systems. Presumptively, it would have been easier to organize a Community-level response, say through the ETUC, had the trend been the other way. Had national confederations been increasing their role in the member states, they might have been more willing to devolve some of this rising influence upon a supranational coordinating body. Instead, they are on the defensive and unlikely to part with anything.

Moreover, many of the issues surrounding the 1992 Package have a divisive impact upon worker interests. Those in the most regulated and protected markets would like to see their rights and entitlements extended by means of harmonization to all EC workers; those in unregulated and exposed conditions may see this less as an unmitigated benefit conferred on them by their more advanced brethren, than as a thinly disguised attempt to deprive them of their comparative advantage in the labour market. Except for symbolic declarations of support for the Social Dimension, it is hard to imagine these issues leading to an integrated response within the EC. What is lacking are sufficient incentives for a comprehensive organizational structure able to internalize the potential conflicts emerging among workers of different nations, sectors, and firms in Europe. Unless, of course, capitalists were to provide those incentives. Here we return to our first assumption. John R. Commons (1932: 682) already took this 'unorthodox' approach over fifty years ago when he affirmed that 'The labour movement is always a reaction and a protest against capitalism (. . .) [and] capitalism is not a single or static concept (. . .). Labour movements reflect these capitalistic movements.' And so, the future strategic and organizational assets of labour in Europe will be in great part dependent on the individual preferences and collective actions of capitalists.

Therefore, we are compelled to return to the four scenarios sketched out above. Whichever one will prevail (or, better, whatever mix will emerge) will determine how labour will deal with the economic and social issues raised by the completion of the internal market. The opportunity for the supranational aggregation and representation of worker interests will be greater, the more homogeneous and concerted is the capitalist proaction in response to the 1992 measures. Two scenarios are most likely to 'provoke' a European-level response by labour. The fourth scenario even depends on it, since the sort of concertation mechanisms it envisages can only function if there is some rough symmetry in organizational format and capability among the contending collective actors. Should European capitalists be compelled to adopt this strategy – say, by landslide victories of social democrats in several key EC countries and/or by severe inflationary pressures linked to over-full employment and corresponding pockets of labour militancy – then, they might very well try to assist national trade-union confederations in giving more bargaining power to the ETUC. Euro-corporatism would emerge with a corresponding macro-Keynesian policy mix for the Community as a whole – and the worst nightmares of neo-Liberals would have been realized.

Since there is very little chance of this happening, the second scenario may the best that labour can realistically hope for in the near future. Here, the impact of trade unions would be felt, primarily, in supranational sectors with oligopolistic markets (such as chemicals, pharmaceuticals, perhaps, armament manufacturers) or special characteristics (for example, air traffic controllers, customs agents, long-distance truck drivers) and, secondarily, at the subnational level in regions that are targeted for special treatment (for instance, those in the Integrated Mediterranean Programme) or affected in some particular way by the new market conditions (like those involved with hi-tech production or dependent on a specific energy source). This may not do much for the ETUC, but it would ensure some presence of organized worker interests at various stages of the deliberations surrounding EC policies.

Should either the first or third scenarios prevail, the labour movement would have virtually no incentives and few opportunities to intervene effectively in EC decision-making. In the former, capitalists would respond in a heterogeneous fashion at the level of individual enterprises. Existing trade unions might attempt to sponsor the creation of alliances among workers in production units of the same firm scattered across EC countries, but that would only undermine their own reason for existence, whether based on craft or industry, and could even lead to the formation of transnational company unions. In the latter, capitalists would react collectively through national peak associations and contribute to undermining the success of the 1992 commitments. Worker confederations could collude with 'their' capitalists in order to help isolate them from the pressures of international competition, but only at the price of rising sectoral conflicts and member disaffection.

None of the scenarios is particularly favourable to organized labour. Admittedly, the fourth scenario would lay the basis for a 'meta-corporatist' arrangement similar to the 'macro-corporatist' ones that prevailed in several European countries in the 1960s and 1970s and resulted in some notable advantages for centralized worker representation and class governance, but there are very few reasons for capitalists to promote such an outcome in the 1990s. Under the other possible conditions, worker interests will be fortunate if they manage to establish a loosely coupled structure of intermediation at the EC level, with a modest capacity to coordinate diverse demands on a very limited range of issues. Their best strategy may be to concentrate on the promotion of the rights and entitlements of industrial citizenship at the level of enterprises (Streeck, 1990a, 1990b), and leave a great deal of autonomy to more specialized institutions and organizations of representation at the sectoral and subnational territorial levels. In fact, for labour to attempt to accomplish more as Europe approaches 1992 would simply increase the likelihood of failure and jeopardize the already thin margin of manoeuvre that trade-union confederations – national or supranational – currently have. Once, however, the integrated market is in place and its distributional effects have begun to be registered, then the opportunity structure is likely to change in favour of new forms of collective action.

Notes

1 Therefore, our impression is that behind Offe and Wiesenthal's article there is not only a class theory of *organizations*, as Streeck (1988) suggests, but, more generally, a class theory of *action* based on the assumption that a generic 'social actor' does not exist but that capitalists and workers are actors *qualitatively* different and that their conduct cannot be analysed by means of a common theoretical framework.

2 Across fifty-six industrial sectors in nine countries, 'there are on the average no fewer than 16.4 business associations to one trade union' (Streeck, 1988: 13–14).

3 However, the more that capitalist interests are jeopardized either by trade unions or by governments formed by leftist parties, the more business associations will come to resemble trade unions. Compare, for example, the weakness of peak associations in the poorly unionized, non-socialist United States with their much more salient role in virtually all European countries. During the 1970s when capitalist hegemony became increasingly questioned, the British CBI, the French CNPF, and the Italian Confindustria all underwent organizational changes aimed at acquiring 'union-like' capabilities: increased member involvement; greater internal democracy; reinforcement of external communications, and so on (Lanzalaco, 1990a). The Swedish SAF, faced with the threat of 'wage-earner funds', in 1983 even took the unprecedented step of calling for a mass demonstration and a strike of capitalists! In the United States, significantly, the collective response was more informal and collusive; namely, the creation of the Business Roundtable, a restricted grouping of CEOs of major firms without a permanent staff or any capability for controlling its members' behaviour (McQuaid, 1982).

4 One of Offe and Wiesenthal's most obvious errors is to restrict their analysis exclusively to the former arena and, therefore, to assume that the only motive for capitalist collective action is class conflict with (previously) organized labour. As we observed above, this ignores the rich experience that capitalists had accumulated earlier when they associated in order to regulate their own relations with one another or to extract advantage from the state.

5 These alternatives are discussed and aggregated into a limited number of 'models' of an eventual European polity in Schmitter (1990).

6 A decision is a strategic choice when three conditions jointly occur; namely, when (1) the parties have discretion over their decisions – that is, when environmental constraints do not bind the choice of alternatives; when (2) the decision determines the range of alternatives among which further and future decisions are to be taken; and (3) when the outcome of the decision alters the the the actor's role in its relationships with other actors. Hence, strategic choices 'are directly concerned with the identities, the structures of, and the institutionalized relations between, social actors' (Kochan et al., 1984: 2). 'Where strategic decisions are at stake, internal lines of differentiation within social aggregates may become potential points of departure for a re-formation of interest structures and identities' (Streeck 1987: 283).

7 Not to mention the fact that many forms of 'flexible specialization' or 'diversified quality production' rest on the contribution of these firms as innovators, component suppliers, and alliance partners. Cf. the works of Piore and Sabel (1984), Bagnasco (1989), Streeck (1989).

8 An analysis of the different phases of the relationships between interest groups and EC institutions may be found in the works of Jurgen Grote (1989a, 1989b) and Schmitter and Streeck (1990).

9 The characteristics and the evolution of the processes of interest intermediation

and policy-making in two specific sectors at the EC level are analysed by Cawson (1990; electronics) and Greenwood and Ronit (1990; pharmaceuticals).

10 From a diachronic analysis of different yearbooks and statutes of the CNPF, the CBI, Confindustria and the CEOE it emerges that offices, committees, and governing bodies specializing in dealing with EC matters are increasingly being created and reinforced.

References

Bagnasco, A. (1989) *La costruzione sociale del mercato. Studi sullo sviluppo di piccola impresa in Italia*. Bologna: Il Mulino.

Berger, S. (1981) 'Introduction' to S. Berger (ed.), *Organizing Interests in Western Europe*. Cambridge: Cambridge University Press.

Bowman, J.R. (1982) 'The Logic of Capitalist Collective Action', *Social Science Information*, 21 (4–5).

Cawson, A. (1990) 'Modes of Policy-making and Patterns of State/Interest-group Relationships: the EC, 1992 and the Consumer Electronics Industry', Paper for a workshop during the Conference on 'The New Europe', Rimini, ECPR (Sept.).

Child, J., Loveridge, R. and M. Warner (1973) 'Toward an Organizational Study of Trade Unions', *Sociology*, 7: 71–91.

Clegg, H.A. (1976) *Trade Unionism under Collective Bargaining*. Oxford: Basil Blackwell.

Commons, J. (1932) 'Labor Movement', *Encyclopedia of the Social Sciences*, vol. VIII. London: Macmillan.

Crouch, C. (1986) 'Le origini storiche dei rapporti tra stati e interessi nell'Europa Occidentale', *Stato e Mercato*, 18.

de Vroom, B. (1987) 'El desarollo de un nuevo "estado" y la evolución de las asociaciones de interés. El caso de las asociaciones de intereses empresariales a nivel de Comunidad Europea', in C. Solé (ed.), *Corporatismo y Diferenciación Regional*. Madrid: Ministerio de Trabajo y Seguridad Social, Collección Informes, pp. 55–69.

Grant, W. (1990) 'Organized Interests and the European Community', Paper presented for the Sixth International Colloquium of the Feltrinelli Foundation, 'Organized Interests and Democracy – Perspectives on West and East', Cortona (29–31 May).

Greenwood, J., Grote, R.J. and Ronit, K. (1990) 'Organized Interests and the Internal Market: Associational Responses to the "Decomposition of the Nation State"', Paper for a workshop during the Conference on 'The New Europe', Rimini, ECPR (Sept.).

Greenwood, J. and Ronit, K. (1990) 'Organized Interests and the Internal Market: Diversity, Cohesion and the Variety of Political Actions', Paper for a workshop during the Conference on 'The New Europe', Rimini, ECPR (Sept.).

Grote, R.J. (1989a) 'Guidance and Control in Transnational Committee Networks: the Association Basis of Policy Cycles at EC Level', Paper presented at the Conference of SOG Research Committee of IPSA on 'Government and Organized Interests', Zurich (Sept. 1990).

Grote, R.J. (1989b) 'Rent Seeking "Without Frontiers"': on Institutional Supply and Organizational Demand for EC Regulatory Policies', Paper presented on the panel on 'Deregulation, Regulation and the International Dimension' of the ECPR Joint Session, Paris.

Ingham, G.K. (1974) *Strikes and Industrial Conflict*. London: Macmillan.

Jacobi, O. (1989) 'The Single European Market in 1992 – Economic and Political Hope', mimeo.

Katseli, L.T. (1989) 'The Political Economy of European Integration: From Eurosclerosis to Euro-corporatism', Discussion Paper No. 317, London, Centre for Economic Policy Research.

Kirchner, E.J. (1986) 'Interest Group Development at European Community Level as an Indicator of Integration', Paper presented to the Fifth International Conference on Europeanists, Washington, DC (18–20 Oct. 1985).

Kochan, T.A., McKersie R.B. and Cappelli, P. (1984) 'Strategic Choice in Industrial Relations', *Industrial Relations*, 23.

Lanzalaco, L. (1990a) 'Pinifarina President of the Confederation of Industry, and the Problems of Business Interest Associations', in R.Y. Nanetti and R. Catanzaro (eds), *Politics in Italy: a Review*, vol. 4. London: Pinter, pp. 102–22.

Lanzalaco, L. (1990b) *Dall'impresa all'associazione. Le organizzazioni degli imprenditori: la Confindustria in prospettiva comparata*. Milan: Franco Angeli.

Lipset, S.M. and Rokkan, S. (1967) 'Cleavage Structures, Party Systems, and Voter Alignments: an Introduction', in S.M. Lipset and S. Rokkan (eds), *Party Systems and Voting Alignments*. New York: Free Press.

McQuaid, K. (1982) *Big Business and Presidential Power*. New York: William Morrow.

Observatoire Social Européen (1985) *L'Europe Consultative. Où en est la participation syndicale dans les Communautés Européennes*? Brussels: Observatoire Social Européen.

Offe, C. and Wiesenthal, H. (1980) 'Two Logics of Collective Action: Theoretical Notes on Social Class and Organizational Form', in M. Zeitlin (ed.), *Political Power and Social Theory*, vol. I, pp. 67–115. Greenwich, CT: JAI Press Inc.

Olson, M. (1965) *The Logic of Collective Action*. Cambridge, MA: Harvard University Press.

Perlman, S. (1928) *A Theory of the Labour Movement*. New York: Kelly.

Piore, M. and Sabel, C. (1984) *The Second Industrial Divide*. New York: Basic Books.

Sargent, J. (1985) 'Corporatism and the European Community', in W. Grant (ed.), *The Political Economy of Corporatism*. London: Macmillan, pp. 189–253.

Sartori, G. (1969) 'From the Sociology of Politics to Political Sociology', in S.M. Lipset (ed.), *Politics and the Social Sciences*. New York: Oxford University Press.

Schmitter, P.A. (1977) 'Modes of Interest Intermediation and Models of Societal Change in Western Europe', in P.C. Schmitter and G. Lehmbruch (eds), *Trends toward Corporatist Intermediation*. London: Sage.

Schmitter P.C. (1981) 'Needs, Interests, Concerns, Actions, Associations and Modes of Intermediation: Toward a Theory of Interest Politics in Contemporary Societies', Berlin: mimeo.

Schmitter, P.C. (1983) 'Organizzazione degli interessi e rendimento politico', in G. Pasquino (ed.), *Le società complesse*. Bologna: Il Mulino.

Schmitter, P.C. (1989) 'I settori nel capitalismo moderno: modi di regolazione e variazioni nel rendimento', *Stato e Mercato*, 26: 173–208.

Schmitter, P.C. (1990) 'The European Community as an Emergent and Novel Form of Political Domination', Stanford, CA: Stanford University (April), mimeo.

Schmitter, P.C. and Brand, D. (1979) 'Organizing Capitalists in the United States:

the Advantages and Disadvantages of Exceptionalism', Paper presented at the Meetings of the APSA, Washington, DC: mimeo.

Schmitter, P.C. and Lanzalaco, L. (1989) 'Regions and the Organization of Business Interests', in W. Coleman and H. Jacek (eds), *Regionalism, Business Interests and Public Policy*. London: Sage, pp. 201–30.

Schmitter, P.C. and Streeck, W. (1981) 'The Organization of Business Interests', Discussion paper IIM/LMP 81–13, Berlin: Wissenschaftszentrum.

Schmitter, P.C. and Streeck, W. (1990) 'Organized Interests and the Europe of 1992', Paper prepared for a conference on 'The United States and Europe in the 1990s: Trade, Finance, Defence, Politics, Demographics and Social Policy', Washington, DC: American Enterprise Institute (6–8 March).

Shalev, M. (1980) 'Industrial Relations Theory and the Comparative Study of Industrial Relations and Industrial Conflict', *British Journal of Industrial Relations*, 1.

Sisson, Keith (1990) 'Employers' Organisations and the Industrial Relations Strategies of Individual Employers', Paper presented at the IREC Conference on 'Employers' Associations in Europe', Trier.

Streeck, W. (1987) 'The Uncertainties of Management and the Management of Uncertainty: Employers, Labor Relations and Industrial Adjustment in the 1980s', *Work, Employment and Society*, 1: 281–308; and *International Journal of Political Economy*, 17: 57–87.

Streeck, W. (1988) 'Interest Variety and Organizing Capacity: Two Class Logics of Collective Action?' Contribution to an International Conference on 'Political Institutions and Interest Intermediation', Universität Konstanz (20–21 April).

Streeck, W. (1989) 'On the Social and Political Conditions of Diversified Quality Production', Contribution to an International Conference on 'No Way to Full Employment?' Berlin: Wissenschaftszentrum (July).

Streeck, W. (1990a) 'La dimensione sociale del mercato unico europeo', *Stato e Mercato*, 28: 29–68.

Streeck, W. (1990b) 'More Uncertainties: West German Unions Facing 1992', Paper presented to a panel on 'One Big Union? Organized Labor and 1992', Seventh Conference of Europeanists, Washington, DC (23–25 March).

Truman, David (1951) *The Governmental Process*. New York: Knopf.

Tyszkiewicz, Z.J.A. (1990) 'UNICE: the Voice of European Business and Industry in Brussels', Paper presented at the IREC Conference on 'Employers Associations in Europe', Trier.

8
Trade Unions and Decentralized Production: a Sketch of Strategic Problems in the German Labour Movement

Horst Kern and Charles F. Sabel

In the last decade liberal or social-democratic observers in the United States and Great Britain have been increasingly drawn to the dual German system of industrial relations as a way of protecting the interests of employees at the company level, encouraging the continuous reorganization of firms required by current competitive conditions, and yet collectively defending the economic and political interests of those who live from pay cheques, regardless of where they are employed. The dual system, in a word, holds out the promise that the efficiency advantages of the Japanese company union can be reconciled with the social-democratic conviction that democracy in advanced capitalist countries requires the participation of a national labour movement.

Seen this way the dual system is indeed attractive. In the typical medium-sized or large firm in the private sector, a works' council is elected every three years by all permanent employees, unionized or not, according to a formula that assures blue- and white-collar workers representation proportional to their numbers in the company. The chief power and distinguishing feature of the factory council is its *de facto* capacity to force management to elaborate comprehensive 'reconciliation of interests' (*Interessenausgleiche*) in the event of any consequential change in the company, including, for example, a major sale of assets or the introduction of new technologies. American unions defend employees' rights piecemeal, and often with little possibility of assessing the competitive effects of their actions, by elaborating and then bargaining the redrawing of rules governing the definition of jobs, eligibility for promotion, and seniority rights. The works' council, in contrast, uses its ability to influence the substantive outcome of reorganization to reach encompassing agreements with management that do justice to the rights of the work-force while respecting the constraints of competitive conditions. At a minimum, the obligation to negotiate reorganization reduces the danger that management will jeopardize the possibility of long-term survival by abrupt efforts to restore profitability in the short term through reduction of labour costs. At a maximum, the works'-council system creates a bargaining regime in which, as in Japan, both parties almost reflexively prefer high-wage, high-skill solutions to adjustment problems as both efficient and just.

Outside the plant, as in the United States, but unlike Japan, the dual system provides a well-articulated structure of collective bargaining. Bargaining is by industry and region, with agreements in each industry typically governed by the pattern set in a key regional contract. General rules governing, for example, working time, training programmes, or the type of wage determination system in an industry, are renegotiated at irregular intervals. Wages are renegotiated annually. This bargaining regime is complemented at the bottom by firm- or plant-level agreements that extend the minima established in the regional contracts, and by extensive, often legislatively mandated participation in the institutions that make and execute labour-market social-welfare, and even health-care policy. In this sense the German labour movement is an advocate for the collective and changing interests of the little people or the average Joe and Jane in a way that Japanese company unions, at least as they have usually been understood in the West, are not.

The firm-level and extra-firm elements of the dual system are linked in at least three ways. First, the vast majority of works' councillors are active trade-union members, and depend on the unions' support in their campaigns for election. Secondly, the most prominent works' councillors in a region sit on the union commissions that establish the collective bargaining demands, and many hold unpaid but influential positions in the union bureaucracy. Thirdly, representatives of the national or regional union may serve together with factory councillors as members of a firm's advisory board (*Aufsichtsrat*). Besides approving major investment plans, the chief responsibility of the *Aufsichtsrat* – often regarded as the core of West German labour-management co-determination or *Mitbestimmung* – is to elect the managing directors of the firm, and through them influence choice of its chief operation officers. Labour's rights to representation on a particular supervisors' board vary according to the size and sector of activity of the corresponding company and are regulated by a body of legislation the extraordinary complexity of which is a constant reminder of the bitter conflicts provoked by every effort to extend those rights. In the best case, labour can always be outvoted by a united management; but even in the worst, labour acquires supplemental information about managerial plans and additional possibilities for coordinating its own response.[1]

The dual system's theoretical appeal is reinforced by the apparent stability of the trade unions in the Federal Republic of Germany despite more than a decade of the kind of industrial reorganization that has shaken labour movements in countries as diverse as Sweden, Italy, and the United States. One indicator is the slight increase in the average percentage of the total work-force organized in trade unions (Baethge and Oberbeck, 1988). Another is the unions' willingness to initiate provocative debates concerning many of the problems with which they are confronted. These include the reduction of work time, the use of new technologies, the reduction of environmental risks, and the recruiting of workers with the kinds of skills and ambitions demanded for success in the most rapidly growing parts of the highly competitive export economy.

But under this unblemished surface, there are forces at work that could create a completely different picture. A closer look at the statistics shows that the trade unions' membership is less and less representative of the work-force as a whole. A coarse but serviceable generalization is that the distribution of trade-union members by occupation and skill-level today resembles the distribution of jobs and skills characteristic of the work-force about thirty years ago. An obvious danger signal is the labour movement's growing difficulty in recruiting young workers. In 1970, 23.2 per cent of employees in the metal-working industries under 25 years of age were trade-union members. In 1987, the corresponding figure had sunk to 17.5 per cent (Mahnkopf, 1989: 5).

Likewise, the debates, stimulating as they may be when taken one by one, appear less promising upon closer examination. Not that each has been a flash in the pan. But each has been conducted in isolation from the others, and organized in such a way as to reinforce rather than reduce bureaucratic specialization of the unions' organization. Thus, 'work time' is a problem for specialists in collective bargaining; 'chips' was the responsibility of the experts in technology policy; 'recruiting problems' was subsumed under the rubric of policies towards white-collar workers, whereas 'ecology' went under the rubric of 'relations to others' – that is, to the state, to the political parties, and to the social movements.

What has been missing is a general concept for reorganizing the trade unions that suggests a coordinated attack on the individual problems. The disorientation which local trade-union activists manifest in almost every conversation reflects the lack of such a general concept. Uncertain of their members' support, and convinced that the national unions' leadership misunderstands or simply ignores them, many factory councillors in the metal-working industry seize the powers to intervene in restructuring that they have by law, or which management has thrust upon them as a last, desperate chance to secure their local position. If, as frequently happens, union officials in the distant national head-quarters later tell them that their decisions violate the spirit or even the letter of collective bargaining agreements, they feel more isolated than before – and more convinced than ever that there is no comprehensive union strategy to guide their decisions. Such experiences are paralysing. Above all, they make it still more difficult to recruit new members and mobilize existing ones. A vicious circle begins, and the anxious, fitful talk of a trade-union crisis that has filled the pauses in the open discussion of recent years suddenly becomes more than just chit-chat.

This chapter is a first effort to connect some of the isolated pieces of this debate. In the next section, we briefly discuss some of the most important trends in the reorganization of industry. Our central thesis is that as the boundaries between the corporation and its environment – other firms and society in general – become more permeable, labour markets are becoming open in unexpected ways. The third section discusses the problems which trade unions face as labour markets open, and section four examines some potential trade-union responses to these dilemmas. These form the core of the chapter. The central argument here is that the same logic of industrial reorganization which is undermining the trade unions' current organization also creates the possibility for a fundamental reformulation of their strategies. We sketch the general conditions under which a reformulation could occur, and we elaborate discussion of these enabling conditions with examples drawn from the unions' current activities. But we do not consider such plainly important questions as how company reorganization has effected macroeconomic policy-making in Germany, or the unions' possible response to these changes. First things first.

Our investigations are based primarily on research that we conducted in German automobile manufacturing companies and their suppliers. With regard to the car manufacturers, we inter-viewed experts in three firms in the areas of production, technology planning, logistics, and purchasing. In addition, we spoke with representatives of the works' council. The interviews were complimented in all cases by extensive factory visits. We conducted interviews in fifteen supplier firms. They were selected because of their central position in the relevant markets. The interviews with the suppliers were less extensive than those with the car companies, though this was, in part, simply a result of the former's more compact organization. The interviews were conducted in January, July, and August 1989, together with Gary Herrigel. Knowledge of other similar investigations in the United States, Italy, and Sweden formed a backdrop for the study.

The central body of research on which this chapter is based, finally, was concluded before the fall of the Communist government in the German Democratic Republic (GDR) and the subsequent incorporation of the GDR into the Federal Republic. We do not offer an account here, therefore, of the specific and enormous problems that the collapse of the economy of the former GDR and the current efforts to restructure it on competitive lines pose for the German trade unions. But the temporal and territorial limitations of our research do not, we are convinced, undermine the urgency of the following arguments. Whatever the latest developments in East Germany may eventually mean for the German trade unions, several preliminary conversations with trade unionists in the new *Länder* in August–September 1991 make one thing certain: these developments will not free the unions from the dilemmas of industrial reorganization traced below. On the contrary, there are already signs that reunification is stultifying within the unions even the hesitant and sometimes contradictory debate about strategy noted a moment ago. The wage earners in the former GDR lack both a language and the institutions for political self-expression; they are all too accustomed to entrust resolution of everyday problems to bureaucratic agencies. It is no wonder that they are by all accounts delegating to the trade unions full responsibility for protecting their jobs, or, failing that, negotiating severance settlements by taking full advantage of the Federal Republic's complex labour law. These tasks are grist for the mills of the unions' traditionalists, who suddenly find a humanly compelling justification for their view of the labour movement as the advocate of the wage earners' rights at the workplace. And those trade unionists in the new *Länder* who would ardently participate in the new debates are simply crushed by traditional administrative responsibilities. One way or another, these preoccupations are likely to make the troubling developments to which we now turn more explosive still.

The Opening of the Firms and the Regionalization of Production

The framework for trade-union action is being redefined by fundamental changes in industrial structure. The substance and scope of these changes is itself a vast subject. (For a précis of our views on this topic and for additional references to the relevant literature, see Kern and Sabel, 1989; Sabel, Kern and Herrigel, 1989.) For present purposes, it is enough to underline two general tendencies which we regard as decisive for the future of trade-union development.

The first concerns the growing diversification of product markets. In stable markets, it pays end producers to integrate vertically. By so doing, they can protect their know-how, appropriate most of the value added in manufacturing, and guarantee regular provision of key components of the final product. This was, of course, the classic strategy of mass producers from the time of Henry Ford until the first 'oil shock' of 1973. Since then, many markets have become much more turbulent. Under the growing pressure of competition, augmented by producers from developing countries, firms in the advanced industrial economies have increasingly begun to manufacture products tailored to the precise wants of consumers who are both willing and able to pay a substantial price premium for goods which correspond more exactly to their expectations. By adopting this new product strategy, the firms accelerated the very differentiation of demand to which they were reacting. Markets became more and more fluid. Even successful products can be sold in only relatively small volumes. Product innovation is becoming ever more important, which means that the costs of product development are increasing. Today, even the most powerful of the large corporations are often unsure which technologies will finally prove to be important for new products, to say nothing of their uncertainty about which variant of all the possible production technologies will prove to be most appropriate. Reducing development costs and time, while increasing innovative capacity – these are the new imperatives.

In order to do justice to these constraints, many firms or operating units are simultaneously reconceptualizing both product and production strategies. This reconceptualization depends on, among other things, redefining the relation between internal development and external suppliers. Complex products are increasingly conceptualized as systems of subsystems or modules. Instead of developing each subsystem itself, the final producer defines the characteristics of the product as a whole, and the functional relations between the different modules of which it is composed. Whenever possible, each of these is then developed in collaboration with a system supplier who possesses the relevant technical expertise and know-how. Final assembly, however, remains the responsibility of the final producer.[2] This collaboration with systems suppliers makes it possible to promote innovation without provoking an explosion of the cost and time of development. The suppliers' advantages in their special areas of technical expertise become more generally available – the more so because supplier firms with customers in different industries can bring the results of one research effort to problems which arise in the others. For this and other reasons, development costs are more broadly distributed; basic designs are diffused more rapidly within and across industries. In short, there is a redefinition of the relation between firms and, at the least, an erosion of the traditional boundaries between them.

This trend reinforces and is reinforced by new developments in the factories themselves. Above all, it is the introduction of the different variants of flexible automation and the increasing network of different technical and organizational units which encourages the reconceptualization of product and process. Managers today no longer hesitate to group several of their internal units into networks. External suppliers may be included in the same kinds of systems. The introduction of just-in-time delivery systems is becoming commonplace – a sign of how rapidly this process of integration is advancing (see Doleschal, 1989b). In principle, every step in the production process, from development to distribution, is regarded as a variable whose effects on all of the others can be measured and regulated. This expansive integration does not, however, eliminate the need for highly skilled human intervention in the production process. Although it may be, in principle, possible to regulate the relation of each sub-unit to all of the others by technical means, it would be in fact unbearably expensive to do so. Network systems turn out to be a paying proposition only when experimentation and improvisation have indicated when and under what conditions particular units can be connected with others. Such (empirical) experiences influence the definition of the machine operators' skills. Increasingly, these skills tend to include complex combinations of traditional craft knowledge and more general theoretical training.

The second tendency follows from the first. The logic of specialization and diversification, which underlies the firms' response to increasingly differentiated markets, also leads to the formation or sharper definition of regional economies: clusters of firms or operating units with different, typically complementary specialities, which collaborate to serve common markets (Sabel, 1989; see also Läpple, 1986: 918; 1989: 225).

The more fluid markets become, the riskier it is to hold or produce for inventory. Hence the attractiveness of just-in-time delivery systems. These require, of course, that suppliers locate their production or warehouse facilities in the proximity of their customers' assembly works, or at least develop transportation capacities which assure a kind of virtual presence. Likewise, the more fluid the markets, the less time there is to develop and evaluate new technologies. It is the more probable, therefore, that face-to-face contact of employees of different firms will be necessary to accelerate the exchange of knowledge. In this way, knowledge becomes local knowledge, fully comprehensible only to those who participate in the day-to-day exchanges in which it is articulated. Once firms have learned to profit from such coordination or come to think that they might, they are determined to maintain or establish a substantial presence in the geographical area in which this expertise is grounded. Call this the localization effect of firms – or of members of a community of producers – on one another.

The more specialized firms become, finally, the more each depends on the collective provision of services which none can provide for itself. Examples are training, research, hazardous waste disposal, supplemental unemployment or medical protection, environmental monitoring, market information, or warehousing. Many of these services can be supplied by private vendors. But in any particular case, some are almost certain to be provided by local authorities or in partnership with them. As firms come to rely on collective and especially public provision of crucial services, however, they become part of the local community. Their survival depends on its prosperity. Call this the localization effect of providing an exoskeleton to specialized firms.

Although the regionalization of production is a direct consequence of the other responses to market fragmentation, the foregoing does not require that all of the key operations needed to manufacture a complex product be located in a single region. Some must be, for reasons having to do with just-in-time logistics and collaboration in the development of particular technologies. But a company often finds it easier to collaborate with a supplier located in a distant network than to try to establish a local producer of a key sub-assembly. Hence, regionalization and internationalization of production may proceed hand in hand; the more robust the local economy, the more it attracts and is attracted to complementary foreign localities. The decisive point is that, independent of the precise distribution of activities among regions, the reintegration of conception and execution leads to patterns of production specialization through which firms in a particular area become tied to one another and to the use of services whose provision depends on the continuing prosperity of a particular locale.

Small Steps to Radical Change

The actual process of reorganization of large firms proceeds, of course, in a more piecemeal fashion, and much less purposefully and peacefully than this sketch of textbook adjustment suggests. Radical change is often the result of a long chain of responses to a few initial decisions taken at best in the spirit of the architecture of the new system.

A few of these chain reactions are particularly common, and two drawn from the automobile industry will do to illustrate the drift of decision-making. Take first the case which results in an increase in subcontracting, but the savings achieved through out-sourcing are offset by the increased costs of administering the more complex supplier system. The obvious answer is to reduce the number of suppliers by making the most competent of them responsible for combining discrete components into sub-assemblies or modules. It is natural to give these suppliers authority to improve the sub-assemblies, provided they still meet the original specifications. But no doubt there will be some highly beneficial modifications which require a (slight) revision of the original design. The customer begins to accept these as well and the example is infectious. If the process goes far enough, the design engineers begin to conceive of the car as a system of systems, each of which might be manufactured by an independent producer.

Alternatively, take the case of car companies that look to new supplier relations for help in mastering new technologies with origins outside the auto industry. Sub-assemblies based on engineering plastics or microelectronics are obvious examples. But here too there is no stopping point. Microelectronics can be, and in some more expensive cars already are, used to control the operation of the engine, the brakes, the suspension, and – through the use of control area networks which make information generated in each such system available to the others – the relation among them. Who is the car manufacturer if all complex systems in the car and even the links among them are designed in substantial measure by suppliers?

High-level managers at companies as diverse as VW, Mercedes-Benz, Fiat, Ford and BMW are well aware of the sources of drift, and in most cases uncertain of what to make of them. One common, provisional response is simultaneously to note and limit the increased collaboration with suppliers by distinguishing systems (such as the motor and power train) which the company *must* make if it is to retain its competitive identity and advantage, and those it *can* make, but might subcontract to suppliers with independent design capacities. But if we asked two or more managers seated at the same table whether a particular sub-assembly might soon be reclassed from 'must' to 'can' they frequently disagreed and said that their differences would be resolved by a committee whose very purpose was to settle such disputes. In principle, they typically added, *anything* could be designed and produced outside. But final product aside, what defines the identity of and gives internal structure to a car company which may not find it opportune to design fully or manufacture any particular part of a car, even the most important?

Adjustment in Small Firms
To grasp better the logic of the current reorganization and take the measure of the confusion with which it is proceeding, it is convenient to examine the process briefly from the point of view of the small and medium-sized firms which it affects. The suppliers' response to the pressures and uncertainties they face depends on their current position. Many of the largest, who are also typically those with the greatest capacity for research and development, are restructuring to become systems suppliers. Sometimes this involves merger of two previously independent companies, as when a manufacturer of wire seat frames and position controls merges with a manufacturer of upholstery to form a company which can build sophisticated seat modules in plants close to automobile assemblers. In other cases, restructuring means the expansion and concentration in one location of research capacity in, for example, air-conditioning or cooling systems, and the construction of new, highly automated green-field production facilities – reconcentrating in the process some previously subcontracted operations in order to ensure quality and steady supplies of parts. (Whether, after a period of consolidation, these firms might not follow the example of their large customers, subcontract some production steps, and reintegrate conception and execution by decentralizing research capacity to the new production facilities is another question.)

Smaller firms are in a much weaker position. Often they must simply accept their large customers' 'recommendations' for the introduction of new technology or inventory systems as a precondition for the renewal of current contracts. They may have to submit to inspection of their production process and quality and control techniques as well. Production schedules may have to be synchronized with the customer's, and changed on demand. All of these forced-draft accommodations may in the end actually increase the firm's capacity to diversify its business and thus reduce its dependence on its current clients, but there is no guarantee that they will.[3]

Restructuring as an Opportunity and Danger for the Unions

There is, we see, a pattern to the industrial reorganization, but nothing like a harmoniously agreed common strategy to realize it. Power struggles in the large firms reverberate with power struggles in the small and medium-sized ones. There is as much confusion as consensus, sometimes as much cynicism as confidence about the feasibility of strategic plans. And all this – the changes themselves, the confusion, the confidence, and the cynicism – undermine the organizational foundations of the union in the firm while creating possibilities for new ways of defending and expanding wage-earners' rights.

In Germany, the current reorganization of industry creates new possibilities for the exercise and extension of trade-union authority simply because German co-determination laws allow labour to block or delay many of the changes management wants. Whether it is a question of more flexible use of labour, including corresponding changes in the regulation of the legal work-week and over-time; lengthening the permissible periods of production, including relaxation of restrictions on shift and weekend work; greater freedom to rejuvenate the work-force, including increased use of early pensions to remove older workers and more aggressive hiring of younger persons with up-to-date technical skills; extensive retraining and continuing education programmes – the factory council's approval is required for the execution of any of these measures. Where fundamental questions of company policy are raised, labour's representatives on the board of supervisors (*Aufsichtsrat*) can demand a more deliberate hearing under the co-determination laws. And quite apart from all their legally secured influence, the trade unions have countless opportunities to intervene in the process of restructuring simply because consensus, however minimal, is almost always the precondition for change. German management is aware that it cannot wage a two-front war against its competitors and its work-force. From this perspective, serious conflicts with factory councillors who make disruptive use of their co-determination rights or even mobilize those workplaces still well enough organized to stand the strain are simply too dangerous to risk. The managers we spoke to know that their careers depend on the outcome of projects whose success would be jeopardized by protracted conflict. They are convinced that change by fiat does not work. They are ready to bargain.

At the same time, it is clear that the day-to-day decisions shaped by the current logic of industrial reorganization work to undermine the unions' positions on the shop floor and in the corporation as a whole. Three problems stand out; and unless the unions discover a way to use their bargaining power to address them in a concerted way, they may cumulatively transform the *de facto* rules of collective bargaining in Germany.

First, industrial reorganization is leading to increasing demand for more technically skilled employees whom the unions have great difficulty organizing. To begin with, the firms are increasingly recruiting university-trained engineers. In Germany, this group has never had an affinity for the labour movement. Perhaps more important, however, are the changes in the career patterns of evening-class (*graduierte*) engineers. Traditionally, this group was formed by skilled workers who spent several years full-time on the shop floor upon completion of their apprenticeship, and then enrolled in evening courses to finish their education. Apprenticeship and shop-floor experience inclined them to union membership; and they typically remained loyal to their origins even when promoted to influential management positions. Today, however, there is less time to form loyalties to labour because the young, skilled workers are abbreviating their stints on the shop floor and continuing their education almost immediately after completing their initial training. The expectation that they will do so, moreover, casts a shadow back on to their experience of apprenticeship, which is now often seen less as an induction into a world of craft work than as a practical phase in an educational sequence that ends far from the shop floor. To make matters more complex, it is precisely these younger, technically skilled workers and night-school engineers who tend to participate in the *ad hoc* project groups which so often create an implicit labour–management counterelite in the firm by their capacity to solve problems which baffle older, more centrally placed managers and factory councillors. In the late 1960s, West German sociologists of work were concerned that the night-school engineers, a crucial link between management and the shop floor, would be displaced by university-trained professionals with indispensable technical expertise, but ignorant or mistrustful of the craft versatility on which the flexibility of so many firms depended. Two decades later it seems more unlikely than ever that the evening-class engineers will be pushed aside or their ties with the shop floor broken. The question today is whether the very success of that group and the strengthening of those ties does not for the first time weaken rather than reinforce the union's role in the plant.

The question is all the more pressing because the traditional union goals are not these groups' most pressing concerns. Collectively bargained wage increases, protection from the intensification of work, formal recognition of skill, and legal reinforcement of job security are of secondary interest to persons who by virtue of their knowledge have a strong position in the labour market, and who, so long as they are young, are unlikely to want to work where they are unwanted. Their chief concerns lie elsewhere, in areas where the unions until now have had little to say: in the opacity of the firm's decision-making process and hierarchy; in the scanty opportunities to influence directly crucial decisions; in confusion about how they themselves are to keep pace with technical change; and, most generally, in worries about the long-term unpredictability of their own careers. Nor are these the problems of a small elite. Multiskilled maintenance workers, highly trained systems operators with responsibility for millions of dollars of equipment, and quality-control personnel whose responsibilities increasingly overlap with those of the industrial engineer, all have concerns which increasingly resemble those of the engineers – the more so, the younger they are. Thus industrial reorganization increases the number of those unlikely to grow into a world of which the union is a natural part, while reducing the number of those who will.[4]

The recruitment problems which these structural changes cause for the union are aggravated by concomitant changes in the typology and geographical distribution of production units. So long as research, marketing, and production were carried out in one complex, the trade unions could use their organizational strength in the last area to win members and exert influence in the first two. But to the extent that large suppliers, for example, even temporarily isolate production in green-field sites away from other corporate activities, this connection is broken. Stripped of contact with production, the labour bastions in large industrial centres could become centres of company or yellow unionism, while the new, peripherally located production centres might remain beyond the reach of a labour movement which tends to be sceptical that smaller firms and workers with little industrial tradition can be organized in the first place – not to mention the additional problems of addressing workers in foreign subsidiaries.

Secondly, there is the problem of the unions' fundamental organizational unit – the company – and, since the installation of industrial unionism, the branch, understood as a collection of firms working similar materials, using similar production technologies, and making related products. In the heyday of mass production the giant firms in the centres of heavy industry and the heavy industries themselves were the central unit of trade-union organization. But the more open the boundaries among firms and branches become, the less relevant these units can be as points of orientation of trade-union strategy. The decentralization of production within a given firm means, for example, that manufacturing operations previously executed in one place are now dispersed to sites in many different trade-union jurisdictions; and the problems of coordinating policy with a greater and greater number of increasingly autonomous plant managers, allied, perhaps, with local union barons, are correspondingly more complex. When local managers make company policy, what good is the union's influence on corporate headquarters?

Increased subcontracting, especially when it concerns collaboration in the development of new products or technologies, obviously multiplies the unions' organizational dilemma. A product previously manufactured by operating units all within the jurisdiction of, say, IG Metall, suddenly becomes an assembly of subassemblies produced by firms within the jurisdiction of, among others, the chemical and textile workers. In so far as these activities are drawn together by regionalization, they potentially form the basis of new organizational entities. But the concentration of firms and branches, we will see, has left the unions ill equipped to make use of even those few existing structures which might be adapted to the formulation of regional policies cutting across traditional industrial jurisdictions.

Thirdly, although the factory councillors are better trained, better protected by law, and better supported by expert staffs than they were in the 1960s, their capacity for action is simply inadequate to the demands of the situation. Try as they will, they simply cannot address, let alone solve, all the questions which reorganization simultaneously poses. The best indication of their limits is the proliferation in the plants of informal, expert 'advisory groups', whose purpose is to assist the factory councils in formulating policy on specific, technically complex questions. Such groups (which may well be anchored in the project teams discussed earlier) are so common that they are discussed as a quasi-official institution in the trade unions' own publications, although no attempt is made to clarify their relation to the legally constituted organs of employee representation (Schwartz, 1989). Under these conditions, it is natural enough for factory councillors to set priorities and dedicate their full energies to the crucial problems. First things first.

But even this apparently straightforward ambition is almost unattainable because industrial restructuring introduces a systematic tension between factory councillors' long- and short-term goals. In the short term, it seems morally obligatory and politically expedient to defend the interests of groups such as poorly paid, semi-skilled women, elderly workers, or the partially handicapped who are threatened most directly by the early rounds of decentralization. The temptation to take up defensive positions here is all the greater given that the union can probably find powerful allies among those managers whose own position also is or soon could be threatened by subcontracting to systems suppliers.

But this is a strategy which at best produces Pyrrhic victories. The more successful the union is in blocking incremental change in marginal areas, the more likely management is to delegate complex, risky development projects to systems suppliers with a freer hand. If the experiments succeed, the manufacturing operations to which they give rise are likely to remain there where they were developed – beyond the immediate jurisdiction of the factory councillors, and perhaps, in the case of collaboration with a foreign firm – beyond the reach of the German labour movement as a whole. To continue with the automobile example: for the moment, determined defence secures in-house production of seat modules, but the development and production of automotive electronics and new plastics prospers beyond the horizon of the factory council. Worse still, in so far as defence of the least skilled means defence of the standardized operations which are most vulnerable to low-wage competition, short-term success increases the plant's and the union's long-term vulnerability; and the effort to increase employment security actually undermines it.

A few years ago, West German observers were warning that, in the absence of a powerful national union able to discipline local activity through broad collective-bargaining agreements, inevitable alliances between factory councils and their respective plants managements would lead to the rapid spread of company unionism. In the light of the reorganization of the corporation, that warning is beginning to sound like a forlorn and perverse hope.

The Reorientation of Trade-union Strategy

To our knowledge, there is no comprehensive answer, theoretical or practical, to the dilemmas of trade-union strategy just discussed. The theoretical answers are flawed by their assumption that unions must learn to control flexibility within closed organizations. Indeed, for many US students of industrial relations, the German factory-council system suggested a model of how unions might address this problem; and they would be disconcerted to learn of the model's vicissitudes on its home ground. The promising practical solutions are incipient and fragmentary – and despite their promise, they may not work. None the less, it is these experiences, in combination with the preceding analysis, which orientate the following efforts to deepen our understanding of the current trade-union disorientation by trying to imagine a way to address it.

First, a conclusion which is just dawning on German unions, but which has become, through bitter experience, the starting point of a new generation of US trade-union organizers: it is futile to hope that the conflicts inevitably provoked by industrial reorganization, and involving engineers as well as production workers, will of themselves drive employees into the unions. German firms, sometimes influenced by US examples, are experimenting with various forms of 'union-free' employee-representation plans which have thus far proved effective at neutralizing potential conflicts, if nothing else. Trade unions and factory councils will be able to turn conflicts to their own organizational advantage when they can offer responses to attacks on employees' interests which are both plausible and feasible: plausible, in that they secure acceptable redress for individual of group grievances, and feasible, in that they encourage the firm to behave in ways which reinforce its economic vitality, and hence increases its capacity to make subsequent concessions. Our discussion of the unions' strategic possibilities is framed by these constraints.

Our point of departure is the effect of industrial reorganization on the very constitution of the labour market. An understanding of the complex, apparently contradictory consequences of corporate decentralization and regional agglomeration is, we believe, indispensable to the formulation of any trade-union strategy whose aim is to turn the new competitive conditions to labour's advantage. We begin by sketching responses which address the needs of highly skilled workers – the traditional core of the unions' constituency in the Federal Republic, and the reservoir from which most of its leaders at all levels have been drawn. Then we will try to show that the same strategy which appeals to them can be further developed to meet the concerns of the unskilled and semi-skilled.

The analysis of the preceding sections describes a double paradox. First, the modern corporation needs a highly skilled core work-force, yet it itself has (almost) no institutional core in which this work-force can be guaranteed secure employment. The whole effort to reintegrate conception and execution depends on the cooperation of skilled persons in sales, design, manufacturing, on the one hand, and in the systems suppliers, on the other – all with an intimate, almost instinctive knowledge of the corporation's needs. But the openness of the corporate boundary to the outside world, especially the constantly shifting but more intimate relation to subcontractors (the systems suppliers) and consultants (the former staffs reconstituted as independent firms, or complete outsiders operating on the open market) make it impossible to say which activities will go on inside the firm and which outside. When the status of whole production or research units can change in a matter of months, or at least when everyone knows that such changes are always possible in principle, production workers, technicians, and engineers must always wonder about how they will survive if they are on the job market.

In particular, they must always be thinking about how to acquire skills in their present position which will equip them for employment if they have to leave it. And they must realize that this is not easy to do within the confines of their current work unit. The smaller and more specialized production units become, the less likely they are to be able to offer in-house the kind of broad, fundamental training at all levels which equips people to meet the challenges of new situations. Broad training programmes, whether organized by large corporations or public institutions, make matters worse. They underline the limiting particularity of the employee's current situation simply by drawing attention to the whole range of crucial developments with which he or she has no direct experience.

Secondly, work in the restructured economy simultaneously increases and limits employees' autonomy in the world of life outside it. The experience of the new corporation increases the possibilities of individual self-expression outside the firm. This is not primarily a result of an increase in the amount of or control over leisure time or an increase in disposable income. Rather, the sense of autonomy and self-respect developed at work seems to bolster employees' self-confidence outside work. Employees who are encouraged to think of themselves as entrepreneurs and to treat dealings within their own firm as market transactions are being forced to manage resources and risks in ways which make it easier to imagine changing the conditions of one's life in many regards. The prospects of going into business for oneself, or simply taking a job in another company, are likely to look less forbidding. Chemical workers who have been instructed about hazardous materials they handle on the job provide another, more surprising example: they are much less tolerant of environmental threats at home than workers without equivalent experiences (see Heine and Mautz, 1989).

But this enhanced autonomy – which can, as the last example suggests, become a source of challenges to the most various and deep-seated assumptions about social life – is simultaneously qualified by the same situation which produced it. Just as the firms must form networks with one another and their environment in order to keep abreast of local knowledge, so too must individuals secure their long-term employability through participation in social networks outside the firm. 'Private' associations – hobby and self-help groups, clubs, neighbourhood associations, single-issue groups, or political parties – are today seldom institutional expressions of a coherent, all-encompassing group life defined by class position, political persuasion, or religious faith. Typically, they are associations of sociable but 'individualized' persons, whose sociability outside the firm often gives rise to, and may be shaped by, connections that reach not so much into any particular workplace as into the world where they work. And increasingly, as the ecological example again suggests, the nominally private and nominally economic spheres of activity are both connected to the world of politics and public institutions.

These private, social networks therefore amount to early-warning and coordination systems which neither public nor private job-placement agencies can provide. Only persons who participate in multiple, loosely connected networks are likely to know when their current jobs are in danger, where new opportunities lie, and what skills are required to seize them. The more open corporate labour markets become, the greater the burden these networks will have to bear, and the greater the economic compulsion to participate in the social activities they organize.

This tendency may well be reinforced by the reconstitution of domestic life, which, of course, is influenced by, but hardly reducible to the reorganization of work. The growing participation of women in the labour force, part cause and part effect of changing gender roles, is creating an increasing number of two-earner households. For such households, with their double dependence on the local labour market, participation in community life – day-care centres, schools, neighbourhood improvement associations – is often a precondition of participation in paid employment.

This is not to suggest that domestic life becomes a mere appendage of economic activity, as it may have almost become during some periods of industrial production. Rather, open labour markets of the kind we are describing depend for their operation on networks which function on the condition that they do *not* mirror the current pattern of economic activity too closely. If they did, they plainly would not help individuals and firms reassemble under new conditions. Seen this way, however, the networks – and with them the part of life which is considered private (from the point of view of the firm) and social (from the point of view of the family) – become part of the public exoskeleton which firms depend on in their constant efforts towards reorganization.

From this it follows that the distinction between a person's interests as an employee and his or her encompassing interest in well-being is becoming so blurred as to be unrecognizable. If unions intend to address the interests of their members and potential members, therefore, they must be at least as attentive to regulating the relation between workplaces and between workplaces and living spaces as they have been to regulating the conditions of work in firms and sectors. Continuing-education programmes; job counselling and placement; planning in the sense of help in finding or creating the institutions needed to integrate domestic and work life – all of these are examples of services directed towards the new field of regulation. Failure to provide them or some equivalent would be for the unions to forgo the possibility of organizing – pun intended – just those experiences which characterize 'modern' employees, and condemn them to representing a social world which is shrinking even as its boundaries become indistinct.

Indeed, to push the point to its logical conclusion and underline its connection to the analysis of industrial structure, the union in an open labour market would in this view assume responsibility for provision of skilled labour – a requirement of production which management can no longer organize by itself. In doing so, the union would become in its way a systems supplier. There are already tendencies in this direction in Germany, particularly as a result of the unions' participation in the organization of vocational training and the administration of labour-market programmes.

Were the unions to assume this role, it would not entail their subordination to the companies. Firms, we saw, collaborate with systems suppliers because they have to, not because they want to. For companies, the price of the cooperation they need is a new and consistently renegotiable dependence on outsiders who can do things the firms can no longer (afford to) do for themselves. Why should firms' relations to union systems suppliers be less ambivalent? There is historical precedent for the claim that they would indeed not be. In the early days of the craft unions, which were frequently socialist, the provision of skilled labour under regulated conditions to specialized firms was a key source of labour's power on the labour market in general, and within firms as well. Naturally, the unions cannot return to the nineteenth century. But, given the direction of industrial reorganization, it is hard to see why control of conditions outside the firm could not become a new source of trade-union strength.

What makes the pursuit of such a strategy especially complex is that services that correspond to novel definitions of interest are often already available, but in a partial and intractable form designed to advance other ends under the current system of interest representation. Reorienting union strategy along the lines we are suggesting requires reconstructing existing institutions as much as building new ones from scratch. Discussion of the possibilities of and obstacles to the use of continuing education as a cornerstone in a new system of trade-union representation will illustrate both the general intent of our programmatic argument and the kinds of institutional considerations which bear on its realization.

Continuing Education as an Example of New Trade-union Strategy

Neither an initial period of formal education, however long, nor constant adjustment to changing conditions through learning by doing today guarantees a person's long-term employability in the reorganized economy, let alone secures a particular job. The more open the corporations and the labour market, the more important become the capacity for systematic (re-)education and the willingness to participate in it. Unions can play a double role in the organization of continuing education. On the one hand, they can help employees understand the importance of further training and how to obtain it. On the other, they can monitor their education to ensure that the skills provided are so systematic, certifiable, affordable, and remunerative that they do indeed increase the employees' chances of prospering not just at a particular job, but on the open labour market.

The situation in Germany, a country widely admired for its comprehensive educational system, clearly demonstrates the need for this supervision. To be sure, the firms clearly recognize the need for continuing education as a concomitant of restructuring. Expenditures per employee for such training doubled between 1981 and 1985 (Mahnkopf et al., 1989: 22). But it is equally clear that many firms understand continuing education as the provision of just those supplemental skills require for a particular job (Mahnkopf et al., 1989: 23); that they are not concerned with the general development of employees' craft or professional qualifications except at the very highest level (Baethge et al., 1989b: 81ff); and that to the extent they can, they define the need for continuing education as a risk to be borne by the employee as an individual.

Here the unions have organizational motives for acting as a corrective. To the extent that they are seen as guaranteeing their members and indeed the work-force as a whole the kind of systematic and well-rounded training which can quickly be put to use in diverse work settings, they acquire both a broad constituency and a place in the institutional order. In theory at least, the firms themselves have an interest that they do so.

This is because individual firms pursuing a strategy of profit maximization through specialization have little incentive to design programmes of continuing education that do justice to the breadth and variability of their own long-term needs. The flexibility requirements of the open labour markets are often at odds with the cumulative results of the firms' short-term planning strategies, although firms need not be aware of the potential disparity. The limits of the firms' capacities in this regard are evident in the fact that in several of the suppliers we visited, the factory councillors had already assumed responsibility for assessing both short- and long-term training needs of every employee. Under these conditions, the unions' efforts to correct the narrowness of the firms' plans (or, more accurately, expedients and vague projections) contributes to the exoskeleton of institutions upon which the collective success of restructuring efforts depends. Naturally, this convergence in principle of trade-union and firm interests shapes company behaviour no more directly than a theoretical account of the advantages of the new subcontracting systems changes the behaviour of purchasing agents. Complex and often unpredictable causal chains, we saw, connect current patterns of behaviour to the realization of such models, if they are realized at all.

A recent survey of trade-union policy in this area suggests, moreover, that the labour movement in Germany is far from making the most of whatever opportunities to influence these developments it already has (Baethge et al., 1989). Take, for example, the factory councillors, the *de facto* though not *de jure* representatives of the union in the plant. Under sections 90, 92, 96, 97, and 98 of the *Betriebsverfassungsgesetz*, they undeniably have substantial powers to influence the organization and provision of continuing education, however controversial the interpretation of their precise rights in particular matters may be. But as a rule, the study shows, little is made of this potential influence. The factory councillors do not generally appreciate the general growing significance of continuing education; and if they do, they are ignorant of their rights to influence it (Baethge et al., 1989b: 422-7). Exceptions, of course, prove the rule. The same study reports the experience of some factory councils in machine-tool and auto-supplier firms – as well as in one major auto producer in the midst of a wide-ranging reorganization – which managed to correct the 'job-specific character of plant-level continuing education measures, and to embed them in a larger context of work reorganization' (Baethge et al., 1989b: 422). Our own discussions with union officials and factory councillors corroborate these findings. Although it might appear that unions have a natural interest in encouraging and generalizing such initiatives, it is only in the last years that the metal-workers' union has begun to make continuing education a central theme of collective bargaining.

The first regional agreement with relevant provisions was concluded in 1987 and 1988 between IG Metall and the entire metalworking industry in Baden-Württemberg (LGRTV 1); in the same period, a related agreement was reached between the union and Volkswagen. The contracts oblige employers periodically to assess their expected training needs and to discuss these with the factory council. On the basis of this assessment, training programmes are to be designed with the concurrence of the factory council. Training is to take place during normal working hours, and those who complete the planned courses are to be assigned work which requires use of their new skills, or paid as though they were performing this more demanding work. To date, there has been no evaluation of the effects of either the obligation to plan training or to pay the successful trainees at rates corresponding to their certified skill level (see Mahnkopf et al., 1989: 41–3, and Baethge et al., 1989: 450–3). But there is good reason to think that these agreements are only the beginning of a broader effort at regulation which could systematize and extend many informal measures in a way which might indeed establish the union as an indispensable interlocutor in questions of further training, if not a system supplier of skilled labour.

From the Outside in and around: Control as a Source
of Influence within Firms and the Regional Economy
Control over local labour markets shades into and requires increasing participation in the formulation of corporate strategy, on the one hand, and regional economic policy, on the other. To stay with the preceding examples: in order to judge which kinds of continuing education will be required, it is necessary to know the firm's investment plans. That is the minimal form of the required participation. At a maximum, joint efforts to define training needs would blur into efforts to reach agreement about all the aspects of product strategy, citing decisions, and personnel planning which bear on the long-term prospects of job security. Although this maximalist programme may seem hopelessly to overstate the unions' possibilities of influencing company behaviour, there are well-known instances at Volkswagen and other important firms

where elements of this kind of joint decision-making are already practised in Germany. Where this is the case, the collaboration is the expression of a broader and often deliberate – though not formal – modernization pact between the factory council and management. The latter guarantees job security for all current employees, indemnifies them for losses sustained as a result of reorganization, and obliges itself to give as many employees as possible a chance to advance into whatever higher-skilled jobs may be created. In return, the former agrees not merely to tolerate reorganization, but to foster it by helping to bring the expertise of the work-force to bear wherever needed. The 'advisory groups' mentioned earlier are often called into being or at least openly recognized for this purpose (see Schwartz, 1989: 448).

This kind of cooperation plainly makes both sides uneasy. In discussion, managers often wonder about what 'rights' they may be trading away in exchange for the work-force's 'constructive' participation. Trade unionists worry that such participation in managerial activities will (or will appear to) compromise their autonomy and political identity. We spoke with one trade-union official in Baden-Württemberg, who was particularly sensitive to the ambiguities of the situation, perhaps because he had entered the labour movement as a result of his experiences during the student protests of the late 1960s. To advance labour's interests through the new form of collaboration, he said, it was necessary to 'worry yourself to death with the other guys' problems'. He defined his own participation in such compromises ironically as 'social partnership from the left' – a formulation that expresses the unionists' persistent fear that the cooperation will end in co-optation, perhaps even loss of the capacity to strike against the firm. For the moment, both parties to these cooperative arrangements seem as aware of the need to retain the power to withdraw from them as the need to make them work.

Simultaneously, however, the exercise of control over open labour markets requires the local union to extend the radius of its action to the region as a whole. As local firms come to depend more and more on one another and on the exoskeleton of locally provided services, the union in any single plant can often best protect the long-term employability of its members by working with firms and trade associations, as well as municipal, regional, or federal authorities, to encourage the establishment or growth of companies or production units crucial to the integrity of the regional economy. This amounts in part to a kind of forward defence against the decentralization of production and development to suppliers outside the region. A more important aim, however, is to diversify the local economy, rendering it less vulnerable to shifts in demand and better able to regenerate itself should there be a dramatic deterioration of any of its key markets. (For an interesting example, see Richter and Zitzelsberger, 1989: especially p. 74.)

To pursue these kinds of strategies, unions will have to adjust their own structures. Here the unions might take a page from the corporations' book on the decentralization of responsibility and the opening of institutional borders. In order to provide the new labour-market services and influence the strategies of both firms and public authorities, they must move beyond their jurisdictional limits to create local, grassroots alliances among themselves and with many actors they have ignored or battled with in the past: municipalities, non-profit groups, social movements, political parties, churches, and educational institutions. The result would be 'networking of trade-union capacities' (Negt et al., 1989: 188). To do this they will need the authorization of national unions, whose authority will also be necessary to institutionalize successful regional experiments.

Many recent commentaries sponsored in one way or another by the labour movement in Germany and often published in its journals in fact emphasize the need to reinvigorate local unions and increase their capacity to act regionally by strengthening their ties to other local groups (see, above all, Negt et al., 1989: especially pp. 184ff; Adamy and Bosch, 1986: p. 502ff; Hoffman and Läpple, 1989: 692–4; von Gleich, 1989: 689; and also Hildebrandt, 1989: 369; Wollmann, 1986: 87ff; Hoffmann and Neumann, 1987: 535). Differences in particulars aside, these commentaries concur on a crucial point: they regard 'horizontal' networking as a subsidiary complement to traditional trade-union activity. The common argument is that groups at the margin of the production process or threatened by expulsion from it – 'housewives, retirees, apprentices, the unemployed, college and high school students' (Negt et al., 1989: 185) – can be won from the unions through 'the incarnation of union projects in local work' (ibid.). The emphasis is, therefore, on organizing defensive activities which demonstrate the unions' capacity to prevent plant closures or, more generally, loss of local jobs, as well as to counter attacks on the local provision of welfare benefits. (Hoffman and Läpple as well as von Gleich, however, also argue for a more offensive strategy, closer to the one presented here.)

Important as they are, from our prospective, these activities miss the strategically decisive point. Corporations, we argued, are experimenting with new governance structures in which headquarters attempts to retain the coordinating authority of last resort, while decentralizing substantial, potentially self-reinforcing autonomy to operating units, and through them to systems suppliers. At the same time, these new governance structures create open labour markets that blur the distinction between jobs inside and outside the corporation, as well as the distinction between paid work and social life. By organizing the open labour markets and shaping regional economies, the unions can influence the new governance structures – not least by encouraging those aspects of decentralization which augment their own capacity to gain further influence. On this view, they ought not aim to exemplify labour's collective power locally, but rather to redefine the very substance of that power – the relation between labour and capital – by changing the extent and goals of local action. Thus understood, localization of union strategy goes hand in hand with its universalization, and is a precondition for that 'broadening of the trade-union mandate' so often mentioned in the German labour movement's current strategic discussions.

The instruments of such a union strategy, moreover, do not need to be developed from scratch. Clues about what institutional solutions might work are buried in the historical experiences of the trade-union confederation's regional councils (the DGB-Kreise and Ortskartelle). In the immediate post-war years these played a significant role in some regions, only to decline into insignificance during the heyday of the large, centralized corporation (see Hoffmann and Neumann, 1987: 540; Negt et al., 1989: 186; Hoffman and Läpple, 1989: 694).

These could be reactivated and redirected in the light of a comprehensive reorientation of union strategy (compare the insightful overview in Adamy and Bosch, 1986: 502ff). But if we are right, it will only be possible to revitalize these institutions if their network is seen not as a marginal complement to current policies, but as a central part of the unions' effort to turn the new industrial structures to their advantage by shaping – through a kind of determinedly self-assured collaboration – their very formation.

The Unskilled and the Semi-skilled

The same analysis of industrial reorganization which suggests a new union strategy at the regional level suggests a new response to the problems of unskilled and semi-skilled workers. Ideally (and unsurprisingly, given that common principles underlie both), the two policies would prove mutually reinforcing.

The unskilled and the semi-skilled fall analytically into two brutally distinct groups. Those in the first group are typically the victims of the corrosive effects of long years of physically demanding, stultifying labour, or of childhoods and educations that make it all but impossible to acquire the basic skills required to master the more advanced ones. Those in the second group have typically suffered a milder form of the same injuries that felled those in the first, or simply resisted adversity better. We take it for granted that society will find it politically expedient if not morally obligatory to guarantee the (decent?) subsistence of the first group. We also take it for granted that almost all interested parties – the firms, tax-paying citizens, political groups – have convergent interests in seeing as many members of the second group as possible enter the high-skilled economy rather than become wards of the state in the first.

The difficulty, of course, is that it is often impossible to say for sure who among the unskilled and semi-skilled is in which group. For one thing, the ability to enter the high-skilled economy depends on the latter's size, which itself depends in part on the availability of skilled labour. For another, it is often difficult to know whether some combination of remedial training and interim support will not allow persons previously treated as marginally employable to learn to teach themselves. In the virtuous circle, improved training and welfare programmes equip many of these once assigned to the first group to find skilled work, which is available – in part, but only in part – because employers expect the new programmes to provide the skill reserves they require. In the vicious circle, the failure of faulty programmes of remediation produces contrary expectations, and the resulting reduction of job offerings pushes some members of the second group back into the first.

The trade unions, we believe, can encourage the formation of virtuous circles by pursuing strategies which would be direct extensions of their efforts to organize open labour markets and regional economies. The structuring principle is to encourage the horizontal connection among local actors in a way which makes the labour movement an integral piece of the resulting system: the networking discussed in the preceding section. One way to see how this might occur is to examine briefly the changing pattern of welfare provision in Germany; a second is to survey more precisely than before how changes in the unions themselves can be related to problems of industrial restructuring at the local level.

In Germany, as in many other advanced industrial economies, the provision of welfare services is a task managed in 'the local political arena' (Wollmann, 1986: 85ff). The central state has reduced its support of both the social insurance and training systems, partly as a result of fiscal pressure (budget 'consolidations'), and partly for political or ideological reasons (attacks on the 'exaggerations' of the welfare state). Under these conditions, local administrative units – the *Gemeinden* or communes – have been forced to assume final responsibility for meeting the minimal needs of the increasing fraction of the unemployed which falls through the tattered social security net. (Correspondingly, the share of the total number of communal welfare recipients who are unemployed has been rising, and in several German cities now exceeds 25 per cent. [ibid.: 85].) However much the *Gemeinden* may have once tried to evade this responsibility, they increasingly recognize it openly in an effort to maintain social peace or – in the large cities under Social Democratic control – improve their political situation.

What is crucial from our perspective is that the assumption of responsibility is accompanied by the growing conviction that the utility of social services, not least those addressed to the unskilled and semi-skilled whose jobs are most at risk, depends on the way they are connected with each other. There is a tendency 'at the local level to look for new (horizontal) organizational forms in order to improve the effectiveness of the social-welfare administration and the services which it offers to combat mass and long-term unemployment' (Wollmann, 1986: 87). Indeed, if needs bundle in the sense that those without jobs are also likely to have housing, family, and medical problems and if potential welfare recipients are incompletely informed about their eligibility for benefits, then 'horizontal' organizations combining services into the bundles needed by particular persons are a precondition for an acceptably efficient and equitable welfare system.[5] To see why, simply imagine two persons needing the same ten services, but with different information about their legal rights. Without 'horizontal' coordination, each will – as is now often the case – receive a different five, with the result that neither is helped (for all services must be provided if any is to work), and each is envious of what the other has.

This brings us back to familiar terrain. The more active the union is in constructing an exoskeleton which protects the currently employed or the temporarily unemployed against the dangers of long-term unemployment, the easier it becomes to imagine and construct the kinds of programmes necessary to move the (potentially) long-term unemployed into the high-skilled economy. Plainly, comprehensive strategies are required which overcome the divisions traditional in Germany (and elsewhere) between measures to create jobs, combat youth unemployment, provide specific social services, and the like (Hjern, 1989). Instead of offering material compensation or short-term remediation, these comprehensive programmes should increase the recipients' capacity for autonomous action by improving their living, learning, and working conditions. Presumably, increased control over open labour markets requires the same.

An analogous tendency towards the articulation of comprehensive programmes and the creation of the institutions necessary to operate them can be seen in the evolution of the unions' 'occupation plans' (*Beschäftigungspläne*). These are typically agreements between a union – usually via the factory council – and firms on the verge of closing plants or laying off large numbers of employees. In 1987 and 1988 there were twenty such agreements, above all in the steel and shipbuilding industries. Their goal is captured in the union slogan 'Better training than lay-offs'. They are financed by a combination of funds which would normally be required for individual severance payments and subsidies from the Federal Department of Labour (*Bundesanstalt für Arbeit*), as well as federal programmes for regional development. They are explicitly intended to provide 'preventive training' to employees who are 'threatened by unemployment, and once unemployed, would be difficult to attract to further training measures' (Mahnkopf et al., 1989: 35).

Surveys of the operation of these plans reveals an ambiguous result (Bosch, 1989). Typically, the *Beschäftigungspläne* are concluded in the midst of a crisis, when room for manoeuvre is already substantially reduced. Hence the chances of identifying and realizing innovative solutions – new products or processes – are slim. The plans, in short, are usually more palliative than preventive, and that obviously limits and redirects their effect. At the same time, despite this limitation, the plans and the activities they encourage have often revealed an innovative potential in the firms which would otherwise have gone undetected. Not least, employees who took advantage of the training possibilities offered by the plans in many cases succeeded in finding more skilled jobs in other firms.

There are signs in the latest rounds of collective bargaining that these developments are just the first steps of a union effort to press the firms to develop 'preventive' training and personnel management schemes which would simultaneously protect the unskilled and semi-skilled and create the possibility of better coordinating employment with social-welfare policy. An example, mentioned earlier, is the April 1987 agreement between IG Metall and Volkswagen. The agreement gives the factory councillors comprehensive rights of consultation in the introduction of new technologies and organizational systems in individual plants. The area of compulsory consultation includes personnel planning and assessment of training needs. On the basis of this contract, for example, thorough reorganization of one parts-production area included a '700-hour programme' of highly systematic training. A quota system gave preferential treatment to applications from unskilled and semi-skilled workers, and their participation was, by the standards of such programmes, disproportionately high. In this connection the LGRTV 1, mentioned earlier, is equally significant. This contract provides for the creation of bipartite, continuing-education commissions in the plants. IG Metall would like to use these to ensure that groups such as low-paid women, foreign workers, and all those threatened by lay-offs receive preferential treatment in continuing-education programmes.

In isolated cases, moreover, particularly active factory councillors have begun to extend the modernization pacts discussed earlier in a way which one of their number described as a 'reversal of managerial thinking'. These activists are pursuing a double goal. On the one hand they are trying to secure their firm's future by insisting on investments in the development of new, more diversified products. On the other, they insist on meeting what they see as a collective responsibility for the protection of the unskilled and semi-skilled by offering special training programmes directed to the latter's needs, rather than simply replacing them with more skilled workers drawn from the external labour market. The benefits of forced-draft, concerted reorganization are intended, in these plans, to produce the supplemental revenues needed to finance the extended training programmes. Projects such as these seem to us to embody the connection between active participation in restructuring and protection, even extension of employee rights – here of the unskilled and semi-skilled – which could become the defining feature of a new overall trade-union strategy.

Towards a New Division of Labour in the Labour Movement

The two conclusions of our argument – the need for a decentralizing relocalization of each union combined with an opening to new groups, including the other unions – are not intended to suggest that the revitalization of the local labour movement could replace the national one. A renewal of local structures, we believe, is possible only on the condition that the national ones are renewed as well. To begin with, the national unions must do their best to assure that the local unions have the resources and competence necessary to minimize the risks of restructuring for employees and maximize the opportunities. This means, for example, that the unions on the national level must use every occasion to extend local co-determination. This requires support whenever possible for factory councils, but also, for example, for the social movements which aim to make the local welfare state more equitable and efficient, as well as for ecology groups which monitor the regional environment. Only the national trade-union entities can organize the exchanges of information and provide the consulting services without which extension of local labour participation cannot succeed.

Just as important, only the national labour movement can, through its legislative influence, help create a system of incentives which encourages the formation and expansion of flexible, high-skilled, and hence robust regional economies. So too is national legislation required to shape the development of the local welfare systems which these regional economies require. The stakes here are enormous. A few islands of flexible prosperity will always be threatened by a sea of potential social discontent. But the more numerous and extensive the regional economies, the greater the probability that unskilled and semi-skilled workers will be able to find places within them through continuing education. The more numerous and extensive the regional economies, the easier it becomes to create national – or state-level – reinsurance systems which facilitate the restructuring of crisis regions by means of subsidies from the prosperous ones.

How exactly the division of labour between local and national union instances will develop – what, for example, is best regulated by a central, uniform rule, and what is best left to the discretion of the local labour movement – will be decided in practice. The division of responsibility between the centre and the local unions in the old system was, after all, nothing fixed. Rather, it was the result of an endless series of contentious, more or less democratic compromises to shifting conditions. Such compromises were possible because all parts of the labour movement came, through their many conflicts with management, to an understanding of their situation and their goals which all could share.

Today, the task is to renew common understanding through conflict and discussion. If we have currently grasped the current logic of industrial reorganization, then the labour movement will come to such an understanding only when it is has succeeded in linking the movement to make production more flexible with a movement to make the reintegration of conception and execution, and life and work on which such flexibility depends, the occasion for a redefinition of democracy.

Notes

Funding for the research on which this chapter is based was provided by the International Institute for Labour Studies of the International Labour Organization. The views expressed, however, reflect only the opinions of the authors. An earlier version of the chapter was published in 1990 under the title 'Gewerkschaften in offenen Arbeitsmärkten. Überlegungen zur Rolle der Gewerkschaften in der industriellen Reorganisation', *Soziale Welt*, 41(2): 144–60.

1 See generally, Berghahn and Karsten (1987). Notice also that the German programmes of vocational training are also often referred to as a dual system in that they combine classroom and shop learning.

2 Note, however, that in Japan the major automobile producers increasingly delegate production of low- or medium-volume speciality vehicles to 'contract assemblers', who may have played an important role in designing some component of the car.

3 There is no doubt that the suppliers, large and small, understand what is at stake. Lured by the prospect of expansion or driven by the fear of exclusion, German auto parts suppliers have begun to invest at a frantic rate. Between 1978 and 1986 West German producers of cars and trucks increased their total annual investments by 134 per cent, while parts suppliers in the industry increased their investment by 162 per cent. The increases in investment in this period measured per employee were, respectively, 109 per cent and 124 per cent (Doleschal, 1989: 27–9).

4 A recent study of the German trade union reached opposite conclusions regarding the behaviour of 'modern' employees – those directly involved with the technological and organizational innovations under discussion. It claims that, far from turning their backs on the unions, such employees may well become one of their most reliable bases of support. This conclusion, we believe, rests on a statistical artefact. In the study's sample of firms, workers in 'modern' companies are more likely to belong to unions than workers in firms where there has been little experimentation with the new methods. Hence the assertion of an affinity between 'modern' workers and unions. Because many of the most advanced firms in Germany are among the most unionized, it is hard to imagine – in the short run, at least – any other outcome. But a comparison of the union membership rates of 'modern' *workers* as against traditional workers within 'modern' *companies* would, we are confident, reveal a different, indeed contrary, result – and one which better indicates the trend of developments (see Bertl et al., 1989: 63; Fröhlich et al., 1989).

5 To streamline the argument we omit consideration of voucher systems, in which the welfare recipients do all the 'coordinating' of programmes without need of any administrative assistance. Note, however, that such systems also depend on implausible assumptions about perfect information.

References

Adamy, W. and Bosch, G. (1986) 'Gewerkschaften in der Region – Impulsgeber oder Dulder regionaler Beschäftigungspolitik', in H.E. Meier and H. Wollman (eds), *Locale Beschäftigungspolitik*, in *Stadtforschung aktuell*, vol. 10, Basle, pp. 502ff.

Altmann, N. And Sauer, D. (eds) (1989) *Systemische Rationalizierung und Zulieferindustrie*. Frankfurt, New York: Campus Verlag.

Baethge, M. and Oberbeck, H. (1988) 'Service Society and Trade Unions', *The Services Industries Journal*, 8: 389–91.

Baethge, M. et al. (1989a) 'Strukturwandel an der Gewerkschaft vorbei? Bedingungen und Probleme gewerkschaftlicher Politik gegenüber hochqualifizierten Angestellten', in *SOFI-Mitteilungen*, 16: 60ff.

Baethge, M. et al. (1989b) 'Gutachten über Forschungsstand und Forschungsdefizite im Bereich betrieblicher Weiterbildung unter besonderer Berücksichtigung der Belange der Mitarbeiter und darauf aufbauend Erarbeitung einer zukunftsweisenden Forschungskonzeption', Manuscript, Göttingen and Bonn.

Berghahn, V.R. and Karsten, D. (1987) *Industrial Relations in West Germany*. Oxford: Berg Publishers.

Bertl, W. et al. (1989) *Arbeitnehmerbewusstsein im Wandel. Folgerungen für Gesellschaft und Gewerkschaft*. Frankfurt am Main, New York.

Bosch, G. (1989) 'Beschäftigungspläne in der Praxis', in *WSI-Mitteilungen*, 4: 197ff.

Doleschal, R. (1989a) 'Die Automobil-Zulieferindustrie im Umbruch', Working paper, Lukács Institut für Sozialwissenschaften, e. V., Universität GHS Paderborn, Paderborn (Sept.).

Doleschal, R. (1989b) 'Just-in-time Strategien und Betriebspolitik im Automobilsektor', in R. Doleschal and A. Klönne (eds), *Just-in-time Konzepte und Betriebspolitik*. Düsseldorf: Hans-Böckler-Stiftung, Graue Reihe, 16: 8ff.

Fröhlich, D. et al. (1989) *Gewerkschaften vor den Herausforderungen der Neunziger Jahre*. Frankfurt, New York.

Hart, H. and Hoerte, S.A. (1989) 'Medbestaemmandets Stagnation', Gothenberg: Arbetsvetenskapliga Kollegiet.

Heine, H. and Mautz, R. (1989) *Industriearbeiter contra Umweltschutz*? Frankfurt, New York.

Hildebrandt, E. (1989) 'Zwischen Bestandssicherung und Gestaltung', *Die Mitbestimmung*, 7: 367ff.

Hildebrandt, E. and Seltz, R. (eds) (1989) *Wandel betrieblicher Sozialfassung durch systematische Kontrolle*? Berlin: Edition Sigma.

Hjern, B. (1989) 'Swedish Industrial Policy: the Demise of the Centralizing State Model'. Paper prepared for the Workshop on 'Research on Decentralization and Regional Transformation', Copenhagen: Vilvorde Centre (17–19 Aug.).

Hoffman, J. and Läpple, D. (1989) 'Kristallisationspunkte regionaler Gestaltungspolitik', *Die Mitbestimmung*, 12: 691ff.

Hoffmann, L. and Neumann, U. (1987) 'Interessenvertretung im Klein- und Mittelbetrieb. Eine empirische Untersuchung über Bedingungen und Prozesse kollektiver Gegenmacht'. Unpublished Ph.D., Fachbereich Sozialwissenschaften, University of Göttingen.

Kern, H. (1989) 'Zur Aktualität des Kampfes um die Arbeit. Strukturwandel der Industriearbeit und Perspektiven gewerkschaftlicher Politik', in H.L. Krämer and D. Leggewie (eds), *Wege ins Reich der Freiheit, André Gorz zum 65. Geburtstag*. Berlin: Rotbuch Verlag, pp. 200ff; also in IG Metall (ed.), *Tarifpolitik in Strukturwander*. Cologne (1988), pp. 166ff.

Kern, H. and Sabel, C. (1989) 'Gewerkschaften im Prozess der industriellen Reorganisation. Eine Studie strategischer Problem', *Gewerkschaftliche Monatshefte*, 10: 602ff.

Läpple, D. (1986) 'Trendbruch in der Raumentwicklung. Auf dem Weg zu einem neuen industriellen Entwicklungstyp', *Informationen zur Raumentwicklung*, 11/12: 909ff.

Läpple, D. (1989) 'Neue Technologien in räumlicher Perspektive', *Informationen zur Raumentwicklung*, 4: 213ff.

Mahnkopf, B. et al. (1989) 'Gewerkschaftspolitik und Weiterbildung. Chancen und Risiken einer qualifikationsorientierten Modernisierung gewerkschaftlicher (Tarif) Politik'. Discussion papers, WZB (Oct.).

Negt, O. et al. (1989) *Emanzipationsinteressen und Organisationsphantasie. Eine ungenützte Wirklichkeit der Gewerkschaften? Zur Erweiterung sozialkultureller Handlungsfelder am Beispiel der DGB-Ortskartelle.* Cologne: Bund-Verlag.

Richter, U. and Zitzelsberger, M. (1989) 'Vom Tornado in die Umwelttechnik', *Die Mitbestimmung*, 12: 713ff.

Sabel, C.F. (1989) 'Flexible Specialization and the Re-emergence of Regional Economies', in Paul Hirst and Jonathan Zeitlin (eds), *Reversing Industrial Decline?* Oxford: Berg Publishers, pp. 17–70.

Sabel, C., Kern, H. and Herrigel, G. (1989) 'Collaborative Manufacturing: New Supplier Relations in the Automotive Industry and the Redefinition of the Industrial Corporation'. Paper for the International Motor Vehicle Program, MIT, Cambridge, MA (31 March); in H.G. Mendius and U. Wendeling-Schröder (eds), *Zulieferer im Netz – Zwischen Abhängigkeit und Partnerschaft.* Cologne, 1991, pp. 203–223.

Schwartz, M. (1989) 'Beratungsgruppen für den Betriebsrat – zur Nachahmung empfohlen', *Die Mitbestimmung*, 8: 448ff.

von Gleich, A. (1989) 'Von der Konjunktur zur Struktur', *Die Mitbestimmung*, 12: 686ff.

Wollmann, H. (1986) 'Stadtpolitik – Erosion oder Erneuerung des Sozialstaats, von unten?' in B. Blanke et al. (eds), *Die zweite Stadt*, in *Leviathan*, 7 (special number): 79ff.

9
Training and the New Industrial Relations: a Strategic Role for Unions?

Wolfgang Streeck

In the past decade, vocational training seems to have emerged as a core subject of what to many promises to become a new type of industrial relations: more cooperative and consensual, less adversarial and conflictual, with fewer costly power struggles.[1] More and more employers have come to accept that a modern economy's competitiveness depends on the skills of its labour force. Many union leaders, in turn, no longer object to the idea that secure employment at high wages requires, above all, economic competitiveness. To deal with what is perceived as critical skill shortages, employers in many countries and industries urge governments and unions to join them in concerted training offensives. Governments, for their part, have moved vocational training to the centre of labour-market policies. As skill formation turns into a central issue of economic policy and labour relations, previously opposed group interests and the general interest finally seem to converge; distributional conflict promises to give way to productive cooperation; and eventually what appears to be outdated political antagonism may be displaced by peaceful competition for the best ideas on how jointly to organize and implement the upskilling of a country's, industry's, or company's labour force.

Still, few unions have yet thought through the implications of the resurgence of training as an industrial relations issue for their own strategy and status. Beyond general acknowledgements of the importance of skill formation, there is considerable scepticism and suspicion, especially on the intentions of employers. Among many unionists, memories of the destruction of the craft tradition under mass production in the name of economic necessity and rationality are still vivid. More recently, unions in many places have observed an industrial restructuring process that was above all aimed at 'doing more with less' – less labour, that is. The training efforts that accompanied this were too often intimately linked with downsizing, speed-up, unemployment, and intensification of work to offer strategic promise from a union perspective. Moreover, the frequent and conspicuous emphasis on 'social' and 'attitudinal skills', especially in firms and sectors that have gone through the trauma of down-sizing, is bound to raise suspicions that the real objective of employers in training is the restoration of unquestioned managerial prerogative. And are there not enough cases where 'retraining' or 'further training' is no more than a cover for outright deskilling? Or where alleged skill needs in fact serve to justify the reintroduction of discretionary wage differentials, undermining the accomplishments in many countries of the solidary wage policy of the 1960s and 1970s?

In the burgeoning 'new industrial relations' rhetoric, all of this is alleged to have recently changed. Employers are said to 'need' high skills – as well as 'good industrial relations' in a participatory work organization – *because of fundamental changes in their competitive environment*. As markets and technology allegedly 'force' employers into high-wage and high-skill production – turning them into 'good employers' *as a matter of economic self-interest* – the implication seems to be that there is no longer a need for unions to impose benevolent labour practices through mobilization and application of collective political power. Now, it is suggested, and not just by traditional unions' foes, that unions can and should instead concentrate their efforts on the implementation of economic restructuring, modernization, 'flexibility', and so on, thereby finally taking on productive rather than merely distributive functions and moving from conflict to cooperation as their main new source of influence and organizational status.

Union reluctance to embrace tripartite cooperation on training as a central new industrial relations subject ultimately derives, I suggest, from its unclear implications for the role of unions and the structure of industrial relations in general. In the following I wish to argue that popular images of a harmonious 'new industrial relations' based on common interests in high skills are dangerously simplistic – mixing truths and delusions, profound insights and business-school rhetoric. The principal flaw is a misconstrued relationship between *productive cooperation and distributive conflict* – or between *cooperative policy and adversarial politics* – suggesting that the benevolent market pressures that give rise to 'flexible specialization' signal the obsolescence of struggles over and for power. This is not just a misreading of the evidence which, as will be illustrated further on in more detail, shows that conflict and cooperation not only do not preclude, but often in fact presuppose each other. In addition, by implying that unions that care about productive concerns can be no more than agents of management-determined economic necessities, it also deters unions from constructive and creative rethinking of present, primarily distributional policies. The point I would like to make here is that one can fully agree with the proposition that unions should embrace skill formation as the centrepiece of a new, cooperative, and productivistic strategy, *and at the same time insist* on unions' need for a strong independent power base giving them, just as in the past, a capacity to impose rules and obligations on employers that these would not voluntarily obey or accept. I will argue that the latter no less than the former is in fact an indispensable condition for a successful joint union–management strategy of industrial upskilling, *even from the perspective of governments and employers.* To do this, I will begin with a brief general discussion of the relationship between unionism and the sphere of production.

Unions and the Supply Side

Mainstream unions in the post-war period have almost universally conceived of themselves as agents of distributive and redistributive politics, not of production. As such, they were reluctant to discuss their activities in terms of their impact on, or their contribution to, efficiency and productivity – and, indeed, usually such discussions were forced upon them by employers, conservative governments, and hostile academics. Nevertheless, the ideological self-stylization of unions as exclusively devoted to distributive concerns,[2] enabling them to decline direct responsibility for the well-being of national economies and individual enterprises, was not only historically new but also factually incorrect. This was because, through their very concentration on distribution, unions in the Keynesian-Fordist world of post-war social democracy contributed importantly to economic performance: both by more or less explicitly accepting managerial prerogative at the workplace, and by helping stabilize aggregate demand and increase the economy's propensity to spend at the macro-level. In fact the very power of unions in distributive politics was conditional on the productive functions that their emphasis on distribution performed for the economy as a whole; and it was only because of these that unionism could come to be regarded by governments and employers as serving not only particularistic but also general interests.

Today the Keynesian configuration is history. For many reasons, the critical problems of the economy have migrated from the macro- to the micro-level, from the demand to the supply side, from the amount of output to its structure – and from distribution to production. In the process, modern unionism has been thrown into disarray. Having comfortably located themselves in the distributive politics of macroeconomic demand management, unions are now faced with an apparently irreversible breakdown of the felicitous convergence of particularistic interest representation and the promotion of the general interest that had in the Keynesian period sustained both their institutional position and the economy.

Why do unions typically have such a hard time asserting themselves in the changed political economy of the 1980s and 1990s? The supply side has been called the 'kingdom of the bourgeoisie' (Przeworski and Wallerstein, 1982: 59). At first glance, production requires above all cooperation and compliance, not conflict and resistance. Likewise, structural change and industrial adjustment have to be responsive to market conditions; if they are driven or constrained by distributional politics, the result is all too often disastrous. Moreover, unlike the demand side, which is governed by politicians, the supply side and the microeconomics of individual enterprises are run by managers; whereas politicians are subject to a similar set of incentives and strategic imperatives as union leaders, and therefore are often sympathetic with them, managers are not. Also, the micro-level is a world, not only of diverse conditions in different sectors and workplaces, but also of competitive market pressures. Unions that get entangled in these may lose their capacity to impose general rules on the economy as a whole; find their internal politics and their organizations fragmented by divergent member interests; and run the risk of being torn apart by identification of their members with the competitive needs and interests of their employers.

Not that there was, even in an orthodox view, no place at all for unions in an economy driven from its supply side. Today, unions are again and again invited to 'cooperate' with management in restructuring, in rebuilding competitiveness, improving quality, increasing productivity, and so on. But typically such cooperation is not meant to entail more than union leaders explaining to their membership why it is necessary to comply with whatever management determines is required – for example, more training and retraining. The rewards held out for such cooperation are improved economic performance, with an uncertain share of the benefits accruing to union members, and perhaps management abstention from trying to break unions and run the workplace unilaterally. Indeed, not a small number of union officials all over the Western world today pursue 'cooperative' policies for exactly these reasons, *and for no others*. Correspondingly, unions in stronger industries or with a more secure organizational base often prefer not to get involved in a kind of cooperation that offers them essentially no other role than that of subordinate agents of management-determined economic necessities.

Drawing on vocational training as my main example, I will argue that just as in the past on the demand side, there are today on the supply side numerous opportunities for unions to combine independent, powerful representation of member interests with a pursuit of general social and economic interests. Exploring such opportunities indeed requires 'cooperative' policies and strategies. But the type of cooperation that is needed here is far from passive acceptance of managerial decisions, or self-limitation of unions to the implementation of these. Quite to the contrary, it requires forceful intervention in, and regulation of, managerial behaviour, with unions potentially and eventually appropriating, *through collective political action*, a significant share of the responsibility for productive performance. This is so, and indeed is 'necessary' in the sense that it is *competitively superior* to managerial unilateralism, because the supply of a modern industrial economy is a kingdom of the bourgeoisie only on the surface. In reality, it is rather a *magic kingdom* full of paradoxes and contradictions, the most important of which is that the king cannot properly govern, neither in his own interest nor in that of his subjects, unless he is himself governed by the latter – a king who needs to be constrained by a powerful citizenry in order to be able to accomplish what he would like to accomplish; a king who, as a prisoner of his passions, faces dilemmas that he can solve only if he is compelled to do so by others.

Skills and Effective Supply

Union involvement in skill formation may well be the successor in the post-Keynesian political economy to what wage formation was for unions under Keynesianism, being as important and performing the same functions for them. Understanding the politics and institutional dynamics of training constitutes a major step towards a theory of effective supply to succeed older theories of effective demand, and may help unions adjust their position in the political economy to new conditions and realities. In training as well as, before, in demand stabilization, the possibility for unions to perform a useful function for both their members and the society at large derives from the fact that their opponents – 'capitalists', 'management' – are confronted with vexing dilemmas between their collective long-term and their individual short-term interests. In the Keynesian world, this was the dilemma between the need for high and stable purchasing power and the desire to cut costs. The solution was cooperation between employers, forced upon them by unions through the exercise of collective power in industrial conflict, and often also by governments through legal intervention. More specifically, unions imposed on employers a more or less uniform and rigid wage pattern, thereby taking wages out of competition and insuring investors against the downward spirals in purchasing power that may result from competitive cost-cutting. In this way, collective action of workers created the stable and growing product markets that enterprises in the era of mass production needed in order to invest and grow.

In a market economy, training poses similar problems for employers on the supply side as did aggregate demand stabilization on the demand side, and it offers similar opportunities to unions to build a base of independent power. What wage bargaining was for distributional unionism, training may become for unions working on and through the production side of the economy and making their peace with it: an opportunity for conflictual cooperation, or cooperation through conflict; for redistribution in the general interest; and for deep involvement of unions in the management of an advanced industrial economy and society. In short, this is for the following reasons:

1 In certain growing but highly competitive product markets, a rich supply of skills, and especially of broad, experientially based general work skills, constitutes perhaps the most important source of competitive advantage for firms.
2 The skills that are most needed in such markets are of a kind that can be generated only with the active involvement of employers. This is because such skills are most likely to be generated through work-based learning in close proximity to the work process, and clearly *not* in schools. However,
3 while the acquisition of today's critical skills requires the utilization of workplaces for non-work purposes, most employers, if left to their own devices, will not by far do enough for skill formation, in part because of individually unsolvable problems of calculating expected returns on investment, and in part because, in an open labour market, skills are, in an important sense, collective goods.
4 Unions, if properly supported by public policy, have the capacity to make employers train, and may well develop the motivation to do so.

I have elaborated these points elsewhere (Streeck, 1989). For the present purpose, I would like to confine myself to a few selective observations.

The Relationship between Modern Technology, Work Organization, and Skills

Modern technology is less than instructive with respect to the skills needed to operate it. The reason is that microelectronic circuitry can support radically different patterns of work organization. Vastly increased capacities to process and transmit information allow for centralization of control and differentiation of tasks far beyond what was possible only a decade ago. At the same time, they *also* enable organizations to delegate decisions to flexible sub-units with integrated, overlapping functions, so as to respond better to more complex and specific demands from their environment.

Different patterns of work organization give rise to different skill 'needs'. A centralized and functionally differentiated organization requires a small number of highly skilled employees located in staff-like departments remote from the actual production process, and a large number of unskilled or semi-skilled operators with narrowly specialized tasks waiting to be eliminated by automation. By comparison, a decentralized and functionally integrated work organization will have short hierarchies and will require a relatively even distribution of both broad and high skills.

Beliefs about a trend towards 'upgrading' of work in modern production systems; about urgent needs for improvements in initial and further vocational training; about a 'skill gap' in the work-force; or about skills as a crucial resource for international competitiveness – all are premised on the assumption that in the future, most productive work will be done, or will have to be done, in less centralized and less functionally differentiated organizations. To the extent that firms will be compelled to exploit the potential of microelectronic information technology for decentralizing and reintegrating work tasks, it is argued that they will have to rely on a large supply among their work-force of a combination of cognitive-technical, attitudinal, and social skills that together form the basis for what has been called decentralized competence – where competence means both the organizational autonomy and the individual ability of workers to make correct and responsible decisions embedded in and related to the context of the organization at large.

The Relationship between Product Markets, Product Strategies, and Productive Flexibility

While the skill 'needs' of employers using new technology depend on how employers choose to organize work, that choice, in turn, is related to the product market in which a firm operates.

Decentralized competence seems to be particularly conducive to, or outright required for, small-batch production, or customized production, of goods or services designed to fit the specific needs of individual clients. This is because decentralized competence provides organizations with a high degree of internal flexibility in general and a capacity for fast retooling in particular – that is, for switching from one product, or batch of products, to another.

Producing a diverse and changing range of products at a high-quality level requires not only a strong engineering capacity that allows for a high rate of product innovation. It also demands close interaction between the organization and its customers, as well as between different organizational functions such as marketing and product engineering, or product engineering and production. For this to be possible, employees in different parts of the organization must be able to understand one another's job, and sometimes to substitute for one another. That is, their qualifications must overlap. Moreover, rapid product change is facilitated by work groups integrating, like small firms, a wide range of tasks and thereby becoming more independent from concurrent decisions or supporting activities of differentiated, functionally specialized units. This calls for duplication of skills across organizational sub-units. Productive flexibility thus necessitates redundant (that is, overlapping or duplicated) organizational capacities that can be economically sustained only if other overheads, like quality control, supply management, or worker supervision, are cut – which again demands integration of previously separate, specialized tasks in front-line production work.

Overall, it appears that *today's product markets place a premium on customization*, and that firms that are flexible enough to engage in small-batch or customized production can command higher profit margins; are less vulnerable in their market position; and are likely to enjoy more long-term stability. Ultimately, this is based on the experience that in the highly competitive 1970s and 1980s firms, or national economies, that were capable of offering more diversified and customized products fared better than more traditional producers of standardized mass products. There is some disagreement as to why this should have been the case; to what extent product markets have 'really' changed; and how large the new markets for what has been called 'diversified quality production' actually are. What seems clear, however, is that the economic attraction for employers of small-batch or customized production is often conditional on the prevailing *wage level* in a given country or region – in that firms which can bring down their wages far enough, may have the alternative to survive as mass producers. The problem is that in a more and more global economy, mass markets tend to be increasingly taken over by producers from newly industrializing countries where wages are so low that firms in old industrial countries may, for all kinds of reasons, find it impossible to compete.[3]

In addition, it seems that the distinction between mass and customized markets is more fluid than is often believed. Given the productive flexibilities made possible by information technology, especially in combination with a work organization that emphasizes decentralized competence, small-batch producers and customizers are often able to transform mass markets into markets for more customized products, in a similar way as mass producers in the course of industrialization transformed craft markets into mass markets. This is because high productive flexibility makes it possible to narrow the cost differential between customized, or semi-customized, and mass production to a point where the (still) higher price of non-standardized goods or services is compensated by their better match of the customer's individual needs. To the extent that advances in customized and semi-customized production methods make this possible, mass markets shrink and differentiated quality markets grow.

In sum, as product markets fragment, the market a firm serves becomes less given and is increasingly subject to 'strategic choice'. Simultaneously, as technologies become more undefined and malleable, the products that are produced with them, and the organization of work that surrounds them, are less than in the past determined by a technology's intrinsic properties; they, too, have to be strategically chosen. Given existing technologies and demand structures, a firm can in principle aspire to be either a quality-competitive producer of customized goods with a flexible, fluid, and decentralized work organization, employing highly skilled workers at a high wage, or an efficient, price-competitive producer of standardized goods with a centralized and formulized organizational structure, unskilled labour, low wages, and high wage dispersion.

The Institutional Sources of Skill Use and Skill Development

The long controversy on the direction of skill development under capitalism can now by and large be considered settled. Whether or not employers prefer deskilled over skilled labour cannot, in Bravermanian fashion, be decided deductively and once and for all. The question can sensibly be answered only when placed in the context of wage-setting mechanisms, the regulation of employment contracts, patterns of work organization, styles of technology use, and firms' strategic product market decisions. Unlike, perhaps, in the era of mechanical machinery, today managerial choices between downskilling and upskilling are clearly *not* driven by technology as such; microelectronic circuitry can be used for cutting costs by eliminating skills and human intervention, as well as for increasing product quality and variety by enriching the productive capacities of well-trained workers. Downskilling presupposes, among other things, downward flexibility and wide dispersion of wages, enabling employers to adjust wages to relatively declining labour productivity, and high numerical flexibility of employment, permitting rapid adjustment of labour input to market fluctuations and making it unnecessary to provide for workers' internal redeployability through training.

By comparison, rigid and high wages, an egalitarian wage structure, limited access of firms to external labour markets, and limitations on the deployment of new technology for 'rationalization' – by making it impossible for firms to be profitable in mass markets for standardized, price-competitive products and forcing them to try and serve differentiated, quality-competitive markets – tend to forbid downskilling and instead force and induce firms to raise the skill level of their work-force.

The extent of downward wage flexibility, the degree of wage spread, the ability of firms to hire and fire, and the shape and extent of the division of labour in production are conditional on institutional arrangements, such as the system of industrial relations or legal rules on employment protection. Where these stand in the way of low wages, high wage differentiation, a Taylorist organization of work, and so on, firms are forced to either emigrate to more sympathetic environments, or give up producing for price-competitive mass markets and invest in, among other things, training. Similarly, where institutional conditions encourage long-term investment in a differentiated, quality-competitive product range, ensure functional flexibility on the shop floor, and facilitate training efforts at the workplace, they may enable firms to adjust to a rigidly fixed, high wage by increasing the skills of their workers. Institutions, that is, can be constraints and opportunities at the same time; in both capacities together, they shape the choices of employers and industries that determine what kind of skills and how much of them they 'need'.

The Importance and the Difficult Economics of Work-based Learning

Consensus is growing that today's advanced work skills are best acquired at or near the workplace. Workplace-based training, where it is up to its new task, is quite different from traditional 'on-the-job training' – which was to impart cheap, narrow, workplace-specific skills supplementing the general skills produced in public educational institutions.

The growing need to use the workplace for training purposes is related to the fact that, with fast-changing and highly flexible technology, and with fast product turnover, work routines can never become so established that execution can be neatly separated from conception. Work in such environments amounts to continuous experimentation with, and permanent 'de-bugging' of, new processes and machine set-ups. On the part of operators, this requires, in addition to high cognitive skills ('literacy' and 'numeracy'), an intuitive 'feel' for the work that can only be gained from experience, as well as a range of motivational, attitudinal, and social skills that cannot be adequately developed outside 'real work' production situations with their pressures and constraints. This is one reason why countries like Japan and Germany, where most industrial skill formation takes place in work settings, are so advantaged by their human capital endowment. It also explains why a country like Sweden, where for historical reasons training takes place almost exclusively in schools and training centres, today complains about critical skill shortages, in spite of vast public investments in training. Put in more general terms, the skills required for advanced industrial competitiveness are most likely to be available where it is possible to *transform the workplace into a place of learning in addition to a place of work* – that is, to place a large share of the training burden on firms and managements and make them accept the utilization of the enterprise not just for production but also for skill formation.

Mainstream labour economics proceeds from the seminal insight that in an open labour market, returns on investment in general skills cannot be internalized by individual firms since such skills are transferable from one employer to another. This is why such skills will not be produced unless the costs are borne by the worker as an individual or as a taxpayer (in the latter case, by the general public). Keeping expenditure on and responsibilities for general and specific skills apart is greatly simplified if general skills are, and can be, taught outside the workplace in specialized training organizations – 'schools' – while specific skills are generated at the workplace.

To the extent that the workplace is used to produce general skills, which is not likely to be typical, workers must be willing to accept a pay cut equivalent to the cost of the general training they receive, or the government must reimburse employers for their expenses. The first solution presupposes that general training can indeed be paid for out of a share of a worker's wage during the training period; both assume that the costs and returns of training at the workplace can be reliably established.

All these assumptions have recently come under heavy pressure. As has been pointed out, today there is for a variety of reasons a fundamental school failure with respect to the formation of general work skills. As a result, to the extent that an economy depends for its competitiveness on high skills, a growing share of its general training effort has to be carried out at its workplaces. Typically, the costs of such training are high and can be recovered by individual employers only over a long period, one which far exceeds the time of training, as well as any reasonable commitment workers can make not to move to another employer. The benefits of workplace training for employers thus become inevitably vulnerable to being 'pirated' by competitors. Unlike previous types of 'market failure', this problem cannot be remedied by unilateral public provision since this fails to produce the desired type of skills.

Moreover, the exact costs of workplace training defy conventional accounting and can therefore not easily be reimbursed. Work-based learning is optimally effective in a group-based or team-centred work organization that is more open and 'porous' than what traditional industrial engineering prescribes. While this may in one sense increase costs, or at least make hidden costs less easy to detect, it may at the same time engender quality improvements and productivity increases. To this extent, workplace training may pay for itself. In any case, an offer by the public sector to pay employers for general training at the workplace is likely to encourage all kinds of 'creative accounting'. Also, employers may feel induced to rely on more traditional, classroom-style training the costs of which are easier to establish. The inevitable conclusion is that adequate utilization of the workplace as a learning site requires that employers pay a significant share of the costs of general training.

The difficult economics of workplace training require public intervention of a kind that makes unilateral provision look simple by comparison. The assumption by employers of responsibility for training in workplace-unspecific skills, as is optimal for competitive performance, demands the effective imposition of social obligations to train, as a substitute for insufficient individual market incentives and as a way of taking training costs out of competition. In open labour markets, employers competing with one another will always be under a temptation to 'cheat' by not investing in general training and hiring skilled workers from their competitors. What is more, the mere prospect that others may behave in this way is likely to deter employers from training even if the result will be a general skill shortage. Societies that have at their disposal institutional or cultural mechanisms by which to oblige firms to cooperate in training are likely to enjoy competitive advantages, as they will be able to protect their firms from the dysfunctional consequences of market-rational behaviour for the production of skills as collective goods.

This principle applies not just to the extent but also to the substance of workplace-based training. Where the skills that are produced at the workplace are so general that they constitute unspecific resources – like the ability to interact with others or the capacity to detect problems – strictly economic decisions on training, based on rational calculations of 'return on investment', are likely to result in underinvestment. Countries like Japan and Germany, however different their training systems may be, testify to the economic uses, in a world of fast technological change, of culturally or politically mandated excess training beyond immediate economic need – of a human resource policy, that is, that increases flexibility by building redundant capacities.

Union Policies on Training: from Consumption to Investment
Unions in advanced industrial countries differ widely in their attitudes towards training as a major concern of union or industrial relations. The spectrum extends from outright hostility among radical unions of unskilled workers (as in part of the communist French CGT); to indifferent lip-service to the idea of shared, public responsibility for skill upgrading; and to long-standing support for, and involvement in, initial and continuous vocational training (for example, in Denmark or Germany). However, even where unions have accepted training as a current concern, there usually is still a long way to go to embracing it as a core subject of union strategy.

This is so essentially for two reasons. For one thing, there is a temptation for unions that support training to do so in the traditional framework of distributive politics, conceiving of training as a basically consumptive, non-wage benefit. Union training policy of this kind would be about creating entitlements to being released from work with full pay for not directly productive activities. Much of the West German *Bildungsurlaub* (literally, 'educational holidays') legislation and some related collective agreements in the 1970s were of this character. Given the overwhelming importance of monetary income for consumption, training thus conceived can never be of more than marginal interest for unions, especially in leaner, less affluent economic conditions.

Secondly, training tends to be regarded even by many unionists as an investment employers make out of economic self-interest, as required by technology and product market conditions. To this, the principal *modus operandi* of unionism, the creation of entitlements for workers, does not seem to apply. As long as it is assumed that employers know what they are doing – that is, that product market signals are sufficiently instructive for employers to do what is needed on training – there is simply no reason for unions as unions to expend scarce bargaining power on making employers train. For this to make sense, union confidence in employers' ability to act economically rationally must be less than complete. An active union policy on training, in other words, presupposes that the limited capacities of the self-proclaimed king of the supply side to act in his own interest are thoroughly appreciated.[4]

A positive union policy on training may also take off from the insight that advanced skills require investment not just by employers but also by workers, and that such investment is indeed more likely to be made if supported by negotiated entitlements – albeit, of course, to invest rather than consume. More generally, the opening for unions becoming agents of a more-than-distributive training policy lies in the *incompleteness*, as it were, of the human resource investment functions of both employers and workers – being due to a lack of resources on the part of the latter, and to the inherent limits of rational return-on-investment calculations for the provision of work-based training in high, broad, experiential skills on the part of the former. Here as elsewhere, gaps in the instructive capacity of product markets and technology have to be filled, and conflicts between individual and collective rationality overcome, by institutional rules and social norms enabling rational economic actors to act in their rational economic interest.

Union Intervention in Training

Independent union intervention in cooperative training and human resource policies must combine the imposition of institutional *constraints* on managements that foreclose low-skill, low-wage paths of industrial adjustment, with the creation of institutional *opportunities* for managements to pursue successfully a high-skill and high-wage policy. Constraints and opportunities must be built simultaneously; while the former without the latter suffocate economic performance, the latter without the former result in a dual economy with widely divergent conditions and performance levels, and very likely an underutilization of productive opportunities due to unchecked temptations for employers to defect from more demanding high-skill and high-wage production patterns.

How specifically unions can deploy their political and organizational capacities to build the constraints and opportunities required to make employers train, and what those constraints and opportunities could be in a given economic and political setting, depends on the situation and, of course, the creativity of the actors involved.[5] What can generally be said is that cooperation on training is not only compatible with conflict, but indeed may require a conflictual capability of unions for its success. Examples where rigorous pursuit of, in part quite traditional, union objectives – if necessary against employer resistance – complements and makes effective a cooperative strategy on training are set out below.[6]

First, defence of *high wages and a relatively flat wage structure*, so as to foreclose as well as possible the option of low-wage, low-skill employment. High and downwardly rigid wages force employers to raise the productivity of their workers to match the given price of their labour, rather than depress wages to the level of workers' given marginal productivities. The more flexible the wage, the lower the interest of employers in skilling. The higher the wage-spread, the more selective employers' training investment will be.[7] Given the inherent indeterminacy of skill needs and the benefits of a rich skill environment for advanced competitiveness, highly selective and targeted human resource investment is, almost by definition, likely to be economically suboptimal.

Secondly, insistence on *obligatory, standardized workplace training curricula* that firms have to follow if they want to train for a particular skill or occupation. These curricula must be broadly defined, so as to prevent overspecialization and provide the ground for future, further training, Standardized curricula also serve the important function of enabling workers to quit and carry their skills with them. This ability constitutes a major source of union and worker power that can be defended only if training regimes are centralized. Moreover, by barring employers from generating skills that are too workplace-specific, generally binding curricula constrain them, as well as giving them the opportunity, to produce exactly the kind of broad, polyvalent skills that they need most.

Thirdly, use of the union workplace organization, or whatever structure of worker representation may exist at the workplace, to ensure that training follows the standardized curriculum and neither becomes too workplace-specific nor is absorbed in productive work. Without an *effective, on-the-ground enforcement mechanism*, unions and workers cannot live with a high differential between training and skilled wages. Effective union supervision of workplace training, ensuring that it remains just that, is an important safeguard against the temptation for management to extract more productive work from trainees, thereby neglecting their firm's own longer-term interests.

Fourthly, defence, or extension, of legal and other provisions that protect *employment continuity and stability*. Employers who can satisfy their skill needs and change the skill composition of their work-force by firing old and hiring new workers, will have less incentive to train than employers who face fewer employment 'rigidities'. An economy where employers have the option of turning to the external labour market for skills, instead of training or retraining their existing work-force, will tend to suffer from a general skill deficit. This is so not least because the expectation on the part of employers that their competitors will seek external rather than internal adjustment constitutes a strong disincentive to train, even in periods of obvious skill shortages and even for firms that feel severely constrained by these.

Fifthly, imposition of a *flat wage regime* with few wage grades and job classifications that *rewards knowledge* rather than activities performed. Wage structures of this kind allow for easy redeployment of workers, which affords firms a degree of internal flexibility that makes the constraints of external employment rigidity bearable. Even more importantly, with the right kind of pay system, workers will not only be willing to acquire skills but will also accept internal mobility – in part because it helps them learn.[8]

Sixthly, active pursuit, as an objective in its own right, of an *anti-Taylorist policy on the organization of work*, aimed at imposing on employers negotiated obligations to move towards broad job descriptions, a low division of labour, long work-cycles, and reintegration of tasks. In addition to improving working conditions, such a policy contributes to making low-skilled labour unusable by eliminating the type of jobs for which it was in the past typically hired. Coupled with external employment rigidities and internal employment flexibility, de-Taylorization of work organization thus constrains as well as induces employers to invest in training.[9]

Seventhly, negotiation of *training and retraining plans* with employers, setting a mutually agreed human resource policy for enterprises, regions, or industries. Such agreements would have to create enforceable entitlements for workers to be trained and retrained at the workplace on a current basis, not just in emergencies, and under general as well as workplace-unspecific curricula. Given that firms lack instructive economic criteria as to what kind of skills and how many they need; and given the advantages quality-competitive firms, industries, and regions derive from a rich supply of 'excess skills', there will be ample space to accommodate egalitarian demands for underendowed groups in the workforce to be included in training. In fact, it will be through *negotiated entitlements to learn at work* that unions will contribute most to the broad and unspecific skill formation that firms in demanding markets need but find so hard to generate on their own.

A Strategic Perspective?

Unions today have a unique chance to return in a productive way to their craft heritage. Craft unions were producers of skills as well as sellers. At the present day, there are industries in the United States where high standards of training at the workplace, and indeed the very provision of such training, depend on strong craft-union presence *and disappear with the decline of unionization.*

But it is also true that in their distributional battles with Bravermanian employers, craft unions often redefined skill in terms of exclusive rights of their members to narrowly demarcated jobs.[10] In that process, the contribution of unions to the production of skills began to take second place to the defence of craft prerogatives. Where craft unionism, or important elements of it, survived, all too often it deteriorated, under the pressure of employers' deskilling strategies, into a reactive defence of status and privilege. In such cases training lost its productivist meanings: at the worst, it became reserved for small groups of carefully selected apprentices, with restricted access serving to maintain a high differential between skilled and unskilled wages, and turned into an increasingly well-paid waiting period for accession to the labour aristocracy, without much of a meaningful curriculum.[11] This, in turn, made it easier for employers to attack unions as special-interest groups impeding both industrial progress and fair access to good jobs. De-unionization and the destruction of apprenticeship could and can thus be presented by employers as efficient as well as equitable.

In a *perverse alliance*, then, industrial employers bent on deskilling and craft unions narrowly representing only their members, often enough played into each other's hands. The dismal results were unhappily reinforced when industrial unionism appeared and found in deskilling the promise of a homogeneous work-force easy to organize in inclusive unions around distributional concerns and without entanglement in the sphere of production. This configuration prepared the ground for the post-war compromise between capital and labour, in which the latter agreed to leave production to management and accomplish its egalitarian objectives through distributive collective bargaining and social policy. With the ascent of Fordism, training was no longer much of a concern.

There is nothing in the present return of skills on to the industrial relations agenda that would compel unions to give up the egalitarian values they inherited from industrial unionism. In fact, in a world in which redundant skills may be necessary for competitive economic success, the two traditions of unionism may now be able to converge in a policy of negotiated general upskilling, conducted and enforced in cooperative conflict with employers and in creative partnership with governments, and indeed much facilitated by the internal organizational dynamics of industrial unionism. Who will be king on the supply side is far from being a foregone conclusion.

Notes

1 This chapter is a revised and expanded version of a lecture given at a conference on 'The Future of Industrial Relations in Europe', organized by the Netherlands Scientific Council for Government Policy in honour of W. Albeda, Maastricht, the Netherlands, 7 and 8 June 1990. I am grateful to Joel Rogers for constructive comment. The usual disclaimers apply.

2 In reality, of course, the matter was more complicated. In all Western countries in the post-war period, there were sporadic demands by unions for involvement in managerial decisions. Mainstream unionists typically had a hard time deciding if these were a right-wing sell-out to capital, or a communist attack on the market economy and, with it, free collective bargaining. The mainstream *Nur-Gewerkschafter*, to use Marx's term, hated both. To keep his distance from the inscrutable ambivalence and the puzzling political contradictions of productivism, right or left, he would insist that the union's proper concern was fundamentally different from management's; that the two were confounded only at the union's and, perhaps, the economy's and democracy's peril; and that while management was in charge of efficiency, or economic issues, the union was to look after equity, or the social questions. Coexisting with this strand of unionism were other, older strategic orientations that sometimes looked 'cooperative', or 'yellow', and sometimes 'radical', or 'red'. Their difference from mainstream centrism was that they saw and sought an active role for unions in the efficient organization of

production. In some countries, these in fact became the mainstream: the 'left' version in Sweden, the 'right' version in Japan, and a peculiar blend of the two in Germany (*viz.*, that chameleon-like institution, co-determination). The matter is made even more confusing by the fact that rhetoric and behaviour did not always coincide, so that one found, for example, distribution-minded centrists supporting wage moderation in the name of economic growth.

3 Firms in high-wage areas that do not want, or are unable, to develop productive flexibility may also, of course, relocate to low-wage countries.

4 Again, this does not appear to be a clear-cut left–right issue. Confidence in the superior economic wisdom of owners and managers can be found both among 'cooperative' unionists for whom cooperation consists of rallying their members behind management-defined economic inevitabilities, and among 'arm's-length', 'adversarial' opponents of cooperation who want to confine unions exclusively to extracting distributive concessions. The latter position implies that the economic basis for such concessions can be safely produced and reproduced without union 'involvement', that is, by management acting on its own.

5 A different but related question that I will *not* address here is how unions with weak or declining organizational capacities, as, for example, in the United States, can use involvement in skill formation to build or protect such capacities. Much depends in this respect on whether employers, and perhaps the state, perceive existing skill deficits as so critical, and their own means to deal with them as so limited, that they are willing to pay a political price to whoever may be able and willing to help them out. This would imply that if unions could come up with an effective contribution to skill formation that only they can make (or that they can make better than others), they could in principle 'sell' that contribution in the same way and for the same kind of returns as they have in the past sold their more traditional 'product' peace at the workplace. As Joel Rogers reminds me, unions thrive if their policies satisfy three conditions: they must be advantageous to their members and possible members; they must give employers something that they want, but cannot get on their own; and they must make a visible contribution to the 'common good'. Promotion of effective skill formation, especially at the workplace, may very well do all of the above.

6 As will easily be recognized, my list draws in large measure on the German experience. However, this is only because I happen to know that experience better than others. To the extent that there may be lessons from the German case for other countries, these would consist of a number of *general principles* rather than concrete institutional cookbook recipes. I believe that most of those principles have to do with the insufficiency of a market mode of skill formation; the crucial importance of using the workplace as a place of learning; the dangers of off-loading training to the state; the need, resulting from this, for mechanisms generating social obligations for employers to train, thereby transcending the limits of a liberal-voluntaristic training regime; and the potentially extremely productive role unions can play in generating such obligations. On the basis of what I think I have learned from the German case, I would be inclined to predict that where such principles are neglected, skill formation and advanced industrial competitiveness will lag behind German (and Japanese) standards.

7 A low wage spread at a high overall wage level induces employers to distribute their human resource investment more evenly. This presupposes relatively *low training wages*, especially for young people – which may or may not be difficult to concede for unions. The narrower the gap between training wages and skilled

wages, the larger the productive component of a trainee's activities at the workplace, as distinguished from its investive, training component.

8 Although a low wage spread above a high wage floor creates an incentive for employers to train, it may constitute a disincentive for workers to learn. The latter seems to have been one of the unanticipated consequences of Swedish 'solidary wage policy'. Unions taking an active role in skill formation will have to search for a 'saddle point' where wage differentials are low enough for employers to be willing to provide training to the work-force at large, and high enough for workers to justify the effort of undergoing training. (To make remaining wage differentials effective with respect to training, they should to the greatest possible extent be based on knowledge.) One would expect that the ideal level of wage differentiation should be found somewhere between the extremely high American and the extremely low Swedish wage spread.

9 To advance more comprehensive job demarcations as well as facilitate the move towards an ability-based payment system, unions could negotiate higher wages for workers who have undergone training, regardless of whether or not their additional qualifications are actually used. This will be a strong incentive for managements to reorganize work in such a way that the new skills can in fact be utilized – which will in turn make it easier for unions to push for a less fragmented work organization. Being forced to use newly generated qualifications by reorganizing work so as to accommodate them, managements will be educated about the possibilities and advantages of high-wage and high-skill production, and in this way unions may provide further training to management on its own long-term interests.

10 That is, where they were given the chance to do so, especially in the Anglo-Saxon countries. For a variety of reasons, the development was quite different in Germany and Scandinavia. Still, the differences are gradual and not categorical, and at least historically the dynamic described here was present everywhere.

11 This was the case particularly in Britain where apprenticeship typically deteriorated into 'time served', at declining pay differentials between skilled workers and apprentices. As a result it almost completely disappeared.

References

Przeworski, A. and Wallerstein, M. (1982) 'Democratic Capitalism at the Crossroads', *Democracy* (July): 52–68.

Streeck, W. (1989) 'Skills and the Limits of Neo-liberalism: the Enterprise of the Future as a Place of Learning', *Work, Employment and Society*, 3: 90–104; also in Paolo Ceri (ed.) (1988) *Impresa e lavoro in trasformazione: Italia–Europa*, Milan: Società editrice il Mulino, pp. 71–109.

Index

activists in unions, 22–3, 74, 75
advanced capitalist democracies, 17–52,
   102–32
AFL (American Federation of Labour),
   82–4, 96, 136
alliances in sectors, 201
anti-clerical coalitions, 73
anti-unionism, 39–42, 73, 75, 95–6, 155, 158
apprenticeship, 228
Argentina, 62, 63, 84–9, 92–3, 96, 97
articulated industrial relations systems,
   169–87
associative action, 190–2
Australia, 18–21, 27, 105–22 *passim*, 137,
   139, 185
Austria: collective bargaining, 171, 173;
   industrial relations, 181; inflation, 176,
   184–6; neo-corporatist concertation, 72;
   strikes, 105–20 *passim*, 125, 175, 182–3;
   unemployment, 176, 184–6; unions,
   18–21, 27, 29, 30–4; welfare state, 134–5
authoritarian regimes, 64, 66–8, 70, 85,
   89–91, 93, 94

Belgium: industrial relations, 175, 181, 182;
   inflation, 176, 184–6; strikes, 105, 107,
   108, 114, 116, 118, 120, 128, 175;
   unemployment, 25–6, 44, 176, 184–6;
   unions, 18–21, 25–6, 27, 30–4, 44, 69,
   93, 178
Brazil, 56, 63, 84–9, 96
bureaucratic-authoritarian regimes, labour
   movements in, 89
business associability, 195, 196–202; sectoral
   differentiation, 201, 203, 205–6;
   territorial differentiation, 201, 203, 209
business cycles and industrial conflict, 102–4,
   115, 121
business interest associations (BIAs),
   188–216, *see also* employers'
   organizations; trade associations

Canada, 18–21, 27, 40–1, 45, 105–20 *passim*,
   125
Catholicism and communist parties, 94
centralization: collective bargaining, 37–9,
   155, 171, 172, 212; unions, 171, 172,
   182
Chile, labour movement, 72–7, 94
CIO (Congress of Industrial Organizations),
   83, 84, 96, 136
clans in sectors, 200
class conflict, 54, 61, 76, 79–80, 83, 95,
   126–7, 159
closed shops, 23, 45
co-optation of labour movements, 85, 87,
   112, 177, 239
collective bargaining, 69, 82, 93–4, 171–4,
   178–9; authoritarian regimes, 89, 90;
   centralization, 37–9, 155, 171, 172, 212;
   decentralization, 210, 245–6; and dual
   system, 218; firm level, 72, 88, 155,
   171–2, 178–9, 181, 185, 218; industry-
   wide, 35–7, 155; pluralistic stability,
   169; shop-floor, 36, 172–3, 174; supra-
   firm, 35–7; supra-industry, 37–9, 170,
   178; supra-national, 203, 211, 212; and
   union development, 56
collective mobilization, 2–5
collective welfare services, 135
collectivism and individualism, 151, 160, 161
collegiate leadership, 77
Colombia, union-party links, 62, 69–70
communist parties, 55, 73, 74, 75, 77, 94,
   156, 162
company unions, 35, 212, 217, 218, 229, 231
competition, 197, 201, 209, 255
concertation, 5–7, 11–12; and consensus, 71;
   neo-corporatist, 70–2, 76, 77, 211
conflict: between unions, 34, 70, 78, 141,
   152; in capital interests, 197; and
   cooperation, 251–2, 253, 255; and
   corporatism, 113, 114, 129, 175;
   symbolic forms of, 123, *see also*
   industrial conflict
confrontational labour movements, 55,
   89–91, 111
consensus, *see* concertation
conservative regimes, 135, 138, 156–7, 179,
   180
contestatory labour movements, 55, 72–7
cooperation and conflict, 251–2, 253, 255
corporate welfare services, 135
corporatism, 70, 90, 94, 113, 114, 129, 169,
   175, 211
craft unions, 35, 82, 83, 159, 160, 163, 175,
   235, 266–7
cross-national comparisons, 17–52, 102–32
customized products, 257, 258

de-Taylorization, 265
decentralization: collective bargaining, 210,
   245–6; unions, 178
decentralized competence, 256, 257
decentralized production and unions, 217–49
democracies, 64–6, 71, 113

Democratic Party (US), 78, 79, 81-2, 83-4, 95
Denmark: collective bargaining, 173; craft unions, 175; industrial relations, 175, 180, 181; inflation, 176, 184-6; strikes, 105, 107, 108, 114-20 *passim*, 124, 175, 182-3; unemployment, 176, 184-6; unions, 18-21, 27, 28, 29, 30-4, 93, 154, 156, 178
departmental unions, 30
depoliticization of unions, 162
deregulation in EC, 197, 201, 203, 209
deskilling, 258-9, 266-7
disabled people and informal economy, 142
disaggregation of interests and unions, 150-68
discomfort index, 176, 184-5
distributional coalitions, 17, 30
diversification of markets and unions, 222
dual system of industrial relations, 217-20

early retirement, 142
economic conditions, 71-2, 112, 152, 158
education, continuing, 236-8, 245
egalitarianism, USA, 80
elites in worker politics, 23, 54
employers and unions, 57, 58, 73, 75, 95-6, 121, 155
employers' organizations, 157, 173, 178-9, 181, 182, 192, 193-5; and unions, 169, 171, 174, 191, 192, 207; *see also* business interest associations (BIAs)
employment, structure of, *see* structure of employment
equal pay, 141
European Community, 197-200, 204, 207, 212; social dimension, 208, 209, 210; welfare states, 135, 142
European internal market, 188-216
European Trade Union Confederation (ETUC), 39, 208, 210, 211
evening-class engineers, 228
exclusive bargaining/jurisdiction, 32, 83

family, care by, 140
financial services sector, union density, 27
Finland: collective bargaining, 172-3; industrial relations, 180, 185; inflation, 176, 184-6; labour movement, 72; strikes, 105-22 *passim*, 175, 182-3; unemployment, 176, 184-6; union membership levels, 18-21, 178
firm level bargaining, 72, 88, 145, 155, 171-2, 178-9, 181, 185, 218
firm level penetration and union development, 55, 56-7
firms, welfare provision by, 145-6, 147
flat wage structures, 264, 265
flexibilization, 145, 223, 231, 256-7
formal economy and welfare state, 140-1
fragmentation: and leadership, 87, 88, 151; of labour movement, 58-60, 63, 72, 73,

74, 95, 151, 155; of opposition to authoritarian regimes, 67-8; of party system, 65, 66, 72; of union confederations, 68-9
France: industrial relations, 174, 179, 186; inflation, 176, 184-6; labour movement, 72-7; multi-employer collective bargaining, 36-7; pensions, 137; strikes, 24, 105-25 *passim*, 175, 182-3; unemployment, 176, 184-6; union confederations, 30-2, 162, 179; unions, 18-21, 22, 23, 24, 43-4, 178; welfare state, 135
free-ridership, 54, 190
friendly societies, welfare provision by, 137, 160
functionalist views of welfare state, 134, 139

gender differences in union membership, 27, 28, 83
Germany: collective bargaining, 69, 93-4, 171; craft unions, 35; dual system of industrial relations, 217-20; employers' organizations, 182; industrial unions, 35; inflation, 176, 184-6; labour movement, 68-72, 217-49; multi-employer collective bargaining, 35; neo-corporatist concertation, 72; strikes, 24, 105-22 *passim*, 175, 182-3; training, 250-69; unemployment, 142, 176, 184-6; union confederations, 30-4, 161; union membership levels, 18-21, 27, 29, 45, 93, 219; union-party links, 62, 70, 93; unions, 32, 34, 35, 178; welfare, 135, 136, 242-3; women's employment, 140, 141; works councils/councillors, 35, 172, 173, 217-18, 220, 230, 231, 237, 246
Germany, East, absorption of, 185, 221
goal formation, logic of business associability, 195, 196, 199
governing parties and labour movements, 65, 71, 74, 76, 77
Greece, industrial relations, 180
guaranteed income, 147-8

heterogeneity/homogeneity of economy, and concertation, 71
hierarchies in sectors, 200
horizontal networking, 240, 243

Iceland, union density, 43
immigrant workers, 146
inclusive unionism, 35
incomes policies, 70, 72, 112, 152, 154, 172, 173, 180
individualism and collectivism, 151, 160, 161
industrial action, non-strike, 104, 123
industrial conflict, 76, 102-4, 121; conjunctural shifts in, 115-18; industrial relations systems, 169-87, 217-20
industrial unions, 35, 74

Industrial Workers of the World (IWW), 84
industrialization, 54
industry-wide collective bargaining, 35–7
inflation, 171, 172, 176, 183–6, 211
informal economy and welfare state, 142
insider-outsider relations, 141, 143, 151,
    152–3
institutionalization of labour-management
    relations, 54
inter-union rivalry, 34
interest aggregation, unions, 150
interest groups, 67, 70, 71, 113
internal mobility, 265
Ireland: collective bargaining, 172–3, 174;
    industrial relations, 180; inflation, 176,
    184–6; strikes, 105–22 *passim*, 175,
    182–3; unemployment, 176, 184–6;
    union confederations, 180; union
    membership levels, 18–21
Israel, union density, 43
Italy: collective bargaining, 172–3, 174;
    industrial relations, 180; inflation, 176,
    184–6; informal economy, 142; labour
    movement, 72, 74; multi-employer
    collective bargaining, 36–7; strikes, 105,
    107, 108, 111–25 *passim*, 175, 182–3;
    unemployment, 142, 176, 184–6; union
    confederations, 30–4, 158, 162; union
    membership levels, 18–21, 27, 29, 178;
    welfare state, 135; women's
    employment, 141, 142

Japan, 18–21, 27, 105–24 *passim*, 260
job security, 265
jobless growth model and welfare, 144
just-in-time systems, 223, 224

labour-management relations: flexibility in,
    7–8; institutionalization of, 54
labour markets, 138, 142–3, 152–3, 160, 220,
    234, 235, 238–9, 244
Labour Party (GB), 63, 70, 72, 78, 95, 138
labour policies, 70
leadership, 57–8, 69, 75–8, 85–90, 97, 151
left-wing discourse and industrial action, 76
legislation, 88, 155, 179
Levy, Albert, 23
liberal corporatism, 129
Liberal Party (GB), 95
linguistic fragmentation of union
    confederations, 68–9, 93
localization of production, 224
lock-outs, 90, 121
longitudinal studies of industrial conflict,
    104–15, 125
low wages in service sector, 146, 154
Luxembourg, union membership levels,
    18–21

macroeconomic demand, management and
    unions, 252–3
managerial behaviour and unions, 254

manual workers, 30–2, 137, 153, 177
manufacturing sector: decline of, 26–8;
    strikes in, 119–21, 125; union
    membership levels, 27, 29
mark-up of union wages, 42
market, and welfare provision, 136
market mechanism for union control, 90,
    179
markets: fluid, 223; in sectors, 200
merger of unions, 34
Mexico, 63, 84–9
micro-corporatism, 72
militancy, 102–32; public sector, 119; and
    structure of employment, 102, 104, 115,
    118–21; and union membership levels,
    23–4
miners and AFL, 96
minimum income, 147–8
moderate union leaders, 57–8, 69, 76
monopoly of union leaders, 58
multi-employer collective bargaining, 35–7,
    155
multinational corporations, welfare provision
    by, 145

negotiation and radicalism, 57–8
neo-corporatism, 70–2, 112, 135, 150,
    169–87
neo-corporatist concertation, 70–2, 76, 77,
    211
neo-liberalism, 170, 185
Netherlands: industrial relations, 181, 182;
    inflation, 176, 184–6; neo-corporatist
    concertation, 72; strikes, 105–20 *passim*,
    175, 182–3; unemployment, 26, 44, 176,
    184–6; union confederations, 30–4,
    68–9, 93, 178; unions, 18–21, 25–6, 27,
    28, 29, 44, 93, 178, 182; welfare state,
    134–5; women's employment, 141;
    works councils, 25, 172
network systems, 223, 240, 243
New Deal, 82, 84
New Zealand, 43, 105–24 *passim*
non-manual workers: strikes, 114, 119; and
    union confederations, 30–2, 34; unions,
    29, 114, 141, 153, 154; welfare
    provision, 137
non-work economy and welfare state, 142–3
Norway: collective bargaining, 171;
    industrial relations, 181; inflation, 176,
    184–6; neo-corporatist concertation, 72;
    pensions, 137; strikes, 105–25 *passim*,
    175, 182–3; unemployment, 176, 184–6;
    union confederations, 30–4, 156; union
    membership levels, 18–21, 27, 29, 93

occupation plans, 244
occupational welfare schemes, 136
oil prices and industrial relations, 107,
    171
Okun index, 176, 184–5
opposition to authoritarian regimes, 67–8

opposition parties and unions, 61-2, 63, 65, 67, 76, 77
organization of work, and skills, 256, 265-6
organizational linking and union development, 55

participation with management, 239
party formation, constitutional factors in, 80
pay, 42, 146-8, 154, 257, 259, 264
peak associations of capitalists, 188, 189-90, 199-200, 201, 204-7
pensions, 137, 143
Peronism, 62, 63, 93, 97
Peru, labour movement, 91
pluralistic stability in collective bargaining, 169
political parties: Argentina, 92-3; and class interests, 61; democracies, 64; formation of, 79-81, 83; and religious interests, 61; and unions, 24, 53, 60-8, 69-70, 72, 74-5, 74-82, 83-4, 87, 88; USA, 77-81; and welfare policy, 138
political systems and labour movements, 53-101
politicization in authoritarian regimes, 67, 93
polyvalent worker, 264
Popular Fronts, 84
populist labour movements, 85
Portugal, 43, 72, 74, 94, 162, 174, 182-3, 184-6
post-industrial proletariat, 146, 147
power, 113, 129, 189, 191, 251
pressure group labour movements, 55, 77-84
private sector welfare provision, 136, 138, 140-1, 144, 147
product development/innovation, 222-3, 256-8
professionalization of leadership, 87
programmatic discourses in opposition parties, 62
prudential unionism, 83
public goods, 204
public sector, 27, 28, 29, 30, 119-21, 126, 141, 154

racial divisions in labour movements, 60, 80, 83
radicalization, 57-8, 73, 93
reformist labour leadership and collective bargaining, 69
regional trades union councils, 241
regionalization of production, 224
reification of capital, 191
religious interests, 61, 68-9, 70, 73, 95
repression of labour movements, 85, 89-91, 93
Republican Party (US), 78, 79
revolutionary syndicalism, 84

sabotage, 104
self-employment, 233

service proletariat, 146, 147, 154
service sector, 146-7, 154
shop floor bargaining, 36, 172-3, 174
Single European Act, 197, 198, 204, 206, 208-9
single European market, 188-216, 209-14
single union deals, 32
skills, 223, 250-69
small-batch production, 257
small firms relations with customers, 226
'social contract' (UK), 174
social corporatism, 129
social democratic labour movements, 54-5, 68-72
social democratic regimes, 112, 133-4, 135, 183, 207, 208, 211
social democratic welfare state institutions, 94
social networks, 234-5
social organizations and party formation, 80
social policy, demographic factors, 144
socialism, 35, 79, 95
Spain, 23, 43, 72, 74, 162, 174, 180, 182-3, 184-6
staff unions, 30
stagflation and strikes, 107
state, and union development, 55, 83, 84-9
state sponsored labour movements, 55, 74, 84-9
statistics, reliability of, 21-2, 103, 119, 127-8
strikes: advanced capitalist democracies, 24, 76, 81, 102-32, 175-6, 182-3; authoritarian regimes, 90; and class conflict, 126-7; duration of, 105-7, 121-4; and economic conditions, 112; and incomes policies, 112; in manufacturing sector, 119-21, 125; non-manual workers, 114, 119; public sector, 119-21, 126; relative frequency, 104, 124; relative involvement (RI), 104-6, 109, 117-18, 121-2; relative volume of, 104, 123-4; shape of, 121-4; and social democratic regimes, 112; and unemployment levels, 102, 103, 107, 115-17, 125; and union membership levels, 24, 102, 117-18
structure of employment, 153, 233; and militancy, 102, 104, 115, 118-21; and union density, 26, 41, 159, 178; and welfare state, 140, 142
subcontracting, 225, 230, 233
subsidiarity and welfare provision, 140
suppliers relations with customers, 225-6, 241
supra-firm collective bargaining, 35-7
supra-industry collective bargaining, 37-9, 170, 178
supra-national business associations, 196, 199, 202, 205-6, 207-8, 209
supra-national collective bargaining, 203, 211, 212

Sweden: collective bargaining, 69, 171, 173; employers' organizations, 181; industrial relations, 181; inflation, 176, 184–6; labour movement, 68–72; neo-corporatist concertation, 72; pensions, 137; strikes, 24, 105–25 *passim*, 175, 182–3; training, 260; unemployment, 142, 176, 184–6; union confederations, 30–4, 156, 158; union membership levels, 18–21, 27, 28, 29, 44, 93, 154, 178; union-party links, 62, 69–70; welfare state, 134, 138, 141; women's employment, 140, 141

Swedocentric fallacy, 134

Switzerland: collective bargaining, 171–2; industrial relations, 178, 181; inflation, 176, 184–6; strikes, 105–20 *passim*, 175, 182–3; unemployment, 176, 184–6; union confederations, 30–4; union membership levels, 18–21, 27, 29

Thatcher regime and unions, 156, 157

trade associations, 193–5, 204, *see also* business interest associations (BIAs)

training, 147, 233, 235, 236–8, 242, 244–5, 250–269; costs of, 260–1

transnational unions, 39

Turkey, union density, 43

two-party systems, 81

unemployment, 25–6, 44, 142–3, 176, 183–6; and labour markets, 152–3; and pensions, 137; and strike levels, 102, 103, 107, 115–17, 125

unemployment insurance and union membership, 25, 177–8

union confederations, 28–34, 68–9, 70, 78, 82–4, 93, 151, 156, 158, 159, 161, 162, 178–80, 210, 212

union density: advanced capitalist democracies, 18–24, 27, 39–42; and strikes, 117–18, 125

union membership levels: advanced capitalist democracies, 18–24, 27, 28, 29, 39–42, 93, 154, 177–8; decline, 18–21; and disaggregation, 151; gender differences, 27, 28, 83; Latin America, 74, 96; manufacturing sector, 27, 29; and militancy, 23–4; and strikes, 24, 102; and unemployment, 25, 26–8, 177–8; and union-party links, 74; and worker mobilization, 23–4, 56

union movements: advanced capitalist democracies, 17–52; fragmentation and decline, 28–32, 150–68

unions: activists in, 22–3, 74, 75; allegiance to, 55, 87, 90, 150, 170, 219; autonomy of, 192; avoidance, 32; decline of, 39–42, 45, 150–68; democracy in, 87; depoliticization of, 162; development of, 55–8; distributive politics of, 252, 262; in Europe, 38–9, 40–2; exclusive

jurisdiction, 32; finance of, 44, 90; local and national organization, 219–20, 229–30, 245–6; objectives of, 17; organizational consolidation of, 55–8; organizational sclerosis, 150; part-time workers and, 164; participation in national policy, 171; peak federations, 37–9, 113; private sector, 29, 141, 154; and production technology, 54; and recession, 18–21, 152, 177; recognition of, 57; recruitment by, 228–9, 232; redistributive politics of, 252; and regional economy, 238–41, 246; and reorganization of industry, 217–49; replacement of, 39–42; representativeness, 150; resistance to, 58, 73, 75, 95–6, 121, 155; and semi-skilled workers, 241–5; and skilled workers, 82, 83, 96, 228, 232; and solidarity, 157, 158, 160, 165–6, 177; strength of, 22–3; structure, 35–7; and strument of employment, 152, 155, 161, 164, 165, 221; and supply-side, 252–4; and unemployment, 26–8, 152, 243–4; and un-skilled workers, 82, 83, 241–5; and vulnerable workers, 231, 242, 245; weakness of, 103; and welfare, 136, 138; and women, 27, 28, 83, 164; and work reduction, 143; *see also* company unions; craft unions; departmental unions; industrial unions; vocational unions; and under separate countries

United Kingdom: collective bargaining, 69, 172–3, 178–9; Conservative Party, 78; craft unions, 35, 159, 160; employers' organisations, 173, 178–9; industrial relations, 178–9, 185; industrial unions, 35; inflation, 176, 184–6; labour movement, 68–72; Labour Party, 63, 70, 72, 78, 95, 138; Liberal Party, 95; local bargaining, 36; multi-employer collective bargaining, 36–7; neo-corporatist concertation, 72; strikes, 105, 107, 108, 113–23 *passim*, 175, 182–3; unemployment, 26, 176, 184–6; union confederations, 31–4, 156; union membership levels, 18–23, 27, 28, 29, 41–2, 93, 154, 178; union-party links, 63, 70, 78, 93; unions, 35, 41–2, 69, 156, 157; welfare provision, 138

United States: class consciousness, 79–80, 95; collective bargaining, 82; craft unions, 82, 83; egalitarianism, 80; labour movement, 63, 77–84; political parties, 77–82, 83–4, 95; socialism, 79, 95; strikes, 76, 105–25 *passim*; union confederations, 78, 82–4; union membership levels, 18–21, 27, 28, 39–40; union-party links, 62, 77–9; welfare provision, 136, 140–1, 145; women's employment, 140, 141

unity of labour movement, 58–60, 76–7, 112, 166
Uruguay, labour movement, 72

vertical integration, 222
vested interests, 163
vocational unions, 30

wages *see* pay
welfare firm, 145–6, 147
welfare networks, 243
welfare provision: conservative regimes, 135, 138; corporate, 135; friendly societies, 137, 160; Germany, 135, 136, 242–3; private sector, 136, 138, 140–1, 144, 147; targetting of, 136; and taxation, 136, 140

welfare states, 133–49; clustered regimes of, 135
welfare state institutions, social democratic model of, 94
women: employment, 140, 141, 142, 143, 146, 154, 234; and unions, 27, 28, 83, 164
work-based learning, 260–2
worker mobilization and union membership, 23–4
worker politics and industrialization, 54
working class, 134, 135, 139, 150–68, 177
works councils/councillors, 25, 35, 155, 172, 173, 217–18, 220, 230, 231, 237, 246

young people in service sector, 146

Printed in the United Kingdom
by Lightning Source UK Ltd.
124998UK00001B/406-414/A

9 780803 979772